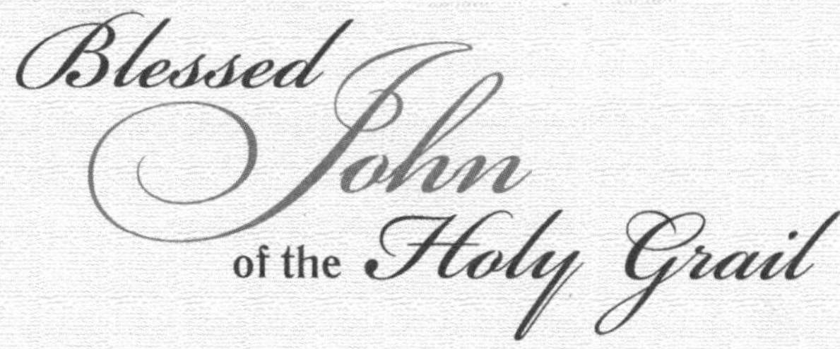

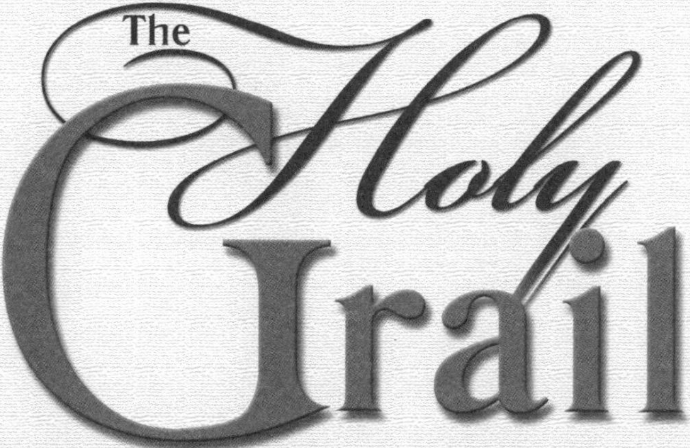

Being in virginal love

Being in love leads to eternity, because love knows no bounds. Being in love is the key to eternal life. I have found the True Church and will never turn away from it. This True Church is the Grail. Oh, the Holy Grail, I gave my heart to you! I became attached to you so much!

I see the sacrifices you have made. You are the twice-crucified Christ. You are the same Lord Who was crucified and the drops of Whose Blood flow into the Chalice.

Blessed John of the Holy Grail

Blessed John of the Holy Grail
THE HOLY GRAIL – BEING IN VIRGINAL LOVE

Edited by Associaciò per l'estudi de la cultura càtar.
Managing Editor: Germán Korneychuk
Translation from Russian: Helen Hagon,
Associaciò per l'estudi de la cultura càtar
Editing and Proofreading: Richard Thornton Smith, John Cliss, Borislav Martemianov, Ekaterina Tsirulina, Elena Ivanova, Michaela Svetlova, Allison Elizabeth Dennis, Svyatopolk Bulgakov, Carol Davies, Arthur Kern
Design and layout: Melchizedec Solntsev,
Alexandra Latisheva, Anna Maria Alekseyeva

Depósito Legal: B-14835-2012
ISBN 978-84-940130-0-3

Impresión y encuadernación: Imprenta Nácher S. L.
Printed in Spain

CONTENTS

PREFACE

BEING IN VIRGINAL LOVE

THE ROYAL GENEALOGY OF CHRIST

THE MYSTERY OF THE MESSIANIC DYNASTY

THE WAY TO THE CASTLE OF THE LOVE-WHICH-IS-NOT-OF-THIS-WORLD

POSTSCRIPT

A Divine Song of Love

Preface

Why am I writing a book about the Grail? Heaven has shown me the treasure of the true Church in the crystal sea playing on the facets of the Grail, so that I may fix my gaze on the Divine Civilization approaching from afar.

Blessed John

'THE greatest mystery of Christianity has been revealed. The angels are applauding. As Mary was conceived immaculately, without sin (Paris, Revelation about Immaculate Conception), so Christ, himself immaculately conceived, begot the Immaculate Conception of Joseph the Sweetest, his offspring, and from him the messianic dynasty of true Christianity (Desposini).

Hallelujah! The Grail is revealed to humanity.'

Blessed John's new book, like all his others, reflects on the imminent coming of Christ. It is so near that we can already see his image. Seeing him, it is impossible not to fall in love with him.

None of the existing religions is even vaguely capable of conveying this image. For a thousand years churches have been unable to teach how to love God, because they have abandoned their own first love (the author uses the words of the apocalyptic angel addressing the church of Ephesus). It is impossible to love the god in which they believe. So this means there is none of the living water of new birth, that miraculous 'love-drink' which, like a unifying circulatory system, will reconnect the hearts of the Creator and His creation.

The author states that the future is that of the new religion of The Most High. This new religion of the transfigured Christ and transfigured humanity is being born and is crystallising before our very eyes as the fruit of Solovki and the GULAG – the real *Second Golgotha* of the 20th Century.

The subject of Solovki occupies a large part of Blessed John's works. In the very face of the great confessor of the faith, the 'Patriarch of the Gulag', St. Seraphim Romanov and his 'Seraphim's brethren', shone the images of Christianity, not just as an ideology or one of the 'traditional faiths', but as a real vision of Christ personified in the thousands of devotees of *divine humanity*. This faith is for the future. It is the legacy of Solovki. And now it has made a new discovery through the prism of the Grail, with its legends about the dynasty of the direct descendants of Christ and the Blood of Christ on Earth, which have been handed down from one keeper of the Chalice to another and multiplied through Knights and Maidens.

'Solovki is connected with *Nightingale Mountain* and the Grail by the great golden luminary triangle. Divine Wisdom brought the last Russian Tsar, Seraphim Romanov, to Solovki, where he was anointed messianic Tsar of the Russian Grail, and given the Solovki Grail of the third millennium, the heavenly altar of *Divine Civilisation III*. Both the Serafimov brethren (the hierarchy of fire), and the church which came out of the *Second Golgotha* of Solovki through Seraphim (one of the last Great Russian Monarchs of the Messianic Dynasty) perpetuated the genealogy of Christ.' (Blessed John of the Holy Grail).

This is not about the genealogical calculations and other contrived means by which European Kings have traced their line 'back to Christ'. This deals with a relationship of another, higher and divine nature. 'Seraphim has become the Christ of Solovki by means of the messianic composition he acquired through the fiery transfiguration of suffering.'

The Grail is, in fact, the return to the church and to human kind of the 'first love', the incredible god-man synthesis which had been lost. It is impossible to speak or write about it without a direct revelation from on high. This very book, which you are holding in your hand, is the fruit of one such revelation. Its source is the Holy Grail.

Around the Holy Grail have accumulated many historical studies, novels, semi-mystic treaties, and attempts to rationalise the mystery or superimpose someone's own theory on it. Do not look for any of that here. We have before us a divine song of love which has been composed during constant contemplation of the Holy Grail.

This revelation was preceded by a period of many days in which the Mother of God delivered Her Revelation on *Nightingale Mountain*, not far from Izmir. There, in ancient Ephesus, Her house has been preserved. She lived out her 16-year Solovki there (from the ascension of Christ until her assumption). There, every stone bears the mark of the yearning for an inexpressible, heavenly love and longing for the Heavenly Bridegroom.

Tormented by the same anguish, Mary Magdalene, the former prostitute, immaculately conceives. Her son is Joseph the younger, hero of grail epic literature, founder of the dynasty of Christ and His son in flesh and blood.

How can this be? The author's explanation lies in the mysticism of the Immaculate Conception and the mystery of virginal love.

In European esoteric literature there is a tradition of 'Desposins': children of Christ by Mary Magdalene. As divine heirs they allegedly gave rise to the Royal Dynasties of the Old World. They hint at a love relationship between the Son of God and the erstwhile sinner. Official theology flatly dismisses these hints: 'no, there was nothing of the sort!' 'Yes, there was', claim the occultists in response. 'Christ fathered Children like any ordinary man.'

Both of these points of view are fraught with fatal consequences for spiritual exploration. The tradition is given a whole new interpretation in the context suggested by Blessed John: the context of virginal love. Yes, Mary Magdalene loved Christ and conceived by Him. However, she c o n c e i v e d w i t h o u t s i n –

out of a great, inescapable love for the Beloved. The earthly gives birth out of a yearning to unite with the heavenly. And the fruit of this conception is the god-man, in the image of Christ.

This is the greatest alternative to the ritualistic religions; to the Roman Curia and the candles of the Orthodox churches! Just as Mary Magdalene, sentenced to death by stoning, became the Bride of the Son of God and the Mother of God's heir, the first divine incarnation since Christ, so too, humanity, betrothed to Christ gives birth to Divine Humanity, as dreamed by Vladimir Solovyov. Blessed John calls him Homo seraphicus; seraphic humanity or Seraphites.

The Divine civilization, about which the author speaks, will be the civilization of those who are in divine love. Some of humankind's most wonderful stories show a glimpse of this.

The author was led to the world of the Grail through divine revelation and prophecy following a long spiritual journey. 'Only now am I beginning to understand what this time was for', he says. 'All the 300 and more books which I have written over many years are 300 ways to the Grail.' Without these entrances, faith cannot exist and religion is reduced to something fruitless. Everything which God reveals over and over again over the course of millennia as immutable, divine law – virginity, the cross, repentance, being from beyond this world, and so on – are nothing more than the large and small gates into the world of the Grail. It combines us with God in virginal love: it is the birth without blemish of a new human; the god-man or Seraphite.

The Grail, like the alchemists' 'philosophers stone', was a central focus of spiritual exploration in the Middle Ages. As the philosophers' stone transforms base metals into gold, so the Holy Grail changes a person, making him incorruptible. This miracle is carried out by the Blood of Christ contained within it. However, a deeper understanding of the mystery of the Grail can be found in its mystical imagery. The Grail is the wedding cup of God and humanity, the vessel of the 'love drink' and a symbol of the eternal bonds of fidelity. As in ancient times, sworn brothers, when making their pact of brotherhood, drained a cup containing a mixture of wine and blood, so God proffers to humanity the Grail chalice; the Covenant of love, the secret Covenant, and the final bonds, captured in the very foundations of human existence.

'This is the new Grail, revealed to humankind for the first time', says the author about his own book. 'The image of the Grail was stolen. Occultists and the Vatican used it for their own purposes. My task is to reveal the true image of the Grail; virginal and purified of any historical interference.'

Using the key of the Grail – the key of Heavenly Wisdom – the author reveals the manifestations of heavenly love in history and culture. The traditions of Egypt and Greece, images of the Middle Ages in Europe and the insights of modern-day philosophers pass before his gaze. Then, taking the author's lead, you come to understand that the Most High did not leave for a second. He was never silent. He was constantly telling us about Himself, and all who came to Him desiring spiritual perfection were embraced by Him; knights and maidens seeking a love which is not of this world.

This is perhaps the most important part of the book: humanity justifies its great search through the wisdom of the Grail. The outline of a new scripture, shown through the whole of world culture, is appearing before us. In the future it will, doubtless, take shape within the new teaching about the Most High – a teaching which befits the Third Covenant. The author calls it Eternal: a Covenant of conjugal ties between God and humanity.

The way to enter this is by being in divine love. This is written between the lines of all the poetry in the world. It is sung about in the White Castles of the Grail from the author's prophetic insight.

'The Grail engenders the god-man,' (Blessed John of the Holy Grail). Never before has the aspect of deification of a person (still one of the central concepts of the mysticism of Blessed John) been so fully revealed. But such are the times we are living in. The Grail is an apocalyptic sign, and a sign of the end of all other paths and programmes. It is the great alternative which can only be seen from the verge of death.

The author calls the Grail the blessing cup to ward against the seven cups of wrath which await the world on the eve of the Second Coming. Like Mary Magdalene who was condemned, humanity has sentenced itself to death by wandering in the darkness and rejecting the heights to which we are called. World disasters and cataclysms, as well as new global threats, are a sign of how near we are to the carrying out of this sentence. However, just like Mary, the world can be put right and saved, in spite of a complete lack of hope, if, like her, we recognise Christ.

To recognise Christ means more than just being saved, though. The Grail brings not only salvation, but also new compositions.

When humanity recognises Christ for what He is, we will be transfigured. The divine potential, which was given to man from the beginning, and has been hidden until now, only to be glimpsed from time to time in Greek myths, Beethoven's symphonies, and philosophers' bold prophesies, will be revealed. The Holy Grail, like the Ark, penetrates the world. Echoes of ancient civilisations are preserved within it. The main mystery of the Grail is the miraculous key which unites the Most High and humanity no matter what.

The Grail is the great unification of Creator and creation, and the meeting point for God's Light and the ascent of humanity. It is bigger than any other religion. It is the source which secretly feeds humanity throughout its long and difficult journey. Blessed John teaches us about the hundreds of spectral facets, particles, rays and Castles of the Grail: its myriad forms.

Leonid Belov
Moscow, August 2005

A Few Words

from the Author

If God gave me liturgies and hours adapted to the Holy Being[1] of the Grail, I would rewrite many of my old books and scrolls which are already covered with a layer of dust.

'Why?' I hear you say. 'Is there not a grain of truth in them?'

I would do it to strengthen their spiritual fragrance.

Books which correspond to the heavenly scrolls begin to emanate their spiritual fragrance straight away. Any other book, no matter how well it is written, or how many copies are printed and categorised as 'best-seller', is not worth the paper it is printed on. Its yellowing pages will gather dust and disappear into insignificance, leaving no trace of either the author (he is probably in a state of sin for having seduced a million readers), or the reader. One day they will say to him, 'It died a mortal death.' It is a mirage. It is nothing at all.

What attracted me to the manuscript (cryptogram) about the religion of the Grail?

It is good for a person to know that the Other Church exists, so that his search may one day be rewarded with the cherished goal.

So that he finds the truth.

It is not in a Lutheran kirkko somewhere on the outskirts of Helsinki, nor in an Orthodox chapel with its beloved ritual nonsense and operatic-sounding rites from the time of Monteverdi and Verdi, but in the True, radiant and transfiguring

[1] *The Holy Being* – in Russian: 'пакибытие' [pakibytie].

Church, where a person can one day unearth a pearl of the Holy Being.

Then the trace of immortality and the infinite potential bestowed on him by the Most High will be revealed.

03.07.2005 Deris Island

The Gospel of Supreme Love Which Cannot be Found on Earth

I have lost count and have been run off my feet... I don't know anything any more. I preach like a madman. I am just talking about a love which does not exist.

It is impossible to talk about it using words. I ask just one thing of You, my Father: light a little candle in my heart! Let its flame be like a silent icon lamp, but let it never go out.

The enemy, that cursed extinguisher of lights, is hot on my heels. His foetid mouth is blowing and blowing both the candle and me from off the throne of Moses and hiding somewhere in a concrete sarcophagus, cursing with black magic of the Orthodox computer, casting a death spell in Antichrist files on the Internet, attaching himself to some kind of virtual 'Orthodox', the likes of whom never existed on Earth...

Father, do not let the tiny wax candle within me go out: the candle of the Gospel of Supreme Love; the Gospel of a love which cannot be found on Earth.

*

It is five o'clock in the morning. Dawn is breaking. The bell tower is frozen in anticipation of its matin chimes: 'Money, money! Bring your money to the church!'

The first scents of morning are already abundant. My goodness, what a beautiful sky! The good souls are sleeping in their stone bedrooms on white beds. They sleep and dream of the Castles of the Grail.

I watch: in Luigi Bianchi's house there are so many stones! There is a collection from all over the world. His wife likes to collect crystal glasses. Here is something else for the collection: guests are few and far between and it is inappropriate for an ecumenical priest to drink. But this is a yearning for a love which is not to be found on Earth. It is a fatal longing, second to none: a longing for the Divine Beloved One.

A crystal glass in an ordinary family is a reminder of the Grail. It turns light into the colours of the rainbow and vibrates with a miraculous sound when touched by the fingers. What is it? The Grail's bell has sounded within a person. The wondrous music of the Kingdom has begun to resound.

So where are our blessed Leonid Bely, Aleksandr Zaokski and Gefsimanski? They are in the White Castles of the Grail by the springs of Higher love, which cannot be found on Earth.

Why does no-one come back from Heaven? Because, in Heaven they experience the love which cannot be found on Earth. Apart from *yurodivy*[2], Heroes or holy and noble Knights who are prepared to sacrifice themselves for the Most Holy Virgin, who would be willing to be sent away from the capital into exile and sentenced to hard labour? No way! Very few return to Earth from Heaven. However, if someone does come back, they do so in order to obtain an even finer pearl of the Grail.

Oh, only on this Earth, where heavenly love is impossible, can we comprehend to what extent it is lacking, even in Heaven.

Earth has a higher calling than Heaven! It is superior to Heaven. Through his calling, man (not a son of Adam, but a Seraphite) is worthy of a higher destiny than the angels. However, it is only possible to achieve this Holy Pollen of *Divine Union* with the Most High in the height of holy passion, in the depths of solitude, in the desert, or in the moaning of the throes of death. This is why Solovetski Special Purpose Prison is known as STON[3] (of the Bride).

*

[2] *Yurodivy* – From the deep-rooted tradition in Russia, see at the Glossary.

[3] *STON* – Solovetskaya Tyurma Osobovo Naznachenia 'Ston' is also a Russian word meaning 'moan', as in the sound emitted during the throes of death.

The place to which the Purest One led me was the Island of Deris[4]. Here, in the centre of the old town, every other house bears a three hundred-year-old carving of the Holy Grail. The Knights of the Holy Grail came here. From here they sang their hymn of the other Church, with its powerful Holy Virgin, and it was here that they led me so that, from the unspeakable heights of Tristan and Isolde, Seraphim Solovki and Blessed *Eufrosinia* I could preach to the world the Gospel of Supreme Love, which cannot be found on Earth.

Not on Earth? Yes, not on this Earth. But, 'the first earth was passed away, and there was no more sea' (Rev. 21:1). It is the New Earth. In it, the impossible has become reality. A love, which is superior to heavenly love, has come down to Earth and this means that the Earth has been raised up higher than Heaven. This is the marvel which awaits humanity.

*

I know, my son: this little book is very precious to you. It is about the most hidden, yet the highest ideal. It is not rational, cosmopolitan or even universal, but, rather, it is on a divine plain and beyond eternity.

Take this command in your hand. Confess it in your heart day and night. Take it like a hot, messianic wine:

> I came into this world
> To become closely united with God
> And through this union with all suffering humanity

This is possible through the chalice of the Grail. This love-drink of a love which is beyond Heaven comes to us from the chalice held by the Most High. The Heavenly Father holds it in His hands and, from it He feeds all those who love Him.

Why does the host of the wedding feast invite the sick, misfits and orphans, yet the healthy seem to refuse, thus inciting the anger of their Lord? This is because the supreme love in this world is felt by individuals who are struggling, who find this world difficult to deal with, who cannot find their place

---

[4] *Deris* – from the Russian 'Devstvennye rizvi', meaning 'robes of virginity'.

in life and who do not belong in this world: they are the odd ones out. They are the misfits, barefooted and the lame (as mentioned in the Lord's parables) who are ready to partake of the love potion.

*

I am a writer who writes about one subject – the love which cannot be found on Earth. And I think... Mankind has already written 300 million volumes about goodness knows what. Someone has written about the adventures of Batman in space, someone came up with the next detective story for a Hollywood blockbuster; someone else invented something completely new, and so on... The time will come, though, when the bell of the Ark will start to sound. Then humanity will say, 'There is no-one except Him, my Beloved.'

Then supreme love will fall on humanity like rain and, like Gideon's fleece, drops of healing dew will come down. Then poor humanity will be purified and will become like the prophecy of Chrysostom, like the Psalter brought to life, like the Mother of God multiplied in her blessed sons and daughters. After many sorrows and dark nights, they will be raised to a new level. The love which cannot be found on Earth will become its only attribute, as everything else will disappear.

They will say, 'the only thing of which this Earth is worthy, and which really exists here, is heavenly love. Everything else will have disappeared from memory, so do not look for traces and descendants.'

01.07.2005 Deris Island

Being in Virginal Love

Being in Virginal Love – the Treasure of the Grail

It is no longer to be found anywhere in the world. The Church has lost it. 'But this is what I have against you: you have lost your first love', is written in John's Revelation to the angel of the church in Ephesus. 'You have endured a lot, you have shown great patience, and you have worked for my glory and were not exhausted. But this is what I have against you: you have left your first love. Remember therefore from where you have fallen, and repent. Otherwise, I will come and remove your lamp stand, if you do not repent.'

What is Christ asking the community at Ephesus (and consequently the Church) to repent for? The 'first love' is to be in virginal love, a young maiden in the castles of the Grail, practising amongst the monks dedicated to a Knight.

What was the Immaculate One teaching about in Ephesus? She simply shared how virginal Their relationship was when Christ came, and how they did not just love but were in love with each other.

Humanity has abandoned its first love – the Most Pure Virgin, the Queen of the Immaculate Conception and the Mother, giving birth from on high. It has abandoned its first love and given itself to another which, in Grail terms, means that the virgin has been abandoned and exchanged for a whore.

Sorrow of sorrow, what great sorrow in the castles of King Arthur! Not one more Knight will be born of the Barren One. What fruits can come from a harlot? Not one more saint will come from the Roman Traitor. The Roman and Byzantine Churches have abandoned their first love. The red dragon worked through Aristotelianism, Thomism, rationalism, dogma and Lateran councils and constitutions.

They have abandoned their first love – the Immaculate Virgin. She has appeared so many times from the 1st to the 21st century! – It is impossible to count them. Falling in virginal love is truly her personification. Countless people have no idea that the sister of charity or the simple village milkmaid who appeared to them is the Divine Mother! Our Queen, as *yurodivy* Theogamy, often appeared in incomprehensible, unexpected guises, so that no-one would recognise Her. She, who shines with heavenly radiance, did not want to be seen.

*

'So remember where you came from, and repent!'

Whence were the Knights of the Grail born? Are they of this world? Are they of earthly descent from Melchizedek's priests? Is the Mysterious Branch, shining and seraphitic, so called because of their many seraphic qualities linking them to the seraphim, the great, six-winged angels?

It is useless to call upon virginal love without Immaculate Conception, and not having any other mystery of another origin. Oh! The gates of the Seraphites are concealed from the unfortunate Adamites. Only those bearing the seraphitic mark on their forehead can enter into the Grail and partake of its Myrrh Holy Being. This, then, is the first condition.

The second (which is linked to the first) is Immaculate Conception.

*

Elsa and Lohengrin, Tristan and Isolde, Louis Lereine and Clothilde... Medieval legends of the Holy Grail are full of images and heroes in virginal love. Oh, how beautiful this is! It is truly sublime and the object of yearning. How this admiring maiden, Virginal Love, ties two hearts together with eternal bonds! She provides such strength for conquering separation, loneliness, despair and death!

The one who virginally loves sacrifices himself with such ease! His blood, which is almost Eucharistic is hot. His countenance is burning with elevated ideas. His heart is full of inexpressible happiness which is not of this world. The devil has no power over him. He is confused by what is before him and slanders such a man, calling him a madman. The ranks of angels bow in great awe, saying, 'The Kingdom of God has come down to Earth! The young maiden, the Virgin Lady, has come into Her inheritance!'

'Romeo and Juliet' (Shakespeare)... In each civilization there are thousands of examples of characters in virginal love, with its unearthly provenance and its romance. Its ideal is incomprehensible and two people who are prepared to die for each other just so that they can be together, require particular strength. Eventually, they will be one day united for all eternity.

Is it not surprising to fall into the chastest of love? Is it possible amidst cloven-hoofed lechery?

Oh! Would you like to take part in the school of the Blessed Virgin and drink from the Grail Chalice? Anoint your heart so that you may be in virginal love and seek to climb the stairway of fire.

The Most Holy Virgin appeared to the Solovki prisoners (to the Seraphimov brethren and subsequently to their successors) as the 15-year-old Mary, dressed in white with a red cross on Her forehead. It was impossible not to fall in love with Her. The first 'genuine' Seraphite on Earth – the Seraphimov brethren, followers of Saint Seraphim the Tender, the last Russian Tsar Mikhail (Romanov) – loved their 'Sister' to distraction. They waited for Her coming like little children. They talked with Her at length, astonished by the chasteness of her mind and the unexpected direction of Her thoughts. She views everything around so wonderfully! She is full of a chaste strength and her gaze shines with such purity! It was impossible not to fall in love with Her.

It is a shame that the visionaries of Medjugorje married! Of course, this fate is better than being a *yurodivy* in a monastery and persecuted because of the apparitions (the usual theatrical farce which always sets the teeth on edge in the history of Catholicism). However, the other extreme is no better with home and family to consider. Is it a cross? Yes. It would have been better, though, for them to remain pure in the world. In Medjugorje the Virgin of the Grail came and reminded Her little visionaries, 'You have abandoned your first love.'

She spreads everywhere the wonderful fragrance of being in virginal love. Is this not why Conchita Gonzalez shone as she contemplated the mysterious Virgin in white who had come down from the Kingdom? Even those who have only seen Her with their own eyes on one occasion are left with the impression of her eternal virginal love which the Pure Maiden spreads everywhere. She has left her impression on Lucia of Fatima, Padre Pio, Conchita Gonzalez and the African visionaries in Kibeho.

The mystery of the Blessed Mother of God is the mystery of the saints.

*

The Roman villains have sealed up this source of original purity, the virginal beauty of heavenly love and the fire of being in God's love! Their diocese is like the bloody baron, Yvon Querbenès, who changed his elegant black dress suit in the Breton style for a dirty robe and a long, grey, wizard-like beard. If you listen to them, every appearance of the Divine Mother (even one of the thousand which have slipped past their censor) consists of the message, 'Build a chapel here in My honour.' Alternatively they may have found, shining miraculously, a wooden icon which is not from our world, so they bowed and prayed before it and took it to the priest. From then on the holy object was given an appropriate place on Earth. It was the source of healing, worship and communication with the Divinity...

Where is the myrrh? Where is the first love? It has been abandoned.

Oh, Church of the Blessed Mother of God Transfiguring, do not abandon your first love! I am doing all I can. I am angered by institutionalism. Like a *yurodivy* I teach my children to live chastely, even within marriage, not to give in to the temptations of Mammon, to be humble, to go against the flow, and always to walk along unpredictable paths which our enemy will not expect. Then the little flock will miraculously enter the Grail, where the billion Catholics (mythical, though) and the unfortunate 3% of the 'Orthodox congregation' in Russia cannot go...

Oh, why have You called me now to Nightingale Mountain and here to the new Eden at Glastonbury? To tell mankind and the Church about the 'first love' of the Purest Virgin for Christ – about the Grail of Christ and Mary and about the most wonderful castle of all time, from Creation until the end of the world. To invite the genuine disciples to the Grail of Nightingale Mountain.

Oh, they have already been transfigured. They are already named Seraphites. They have no connection with the cursed heritage of 'original sin' and the incurably bad origin. They were born from on high and are received into Your Heart. They know the secret of the 'second birth' of virginal water and the Holy Spirit: the seraphitic spirit, the white font and the drops of myrrh.

*

My child, we digress...

So, there is nothing more wonderful and more exalted on Earth than to be most chastely in love. As Christ of Nightingale Mountain told the disciples in Ephesus, it is based on a burning repentance and recollection of one's origins. Here, he associates the fall of Ephesus with a mysterious Light in the heart.

This light is the 'Inner Sun'. In the Adamites it has been

extinguished. Alas! There have been more than enough people to extinguish and destroy it. In the two thousand years since His coming, time spent on Earth and His return to the world through disciples and messengers, is there but one living flame to be found, which has not been extinguished in the damp dungeon? Is there just one font which has not been desecrated? Just one vessel which they have not maligned? Just one shrine which has not been brazenly plundered by these 'pirates', as we would now call those to whom was ascribed the earthly status of robbers and thieves, false pastors and first-class liars, mercenaries, but not selfless servants of love?

Therefore, adopt the mystery of being in virginal love like the 'key of David', opening doors which no-one can shut.

Lord, what a door you have opened in front of me, which no-one can close! Not even 'that group that belongs to Satan', those liars who claim they are Christians but are not (Rev. 3:8-9).

'Oh, I will make them come and bow to you and they will know that the wonderful virginal love is amongst Us – We are in virginal love.

I have not spoken a word about her in my days on Earth but, My child, she is the 'key of David' and the golden 'key of Solomon'. It is said of the door to the Grail that, 'Whoever opens it, no-one will be able to close it, and whoever closes it, no-one will be able to open it.' It is only possible to enter into it with the unblemished sign on the forehead – the mark of the Seraphites.'

Therefore repent with fire and throw off the yoke of the ordinary person and the vulgar ideals of the modern world: lust, polluting cars, Hollywood cinema, instability, Mammon, the mafia etc... Civilization has perished for one reason: the tiny pieces of Original Immaculacy (being in virginal love with Christ) have catastrophically run out and have been outweighed by another cup on the apothecary's scales.

Just read from one of the trails left by of the history of

America, Europe and Russia in the Middle ages or later. So many abominations were carried out by endless streams of Spanish Conquistadors, conquerors, merchants, metropolitans, inquisitors, reigning Caesars, hooded gendarmes and the double-headed eagle governed by the principle of Symphony! The only cup they drank from was that of lust. They came to know such depravity! And so the gates (the very ones which only He, El Elion, can open) are closed to them.

Therefore leave behind these ideals: TV, holidays, career, night clubs, transcendental music, transmeditation, Upanishads, yoga, the Roerichs and other things which are luminescent in the night glow of Tibet (a different mountain, a different love, a different origin and a different branch) and seek out the Most Pure Virgin. Fall in Love with Her as your father and his sons and daughters have loved Her.

The Church of the Seraphites

The mystery of our Church (of the easy assumption into the blessed destiny of the Mother of God) lies in being perpetually in love with Her.

I recall that, at the XVIII Council, upon seeing this, some well-travelled Italians and French exclaimed:

'We have travelled through over 80 Christian countries and observed how the Virgin is worshipped. However, we have not witnessed anywhere else such love as that which you have for Her in the Church of the Mother of God!'

What is this? Father John, together with blessed Paisius, Makari, Ilya, Joachim, Theodosius, Athanasius, Timothy and Mikhail Tverski bows like a knight before the Virgin. How beautiful their movements are! They are so sublime and enraptured! Who are these Knights of the Grail who are not of earthly origins? It is impossible to describe them. They have no certification such as a baptismal certificate or guardianship documentation to confirm their right to episcopal consecration. They are the priests of Melchizedek. In their hearts they are in virginal love with the Virgin of the sweetest joy, and this love never fades. They are madly, head over heels, in love with Her. They cannot take their eyes off Her. They are so captivated by Her image and so mad about Her that they can think about nothing else. They only want to honour the Virgin and profess themselves Her guardians, Her Knights and her army. They want to follow Her and carry out Her every command.

This is the knighthood of the future: the knighthood of the Grail! Look at the beautiful faces of our fathers. Their secret is unfathomable. They are rather like priests. They are Orthodox, yet look like Catholics. They are better preachers than the protestants. They are peacemakers. They hear the Word. They partake of the myrrh scrolls.

Where does their burning faith come from? Where does this virginal power come from? Who extinguished their sexual furnace? How could they so quickly leave behind the shadows of this world and turn their gaze heavenward? Why do they only think about Christ and Mary? Why do they thirst for the Divine Revelations time and time again and ask, 'What did the Mother of God say?' (this was the first question that mother *Eufrosinia* asked me when I visited her at Pochaev and Kremenets).

They are saturated with the essence of Eternal Virginity. They are eternally and virginally in love with the Most Pure Virgin – eternally because they cannot satisfy this love. It always presupposes separation (Oh! even in the future...) but there is nothing sweeter than returning to the Grail, the palace of the Eternal Virgin Mary.

Today, Theogamy has provided such an experience of revelations, for example the *yurodivy* maiden Cundry, the 'village milkmaid', the sister of mercy of Solovki and so on... The Virgin Mary Mother of Mercy in the Gate of Dawn, dressed in a mantle of the stars of Heaven and the gold crown of the Queen of the Universe.

But remember this, Church of the Seraphites: do not abandon your first love! Do not indulge in the debauchery of 'another love', no matter how attractive it may seem from the outside. There are plenty of substitutes. Look at the others – they seem to have priesthood, faith and the Eucharist... But they have lost their first love and their faces are like those who have been damaged.

I hope that the Saviour, in His Judgement, will not say, 'I have just one thing against you.' Patience, victory, asceticism, bearing witness to faith, and even martyrdom are important to Him. Much more important, though, is the first love.

The judgements of the Grail. Their criteria are irreproachable

John's Revelation is full of images of the Grail. The 'key of David', which was given to the church in Philadelphia (which literally means 'brotherly love'), means that they are in eternal, virginal love. In Sardis there are a few who 'have kept their clothes clean' (Rev. 3:4). Their prize is, 'You will walk with me, clothed in white' (the Seraphites)...

It is at the door of the Grail where the symbol of original purity is carved – the octagon, the Immaculate Heart, the Pure One's spear and sword. The Lord stands there and says, 'Whoever comes by (whoever preserves the flame of the first love for the Heavenly Father within himself), I will give them mother-of-pearl, the ivory of the Grail and a White Castle built from it.' 'Behold, I stand at the door, and knock: if any man hear my voice, and open the door, I will come in to him, and will sup with him, and he with me. To him that overcometh will I grant to sit with me in my Throne, even as I also overcame, and am set down with my Father in his throne' (Rev. 3:20-21).

Oh, Eufrosinia, maiden of the Grail. Is this not why, having left behind the enemy, Lucifer, Moscow's beau monde, high society, my studies, and all that was dear to me in Moscow, I then came running to you in a distant land?

My feet brought me there against my will. I hurried to the

Grail. How mystical it was. Pochaevskaya Lavra was built for ignorant lay people (fools). It was built by Prince Pototski for his mistress. With its luxuriously painted churches, wide towers and substantial cupolas, it is a caricature of the belfry of Heaven. However, about fifty metres away, in an overgrown garden, there is a little straw hut and, inside it, is Eufrosinia, Queen of the Grail with the simple nun, Natasha.

Blessed is he who enters through this door! Verily, it is only visible to those to whom our Lord, the King of the Grail, shows the way.

Saint Eufrosinia's door was wide open day and night. The dear Mother was not hiding from anyone. Anyone could come to her. And they did come: from George the priest (the former dean sacristan with the 'Holy Spirit'), and Elevferia, a simple old woman from Novosibirsk, to people from Tumen, Kamchatka, Lake Ilmen or Kitezhgrad.

'The messengers have come to me today.' Where have they come from? She is very mysterious, sheds myrrh, and refuses no-one. Have many people come through her door? They can be counted on the fingers of one hand.

They saw something, took a closer look and tried to follow... However, burly monks in black hoods and silk robes, with rosaries in their right hands, paraded next to the golden gates which were 'evident' for tourists and pilgrims. The holy *yurodivy* elder of the Grail blessed *Eufrosinia*, lived among them. God honoured her relics with the ability to shed myrrh – a sign of a saint of the Grail. There was also a *yurodivy,* an elder in the monastery who gave her the seals from the casket of the Grail – Amphilochius. She recalled how he beat her almost to death with a stick (she was completely covered in bruises) because she obtained the Holy Spirit and she revealed to the father, how a white dove had sat on her back during prayers.

There were about twenty worshippers, but the dove, its wings fluttering, sat only on her. From that moment her mind was enlightened and her heart was reborn.

Her sickness was gone and her former self melted away. She had already forgotten her father, Nikiforov, her mother, her family and others. Then an unseen world of angels and demons was revealed to her. She wept when she saw how much control the enemy had over people. Then she prostrated herself even further when an angel of the Most High handed her the keys to victory over sin, the Psalter and a mysterious curse.

Shrewd seekers frittered their time between Optina shrine and KGB office. Simple ones, though, went to holy Eufrosinia's hut and the dear mother explained to them the mysteries of the Grail.

'Make 5000 genuflections and read the Psalter. You must obtain the Holy Spirit and bathe in the holy spring.'

'So where is the spring, mother?'

'Where?' exclaimed the one who is in love with the Virgin and the Lord. 'Saint Anne's spring on Holy Hill.'

'Where is that?'

'Let's go. I will cure you!'

It is useless to go without her. She anoints with the seals of the life-giving Svyatogorsk spring (a plain concrete ring, from which flow the mysterious waters of the Grail), and you can no longer live without holy springs. Wherever you go you will always look for them: 'Tell me, is there a holy spring near here, like the Kazan spring or the spring of Nikolas of Myra-in-Lycia?'

It does not matter if there is none, if you are misled or if you end up in a puddle which cattle drink from and which is surrounded by cow manure. The Grail is everywhere – and it is nowhere.

I recall Eufrosinia bathing us in a holy spring on the outskirts of Moscow. In reality, it was a dirty well from some kind of reservoir. But when the Queen of the Grail bestowed herself upon it, steam began to rise from her ablutions. She stood regally. She prayed, immersed us in the water and washed our heads. We emerged as if we were newly born, with angelic countenances.

Why did I hurry to the liturgy in the cave church of Job Pochaevski, where the relics of her teacher Amphilochius now lie? Eufrosinia treated us with the generous Mystical Meal. The liturgy with her was indescribable. I understood that it is better simply to make genuflections in a vestibule of a church with no-one watching than to take communion from a chalice with a priest at the altar. The dear mother and I took communion from the other Chalice. She wanted me to become a priest so that I could give her a whole spoonful of communion from the Grail Chalice. So I became one in some god-forsaken region in the village of Makhoshevskaya.

There have been three metropolitans of the True Orthodox Church (in catacombs): the first was the *yurodivy* holy Gennadi, the second was his nephew, also a fool-for-Christ, metropolitan Grigori (assigned by Genadi a year later), and the third was Theodosius (he completely missed the Knights of the Grail). The KGB sent its bishop to bring about a reprisal. An army of wolves with fearsome claws rushed to Theodosius at the site of the desecrated shrine.

The Grail lit up the village Makhoshevka, where the three secret metropolitans of the True Orthodox Church dwelt (in grey woollen scarves and women's skirts they went into the toilet so that no-one would recognize them being a male; the toilets in the villages of Russia are often outside, and nosey neighbours can spy on them). It visited them and disappeared for ever. There only remained the *anointed* sovereign – the King of the Grail.

Makhoshevka had long since been destroyed. Only fools and vampires, those who have committed patricide and good old-fashioned traitors hurry there like the medieval 'Ladies' Knights' – lustful do-gooders seeking out the Grail in order to satisfy an idle interest and achieve fame in the world.

Such are the judgements of the Grail! Their criteria are irreproachable. The King of the Grail, King Solomon of Israel, gained the respect of the whole world through his wise judgement. We have been given the judgement of Solomon over the whole world – the judgement of the Grail.

Somebody came with the request that the wasting disease should be eradicated – this is essential for the judgement of the Grail. Only a Virgin of the Grail can apply a moist ointment, a white plaster, and then, with a touch of the rod, you will be healed. Only pure, virginal grace, only the purest virginal love and ardent faith, the sword of the Grail (it is known as the gift of discerning spirits) and other divine judgements.

The villains organised persecutions. Three times they sprinkled a fine yellow, slow-acting powder. Useless! The mysterious taking of monastic vows was connected to another, divine, mysterious one, of the order of the Grail. Stalin's State Political Directorate could only be defeated by such a great Tsar as Seraphim the Tender, the last Russian emperor, who brought the Grail to the empire of Peter the Great.

Exegi monumentum. I erected a monument which is more solid than brass: Immaculate Origin, Conceptio Immaculata, the virginal service, ex toto (with her whole being).

The Romans said, 'Ex malis eligere minima'[5]. The world outside of the Grail can be understood through the principle, 'ex malis minima' – the lesser evil. There is worse than its tyranny, capitalism, fascism, communism and other traps. Alas! In the fallen order, there remains only the principle of ex malis minima. However, it seems that the time of this oppressive world order is already at an end. The king of the Grail is assuming power. He bears the Rosicrucian Rose which is on the wonderful sarcophagus where the young Louis Lereine sleeps: his white remains in an elegant black suit remained uncorrupted for fifty years after his martyrdom during the Inquisition.

The Church of the Grail has shone!

*

[5] (Latin) Choose the lesser of two evils.

Tristan, a Knight of the Grail, looks for Isolde, a virgin of eternal love. On the way to see the king of Ireland, where this wise beauty dwells, he fights with a dragon.

This is how the legend of the Grail describes the monster: its head is that of a bear (the ignorance of hypocrites), its eyes are red (the bloodthirstiness of an executioner), like burning coals (the fires of hell blazing inside it), it has two horns on its forehead (a sign that it comes from the devil and Baphomet), it has long ears (so it can listen to the Inquisition gossip), it is hairy (it is covered in thoughts), it has claws like those of a lion, it has the tail of a snake (it hatched from out of a snake's egg), it has scaly skin, and it feeds on carrion (it lives on dead saints – Knights of the Grail).

Tristan's lance (the lance of the Grail) broke. His armour (the shield and the armour of the Immaculate Conception) turned black, like burnt coal. His horse fell under him. His sword helped him: Tristan excelled by thrusting it into the jaws of the monster, stabbing it and slicing its cursed heart in two. Tristan cuts out the dragon's tongue: the Roman beast can no longer promulgate its innumerable catechisms or spread its spurious faith. He was almost poisoned to death by the venom which oozed from the dragon's tongue (the malice and curse of their anathema).

The golden-haired Isolde, the maiden of the Grail, healed the Knight and their wonderful romance continued in virginal love. They remembered each other through their wanderings in different lands until they were united in the indescribable bliss of the Covenant of the faithful – the marital bonds of the Most High.

*

Oh, come, Tristan and Isolde of Russia – the holy Virgin Fevronia and prince Petr Muromski! Come, holy Virgins of the Grail: holy Yuliana Torzhetskaya, Virgin Mary Solovetskaya! Free Holy Rus' from the dragon's heathen temple! No longer will the dragon whine plaintively or read its sermons 'on the holy fathers'. Its torn out tongue is in the pocket of a knight of the Grail. Tongues of fire will descend on the Knights of the Most Pure Virgin and carry news of the sweetest and righteous victory of Christ their King.

The path to the Grail is revealed to the righteous!

18.06.2005 Deris Island

Oh Mary Magdalene,
Mother of the messianic dynasty of the Desposins.
Having immaculately conceived Joseph the Sweetest
The supreme Evangelical Wisdom.

Oh origin of Christ, brought about through transubstantiation
The Eucharist is continuously realising
The Love which is not to be found among us on Earth
Infinitely high on the Throne of Theogamy.

Oh Sweetest Mary, Mother of the Most High
Co-saviour and co-redeemer
The Second Divine Mother, giving birth to the likeness of Christ
Triumphal Arc of Heaven.

*

Oh Mary Magdalene,
Mother of the messianic dynasty of the Desposins
The old history of the world has been erased
With its false gods and idols.

A harlot transformed into the one who is anointed with myrrh,
A chosen Mother of sons of Christ
The kin of heirs, apostles and bishops'
Is damned!

Another branch.
The mystery of divine matrimony is revealed.
From Mary and Christ
Is born the civilization of the Seraphites.

Inherit His God-Human compositions,
The seals of the prayer 'Ave, Father, Ave!'
They walk in heavenly bodies
During the Sunday liturgies.
In resurrection liturgies.
In the house of culture of 'Three Fools' they divinize.

And their numbers multiply with every passing day.
Their race is like a new monarchy from Heaven.
A messianic dynasty,
The hierarchy of Melchizedek.

Fathers and sons are united by the conjugal ties,
of the heavenly love like ineffable lambs.

The Bloody Baron

The Inquisition and the Triumph of the Grail

I heard about the 'Bloody Baron' a long time ago by word of mouth... There was the Inquisition and people were afraid. All around there were distorting mirrors. Up against the Divine Castle of the Grail, Korbenic, is the underworld of Querbenes. Up against the most gracious Knight of the Swan, the enlightening Lohengrin, is the monster Yvon, Lord of Querbenes and heir of 'Blue Beard' through seven generations. Up against the gates of the Virgin is the evil kingdom in northern Brittany in France and a terrible castle in the region of Port Vièrge...

Oh, perfect Church of Christ! How you are longed for today!

Are any of the passengers who are looking for Most High on the sinking ship that is the modern world, aware that beyond the Roman thieves and the Byzantine rogues, there exists the Perfect Church? Christ has come to her.

Who was she? The Most Pure Virgin, His Divine Bride, whose Altar of Union was extravagantly decorated at the Assumption. Orders of Knights and Hermits living in solitude or somewhere in barracks.

The Perfect Church conducted liturgies and divinised and bore the Christ-child without the need for black books and four gospels, the 'Bloody Baron' and the Inquisition, Paschal services and a calendar of rituals, leeches and tarantulas, hunting with hounds, malice or judgement.

Christ has remained miraculously concealed. His followers should know about this! Another Church did exist beyond the boorishly titled 'Orthodox', 'Catholic', or even 'Lutheran', 'Jehovah's Witnesses', etc. It is more than just another Church: it is Perfect – an unblemished mirror.

It did not have any resources or a printing press. It paid no heed to imprimatur or censors. It was elusive. Its noble Knights were burned to death, like the leader of the Knights Templar, Jacques de Molay. They unquestioningly followed the will of the Most High. Angels appeared to them. They drank from the Chalice of the Grail and the Most Pure Virgin did not withhold Her merciful Protection from them. They were born from on high and Christ grew within them through His wondrous mysteries.

This was the Church which had not been defiled by a monarch and a monarchy, priests, popes and other worldly impurities, boasting of their imagined precedence and setting up mystifying offices under the guise of regulating the work of a religious institute. Now, it is all about her – about the one who bears the seal, who was concealed and then miraculously revealed; the perfect Bride of Christ, without blemish, not succumbing and preserved by Him for millennia.

She had no press and no broadcast at her disposal. However, she possessed mysteries which surpassed the capabilities of everyday printing houses producing thousands of publications by Dominican overlords or butchering monks. Her language was much more accurate and allegorical.

One such medieval legend of the Grail is that of the 'Bloody Baron'.

There is no doubt whatsoever that, the villain's castle of Querbenès, owned by the sullen knight of Port-Vièrge, and inhabited by black crows and moaning vampires, was where the Roman Inquisition was planned – that insanely jealous rogue and a blatant thief. The Knights Templar were required to enter relations with the Pope. However, they knew more than anyone that the Eucharist is to be found wherever the Grail is. The Holy Lance still weeps blood to this day, down to the very

Last Drop, and hearts will melt at an unthinkable temperature of several million degrees of this heavenly love. The key to victory over the Saracens and other enemies of the Most High is to keep the heart's flame always burning, rather than a sharp sword with a spear and shield, or a cudgel and club.

*

...The Baron was the heir of malice through seven generations. News of the evil deeds which took place in the castle, have been passed on from generation to generation. Dozens of servants disappeared without trace. Knights from the surrounding area were horribly afraid of Querbenès. They could be attacked, tortured and branded in the castle, then eventually burned alive. The owner of the castle had evil connections with kings and dukes, bishops and cardinals. Ludovic and Richelieu, Torquemada and Olivier were on their side. Therefore it was impossible to seek justice for the evil deeds carried out at Querbenès, that evil kingdom in northern Brittany. Everyone knew about it. All the authorities were on the side of the villain.

No-one could consider himself safe with a neighbour like that. His watchful eye was always open. Brittany was under threat from the dreaded symphonist Ludovic XI.

This lover of Catholic monks and who practised such terrible morals, forcibly gave his daughter to a hunchbacked Duke, striking fear throughout the land. Ludovic's court was full of flatterers and adventurists such as Olivier, the favourite of Yvon Querbenès. Having enlisted the support of his favourite courtier, Querbenès no longer felt bound by laws or the advice of insignificant monks and exercised his own judgement on poor vassals who had been stripped of their rights.

If found guilty, Yvon Querbenès could count on the protection of the Justice in Brittany. No-one could count any longer on the protection of the law or the Protection of the Most Pure Virgin in that unfortunate country. Everyone had just one aim – to avoid the gaze of the evil villain. If they were suspected, they were imprisoned. The patrol vehicle worked day and night and Yvon the vampire drank the blood of his transgressors, instilling in them great terror and a mortal fear.

The legend of the Grail unveils the stench of the symphonic model: tyrant kings surrounded by flattering adventurists and court cardinals who were prepared to cover up any corrupt practices. The Virgin of the Grail insists that it has always been this way.

What kind of a church, a propagator of lies, could indulge such monsters! No-one believed in anything. In the Castle of the Grail, Korbenic, it was said of the Roman villain that, 'No trace of Christ remained.' Today there remains no trace of the castle of Querbenès. It is just a reserve arsenal for damp gunpowder and a store for State customs. The dungeons, where innocent victims were tortured, are covered in mould which has been sprinkled with sand.

*

...Yvon's younger brother, Claude, was found dead in a reed bed with 16kg weights tied to his legs. Fishermen (the Fisher King is the keeper of the Grail) discovered the leader of the army bound hand and foot at low tide (an allegory which helps to uncover the truth).

Claude had turned his back on Querbenès. Claude is from the Mysterious Church. He is the symbol of the saints who were mutilated by the blood-red Baron. The heavy weights on his legs are the earthly burden, the sign of mortal ties, ties of holy union and repentance for someone's sins. Tied to his legs is the burden of a hundred million cries of anguish from the Second Solovki.

Now there lies the heavenly treasure: Claude, brutally murdered by his own brother. His property was taken illegally by the villain. Claude, who was found in the reeds by the fishermen (the true Christian spirit), is the holy Church, persecuted by the enemies of Christ, the Inquisitors. To this day, the Mother of Mercy mourns for him and accuses Cain of the murder of his brother, saying, 'What have you done with your brother? His blood will be on your hands for eternity.'

*

Oh, eternal tears! Oh, heart burning with a candle flame!

The Knights Templar are mourners. Who knows the secret of the Knights Templar? Under the guise of guardians of the Temple of Jerusalem, they protected the mystery of the other Temple.

For centuries the Templars have been in love with the Most Pure One and with the Lord. The fifteen steps on the path to the Grail propose the following:

1) A burning faith.

2) Vows of eternal and fervent virginity, to be renewed every month.

3) The mysteries of the Chalice, the Sword and the Grail: the army of Christ and the laws of the invisible battlefield.

4) Renunciation of the world (giving up possessions), entering into the Holy Being, the rods of Christ and the strengthening of spiritual fortresses and castles.

Christ never left them, but granted them more and more. However, the army of the Grail remained secret, as they understood that the way to the secret entrance to the Kingdom and the Reign of Christ is not through the visible paths in today's fallen world. They guard it and prepare for the coming of the Temple of Jerusalem.

5) Communion from the mysterious Chalice and its seven forms of transubstantiation. Partaking from the heavenly springs.

6) The miraculous brotherhood and sworn brotherhood, ministering to the poor and downtrodden. A heart burning with supreme love.

7) Dedication to the cross, anointing and holy passion. Victory over the seven enemies: sin, death, sickness, lust, the world, the devil and hell.

8) Putting on the robes of eternal virginity and the armour of a soldier of Christ. The banner flies showing:

Led by,
Perceptive
Invincible.
The Temple of Solomon,
Holy Israel.

9) The martyrdom of Supreme love and betrothal to Christ in the Kingdom of the Holy Spirit. The inaccessible Glory of the Only Son of the Most High around the Grail, which is kept in Glastonbury, Monsalvat and Korbenic. There were much more than this, though, around 150. More and more were added wherever the Chalice appeared, wherever fate had led the warriors. The Grail came, fed them and enlightened them.

10) Commitment to the secrets of the dynasty of Christ (not the 'Desposins', but the *anointed* followers and the spirit of His maidens and warriors). Virginity as a condition of victory on the battlefield. The skill of virginity, the burning candle of the heart, is capable of fighting against lust. Putting on the spiritual robes of the Most Pure Virgin, honouring Her through spiritual improvement and prayers.

11) The theogamic apotheosis of holy union with Christ is revealed to martyrs.

The Altar of Union is their secret element. Not only the wedding wreath, but also the Bridal Chamber awaits them. So the Templars burst into action to fulfil the inspiration of the Most High. Like brides of Christ they rushed to the spiritual palace of ineffable beauty, where the most perfect happiness is to be found.

12) To obey the beloved father (the most important). Obedience of the brethren: 'My heart belongs to another.'

13) The art of fighting.

14) The art of management and subordination.

15) The secret of understanding the Most High and one's neighbour.

The keepers of the mystery and the Keepers of the Grail... However, the chosen one and the chief guardian of the Grail lay with two weights tied to his legs with the pale face of a martyr, turned towards Heaven. The Roman vulture found Claude's fortune; infinite treasures.

*

The evil villain, Yvon Querbenès wanted to find himself a Virgin Bride.

Is that so surprising? The devil himself wanted to take the Bride of God; the purest of the pure! It is customary to say that Christ is the Bridegroom of the Church. The wisdom of the Grail tells of how Yvon Querbenès hunted down the Church, the Immaculate Virgin. Untroubled by his conscience, and not even finding any comfort in drinking wine, Yvon travelled around the neighbouring castles looking for a bride for himself, until he eventually heard about the only daughter of a rich knight who lived nearby.

Clothilde (that was her name) was terrified. How could she marry this Mephistopheles who brought fear everywhere he went? 'Father', she said, 'you want to hand me over into the clutches of a dragon, like a sacrifice. Have mercy on me! I do not want to marry!'

'Clothilde yearns to devote herself to the Most High. Any day now she will go away to the convent', her father responded to the matchmakers.

'What?!' screamed Yvon. 'How dare she refuse me? I will give you three days to change your mind!'

The legend says that the Most Pure Maiden Herself then came out from behind an icon and stood in front of him. Yvon was struck dumb with rapture. On hearing her refusal, though, he laughed wickedly.

A few days later he came with his armed men, tied up

Clothilde's father and tortured him and his servants to death. He ordered the castle to be set on fire from all four sides.

Clothilde was not there. The villain could not find where she was hidden.

*

Clothilde, the third character in the legend, is the Church of Christ. A kind abbess harboured her. Querbenès began to plot against her. He convinced his friend, Olivier, that both nuns (Clothilde and the abbess) were taking part in a conspiracy against Brittany on behalf of king Maximillian of Austria, and so he requested permission to have them arrested and tortured.

The old abbess was subjected to brutal interrogation on the rack. The villain, who was distracted by the vision of his bride's beauty, forgot to give the order to cease the torture and so she died in the most terrible suffering.

The abbess represents the patriarchal order of the old church. The great images of this were destroyed by the Inquisition, which was only interested in terror, blood, evil deeds and persecution, suspecting and hating all. The old woman represents the elders of the church and its patriarchal customs. They no longer have a place in the church. When the Inquisition came to power, these holy people fled into the wilderness.

Clothilde agreed to marry the evil villain (in 4th century Christianity the church was run by the state). She did so in spite of the fact that Querbenès had killed her father, tortured to death the abbess, whom she loved, ruined her fate, crucified Christ, to whom she wanted to dedicate herself as an Eternal Bride, murdered the servants who were dear to her, as well as her closest friends and her mother, and burned down the family home where Clothilde had spent her childhood!.. How many more threats and how much more blackmail would the evil baron have been prepared to carry out to persuade her to marry him?

The marriage was such that, after a year spent with him, Clothilde had not once smiled at him, not uttered a word and not even glanced in his direction. She humbly bore her cross until she died shortly after childbirth, when she smiled for the only time, saying, 'One life has come in exchange for another.' This single smile, though, was directed not at her evil husband, Querbenès, but to her daughter, Clothilde the Second.

Clothilde died of a broken heart: having been handed over to the State, the church had died, while another was already being born.

Clothilde II possessed the spirit of her mother. She was under the power of her inquisitor-father, though.

'Here, the saints are silent', the Apocalypse says of the two Clothildes, the two churches – the True Church and the false church. The attitude of the true Church to the Inquisition is that She did not utter a single word and did not look up, however much the latter tried to grab it and take the recognition for its services before the Most High. The age-old, eternal thief stole the services of holy people, stole the Chalice, stole the liturgy and stole the presence of Christ in the Grail.

Rome is a vulgar, cheap version of the Grail. The Templars were aware of this and guarded their temple in the knowledge that the hour will come when there will be a new, Shining Eternal Temple, when Christ comes to reign in His Kingdom and they will die for this golden Temple, ascending to the Altar of Union like fiery brides of Christ.

*

Following the death of his wife, Yvon tore around the castle, blasphemed and banged his head against the wall. It was too late! Did he feel the need to repent after such a shock? Not at all. Yvon became even more sullen. So it was on the inside of the Inquisition. That was how the Grail saw things through the eyes of the Most High.

Now the sadist turned his sinister attention to his daughter. He saw in her the perfect likeness of her mother. Yvon wanted her to remain pure. He wanted to share his heart with her and to make her see him as a kind and loving father. Clothilde II should not know anything of malice, execution, torture, dungeons, wailing day after day or any other kind of terror. She should grow up in innocence like a young Buddha in the castle of his rich father.

However, Clothilde II (monastic asceticism) was the child of Clothilde the First (the Church had lost its senses out of despair, not love, having entered a marriage with the monarchy and left behind the heart of Christ). Clothilde, sees her father through her mother's eyes – with terror and repulsion.

The Grail shows the paradox of this church, which is a source of bewilderment for angels and demons. Who are these Roman politicians and inquisitors? They believe in and love God and they are prepared to die for Him. At the same time they hate Him and crucify Him. There is no simple way to describe them. They can be called neither friends nor enemies; neither admirers nor inspirers. The Most High, in His purity, gave the commandments to those who love Him and those who hate Him. Those who hate Him will be punished for four generations. Those who love Him, He told Moses, will be shown His love for a thousand generations. Here, though, were those who both loved and hated simultaneously! He worshipped his daughter and watched her like a hawk guarding its prey, never removing his Mephistophelean gaze so that she would never find out the truth about who her father really was.

However, Clothilde I passed her spirit on to her daughter. The daughter was not only the very image of her mother on the outside, but also in terms of her character. She is just as pure and wonderful.

Yvon was losing his mind. He had almost fallen in love with his daughter. He was ready to sacrifice everything for her, but he hated her and was plotting against her. He was ready to torture her in the dungeon of his own castle because she responded to his tenderness with coldness and repulsion, saying, 'Where is my mother? And where is my uncle (Claude)?'

'Where did the little bitch find out about her mother? Who told her the secret?' The Breton villain ground his teeth and tore his clothes in frustration at not having found a solution. This paradox of love and hatred, and murder out of love is described by the Grail in the legends of the Roman Villain.

*

...A new character appears in the legend – Louis Lereine. As well as his murdered brother (the sacrificed holy lambs, the spiritually aborted church, the persecuted *anointed* ones), Yvon also had a defenceless sister. Stripped of all her rights and her fortune, and essentially imprisoned in her own home by her brother, she maintained a wonderfully innocent view of the Grail and did not even notice her brother's evil nature.

The sister of the evil villain represented an innocent guiding light; the virginal Grail.

From her ever innocent viewpoint she did not believe the rumours about her brother's outrages. She literally worshipped him and was raising an heir for him – her son Louis (a Knight of the Grail).

Yvon had no male heirs and, on his sister's advice, he wanted to pass his estate on to Louis Lereine. But this was not to be. Clothilde was in love with her cousin, and Yvon, who watched them constantly, overheard the following conversation:

'My dear brother, you must leave this place! Leave as quickly as you can! You do not know my father. This evil villain murdered my mother, my uncle and my aunt. He has disposed of all who were close to her. My mother was wonderful, like the Most Pure Virgin, but she died of a broken heart and in suffering. I hate my father, but I do not know what to do. I am afraid of him. The doors of the castle are kept locked and I know that, if I try to escape, I will be caught and subjected to brutal torture. My unfortunate father will stand over me and torment me all the more because he loves me ineffably.'

In the eyes of the evil Inquisitor, the Church wants to marry

Christ! Ascetics are inclined to drink from the Grail Chalice. Clothilde II wanted to marry Louis Lereine.

Yvon's sodomite instinct doubled the evil and treachery within him. The next day he fixed a date for the wedding. However, the wedding would never take place: Yvon wanted to deal his daughter a fatal blow.

Everything was ready. The table was set, the guests had been invited and the bride was dressed in white and ready for the ceremony. But where was the groom? He was not there. He had disappeared without trace.

Louis Lereine, bridegroom of the Church and Knight of the Grail, had been torn to pieces by a dragon. According to the wedding song of the Grail, the pieces were incompatible. The knight's quest was to kill the dragon. The dragon's triumph was to kill the Knight. Who was to kill whom?

This time the army of the Templars was driven away. Louis Lereine (prototype keeper of the Grail) was found dead. His bloody body was stretched out on the floor of the castle, staring up into the sky.

Clothilde had a shock from which she could not recover. Like Shakespeare's Ophelia, she went mad and started sleepwalking. At night she crept into the empty rooms of the castle and blindly sought her beloved. 'Where is he? Where is my sweetheart? Come, my beloved, and comfort me.' She talked with Louis for hours at a time, refusing to believe that her intended was no more. No, the wedding did take place! – so she believed. They were happy and her husband would return shortly. She could already hear the hooves of the horses in his retinue and proclaimed her joy at his arrival. She was ready to order the servants to get out the best wine... But, as before, he was not there. What is it? What is it?

Over the years, the incarcerated Clothilde turned into a grey-haired, senile old woman. The inhabitants of the surrounding villages recall the terrible moaning and wailing which used to come from the castle dungeon, until finally there resounded one terrible, despairing cry of anguish, encompassing all one hundred thousand cries of anguish from the Second Solovki. When Yvon's servants entered, they discovered the blood-covered body of Louis. What had become of his mother, the sister of the evil villain? No-one ever speaks of her.

*

The 'Bloody Baron' vanished. He disappeared from the memory of subsequent generations. His castle became overgrown, deserted, wild, forbidding and sinister. At night, many ghosts wander the halls and the gloomy dungeon, filling them with the groans of innocent victims, as if they had never left. The Grail teaches that the atmosphere of Roman Churches is like this.

The walls of the castle of Querbenès contain an unsolved mystery. According to the legend, Yvon left some treasure in the walls of the castle – this treasure is the mysterious Church, the Divinity of the Grail and the true Christ. It is guarded, though, by the ghost of a woman who sometimes appears in the castle.

The nature of this treasure is revealed by the wondrous legend of the Grail. This treasure is Claude, risen from his martyr's death at the hands of the Inquisition; the church of the saints.

...Fifty years went by. On the feast day of John (because this is the Church of John, not Peter), the area witnessed a terrible storm, the likes of which no-one had ever seen. Lightning struck the castle and it burned to the ground, as if it had been set alight on all four sides. When the fire eventually died down, the inhabitants of the surrounding villages noticed a great fissure in the wall. 'The treasure! The treasure!' suddenly declared one bold person. Hardly able to contain his excitement, he began to pull the wall down. Imagine his surprise when he reached the hiding place deep down and saw a fine, young, perfectly preserved Knight, who appeared to be in a deep sleep. His face remained divinely young and fragrant.

The relics! The myrrh-scented relics! The sweet aroma of the Kingdom emanated from him and a fragrant, bright red rose was lying on his breast, which had lost hardly any of its colour.

The fragrant red rose is the immortality of the Grail, the triumph and the glory of the approaching Grail and the treasure of the Grail.

But, what was this? A cry suddenly rang out. The crowd parted and a mad old woman came into view. They were quite afraid of her: the local people thought her to be a witch. What did this grey-haired, ugly old crone want? What was the meaning of this terrible, heart-piercing cry?

As she approached the Knight, the old woman exclaimed, 'Oh, my Louis, my sweetest Louis! At last I have found you, my betrothed! I have found you on the feast day of John, which was the day set for our marriage! For fifty years I have waited for you and now I have found you, perfect and fragrant. The Most High has anointed you for our nuptials. How fragrant you are, my beloved betrothed! You are eternally young!'

It was Clothilde, daughter of the Bloody Baron.

Suddenly, veiled in Light, she raised her eyes heavenward in ecstasy, fell silent and dropped to the ground, her arms outstretched.

Finally Clothilde was united forever, and had found her eternal rest. Their beautiful bodies were placed in the small church to accompaniment of the triumphant strains of the organ and they were both laid to rest in some humble village cemetery. It is said that, in the coffin, Clothilde's body regained its youth and she was just as beautiful as her betrothed. All signs of age had vanished and the memory of the evil villain and his castle faded away.

During the funeral a mysterious star shone in the sky. It shines especially brightly on the feast of John. It is the new star of Bethlehem – the perfect Church of the Grail, which, through the image of Clothilde and Louis, foreordains the union of Christ and Mary, the Wedding Feast of Christ and His Bride – the Church, the Virgin of the Grail.

Over the thick heather, which covers the wedding tomb,

hover fireflies – divine souls, burning with love for Christ. The world around breathes in the silence and the sweetest strains of music are carried along, as if the eternal wedding is still taking place in Heaven.

08.06.2005 Deris Island

❧

The Gates of Aten-Ra

OF THE INNER SUN AND THE WINDOWS TO THE SOUL

The Egyptian soothsayer and Pharaoh Akhenaton (14th century BC) reformed the Egyptian pantheon. Having abolished polytheism and Amon-Ra (the superior of all the sun deities) he established the cult of Aten, the manifest, visible sun. He composed songs to him and called him the universal and most high Divinity...

Heathen (in Judeo-Christian terms) Egypt at the time of the blessed and spiritually inspired martyr-reformer, Akhenaton, comprehended monotheism more deeply than Israel during the time of Moses!

Akhenaton was not understood by his contemporaries, let alone the generations which followed. Having built a marvellous city of the sun and changed his name from Amenhotep IV to Akhen-Aton (servant of the Most High), this Egyptian ruling Pharaoh, Divinity incarnate on the throne, was millennia ahead of his time and a prophet of the Divine Civilization.

Researchers studying only the superficial aspects interpreted the switch from Amon-Ra to Aten-Ra (from the 'outer sun' to the manifest and visible Sun) as a move from polytheism to monotheism or religious reform. Akhenaton was mysteriously enlightened by the Most High. The king of 'Divine Mercy', as they said in Holy Rus', understood monotheism to be like the Inner Sun – like the gift of supreme love. Queen Nefertiti, his beautiful wife, shared the views of her husband. The sun of Love, which does not set, burned in her heart.

The one God of the Egyptian Pharoah's theology (unlike

that of Moses, the Jewish reformer) was not a lawgiver, declaring statutes and commandments and leading the people, but rather an Inner Sun, an Undying Divinity of the inner self, and a secret altar. Aten-Ra surpassed the other deities by virtue of the strength of his unprecedented love. He reigned alone because he captivated the mind of the religious poet and Pharaoh, Akhenaton.

*

Researchers cite the naturalistic verse and mystical odes which Akhenaton composed in honour of Aten-Ra. Egypt attracts inquisitive and brilliant minds, such as Vasili Rosanov and Dmitri Merezhkovsky... However no-one can understand the Divinity of Divinities, the Most High and the Universal All-Powerful, who is like an inner sun which never sets. They lacked a virginal mind, virginal ecstasy, virginal reasoning and enlightenment of the mind, or the state of being in virginal love which goes with them. European consciousness is tangled up in rationalism, aristotelianism, Greco-Roman culture and philosophical fiction. There is no question of a global inner transformation on the part of mystic writers.

Is this really surprising, though? *Startsy*[6] remain somewhere at the distance in seclusion, but how much can you learn from such stagnant, static people, like Metropolitan Sergius Stagorodski, the bookish theologian?

*

The great Akhenaten despised world pharisaism, such as complex funereal rituals, magic and mummification. He would have replaced the mystical concept of combining 'Ba' and 'Ka' with more *yurodivy* ways. He allowed himself to be portrayed as rather plump, with a double chin. He was a highly religious man who did not want to be worshipped as a deity. Akhenaten regarded himself as a divinely inspired prophet of the Sun, spreading a new, true religion, and as high priest of a faith in a Universal Deity.

---

[6] Elders from the deep-rooted tradition of Russian or Orthodox, spiritual mentors.

Akhenaten brought about a revolution in the consciousness of the Egyptians. His predecessors, together with the Egyptian (and Jerusalem) priests, believed that only they came from God and that all others were 'sons of the devil'. Akhenaten arrived at the belief that God embraces the whole of creation with his love, and there is one God over all.

'All eyes look to You, Divine Aten! But in the whole world only Akhenaten has understood and recognised You.' For Akhenaten, Aten was the universal God of the world. The Pharaoh was His chosen one (his beloved son).

Without the Sun all life will die. When He rises everything comes to life. 'When You disappear the earth is enveloped in pitch darkness. One eye cannot see the other, and men sleep in the burial vault with their heads wrapped up: dead. If a valuable possession were stolen from under their heads they would not notice.'

Here and everywhere else Akhenaten teaches about the Inner Sun. If it is not released into a person's secret source, then counter-forces will begin to grow within it.

Akhenaten liked to be portrayed as ugly. He bestowed the image of his wife, Nefertiti, and that of his daughters, on the new schools which he had set up. His expressionless figure, his large belly and his protruding jaw were often caricatured. Akhenaten smiled gently: they could do what they liked but without the vulgar pomposity or that old fetish of the double crown of Both Lands, which his ancestors had worn since ancient times. Akhenaten begged the architects, who had built his City of lovers, to ignore the dead clichés and canons of the old school and 'strive for the truth'.

No-one understood his genius. He acceded to the throne at 15. He reigned for 18 years. In the latter years, though, he did not appear in public and nothing is known about how he spent his time. My friends, more than just the indescribable sun of the Highest One entered the heart of this Pharaoh, the architect of the City of the beloved! This Sun burned in him so much that he could no longer think about anyone or anything. Being in blissful enlightment of his spirit he communicated with Queen Nefertiti and his daughters through thought. Soon, though, he withdrew completely.

The Inner Sun did not leave him. It went around with him and served as a divine mirror. In it Akhenaten could see the reflection of his dearest protector, Aten (the Divinity of the Inner temple).

*

Thebes, Akhetaten, the gigantic colonnades of the sanctuaries of Karnak and Luxor, the construction of an irrigation system in the Nile valley and the erection of a temple in honour of the God of the Inner Sun... Akhenaten created a temple of comparable proportions to the one in Jerusalem. The Temple of the Sun Deity is 800 m long and 300 m wide.

The mystical architectonics of the temple are even superior to the mysticism of King Solomon and depict the hierarchy of the celestial spheres. It is impossible to enter the Inner Chambers without the illumination of the Inner Sun. How does this come about? Through the mystery of initiation. Through the lighting of Divine Love, through selection and the inspiration of the spirit.

The priests hated Akhenaten because he rejected their magic and endless rituals, their funereal religion with the ancestral cult, their venality and corruption. The priests' hearts were closed and Akhenaten did not desist from denouncing them because they only understood Aten-Ra superficially as the 'apparent sun'.

'It is not about the luminary which lights up the Earth, but about an inner sun!' he reminded the priests. They did not hear him, though. So, the mystical enshrouding of the poet-reformer, the reigning Pharaoh, the lamb of the Most High on the throne, who was sacrificed by the priests, rather like Christ, at 32 years old, was seen as a 'exchangeable component' in the Egyptian theocratic system.

The Divine Hierarchy was changing! Amon-Ra and the other 'deities' were replaced by Aten-Ra, a usurper and a despot (to the heathen priests the One Divinity was synonymous with an authoritarian despot and failure to recognise the qualities of the other 'deities')!

Akhenaton was slain like a sacrificial victim and he was said to have sadistic tendencies – he who was the kindest of angels, whose heart shone like a celestial light for the Wise Virgin. They called him a 'great tyrant' and a schemer, who had defiled the memory of his ancestors, and said he had destroyed Egypt. The richest empire in the world at the time of Akhenaton, was essentially crumbling.

*

The divine prophet, high priest (here is where the ideal of universal theocracy came to fruition – not in Israel, but in Egypt!) was so absorbed in the mysterious incandescence of the Inner Sun, that he wanted to enlighten all his faithful followers. At night he walked about like a shadow, burst into houses and lit candles. People thought he was a madman and chased him away. Finally, at the age of 32, he died at the hands of those close to him; hated and cursed by the priests.

The Pharisees did all they could to erase his memory from the face of the earth. Such was the malice of the priests towards the Pharaoh-messiah that they incited his brothers-in-law, Tutenkhamen, Smenkhkare and Ay to remove from the face of the earth the city of the beloved, Akhetaten (Horizon of the Inner Sun) which had been built by Akhenaten. The name of Akhenaten became a curse. Images of him were smashed to pieces and his burial pyramid was defiled. Thus began the end of the messianic dynasty.

The grace of the Holy Spirit had shone in Egypt for a short while and Shekhina, the Holy Being, had gone somewhere else. It had gone to the temple of Jerusalem, built three centuries later by Solomon and which was a likeness of Akhenaten's sun temple. It wandered through the darkness of world history until a great new eternal sun, the size of half the sky, burned in the heavens over the Second Solovki and set alight the hearts of millions.

This is where, on the archipelago in the White Sea, the ideal of the prophet and messiah was realised, the Pharaoh of the greatest power, the lone sacrificial lamb, Amenhotep IV, Akhenaten and 'servant dog of the Most High', as he referred to himself in his writings and his epistles to his people!

*

Akhenaton, divine messiah and Egyptian, could say of himself the same as Christ: 'As the Father knows me and I know the Father, in the same way I know my sheep and they know me. And I am willing to die for them.' (Jn 10:15). This shows the other image of the Most High: the loving Father, sacrificing himself for love. This is the image which remains after sweeping away royal titles, magical ceremonies, mummification rituals and the secrets associated with them, lengthy funeral services, and the boasting of priests ('the others are sons of the devil and cursed by our deities').

What is this Love which sacrifices itself? The Father is the celestial Inner Sun. The heart of Aten-Ra, the Heavenly Father, is the Royal Lamp, Supreme Love. Here it is; the altar of the approaching sun-filled Divine Civilization of Supreme Love!

The gates of Aten-Ra (the inner sun and the shining eye) are marked by today's ceremonial priesthood. However, the Most High and the Great Wisdom never tire of sending Their Akhenatens, Moses, Orpheus and Dionysus. The divine singers essentially sing one and the same song.

The old styles of religion (forceful-parochial and authoritarian-fanatical, built on slavish fear by a heathen generation) have been abolished. Two images are apparent from world history: a divinity, such as the loving Father, and a devil, like the Evil, Vindictive One, who erases from the face of the earth, he-who-is-not. It is the Divinity 'who-is-not', the person 'who-is-not' and the world 'which-is-not'. I, too, am subject to the same internal elimination, annihilation and being consigned to oblivion.

However, He Who is mysteriously revealed and secretly reveals a person's Divine Origin, uncovering one after another the twelve inner gates and entering the Light of the Inner Sun. And so the lamp of a Virgin Bride is lit. At midnight she rises up and joins in the nocturnal procession of all humanity.

18.06.2005 Deris Island

❧

Orpheus, or the Strength of being in Virginal Love

Oh profound virginal love! The greatest key to deification (Theosis), the key to *divine union*!

The one attribute shared by Hermes Trismegistus, the apollonian-dionysian principle, Orpheus, Pythagoras, Moses, Zarathustra, Christ, and prophets and anointed ones of all eras, is that they were in indescribable love, which is greater than that of ordinary mortals.

Profound virginal love keeps the peace amongst the deities of Olympia. The Egyptian and Greek (Eleusinian) mysteries and even the dionysian-bacchic dances performed by women to the great deity, display a thirst to find an outlet for the particles of unity with the Divinity. It was revealed to Moses, as if for the first time, and placed in the ark. It contains the essence of all existence, the origin of all origins.

Every civilization has its own ark, and, in it, is a vessel containing manna (crystallised myrrh), a tablet, writings from on high of two parties who love each other (divinities and mortals, the Most High and man) and a miraculous flowering staff (the rose of resurrection and eternal life).

*

Orpheus was a divine singer from Thrace in the Achaean epoch, and son of the sweet-voiced muse, Calliope, and the god Apollo.

What is the mystery of the lyre of Orpheus? Why did it charm the evil three-headed guard dog, Cerberus? Why did the monsters of hell and the fierce old witches, with tangled snakes instead of hair, become calm and pay heed to the lyre of Orpheus?

Orpheus is a messenger of the Most High and anointed one of the Bridal Chamber. Orpheus brought the religion of the Kingdom into the world. It is the one Gospel of all time, or the true news.

There was nothing messianic, redemptive or relating to the restoration of Israel in the religion of Christ. Mohammed was one hundred percent correct when he spoke of the Revelation given to him by the Archangel Gabriel, the divine herald of all world religions who revealed the truth about the Most High, bestowing heavenly love through Immaculate Conception: 'The news of Christ is different to that laid down in the Gospels! It is misinterpreted and distorted!'

Let us return from Christ back to Orpheus. He was a divine singer, prophet of the fates, musician with a divine gift, priest of Melchizedek and twice born. He was a singer of the radiant 'protogonos' (a perfect Adam) and the Seraphite who cannot fall. Having no connection with the coldness of fallen creation Orpheus is filled with the aroma of supreme love. The music of the Kingdom and perfect peace resound in his harmonious vibrations and perfect peace.

The mystery of Orpheus is that he was perpetually in profound love. This profound love creates wonders. Orpheus is madly in love with Eurydice, his virginal wife. He literally worships her and sees in her the face of divine virginity, intercession, and the purity of the Christian Virgin Mary.

Orpheus comes from the ancient Hebrew 'or', meaning 'light'. He is the radiant light of the Kingdom.

Eurydice dies after being bitten by a snake in the forest and descends into Persephone's kingdom of shadows. However, Orpheus loves her so much that he transcends the boundaries of life, death, finding and loss. His joy and his sorrow are combined in one eternal holy passion in the hymn of Divine Love.

Orpheus sings the hymn of praise and, in so doing, he desperately pours out his grief over his Divine Beloved. He accomplishes unheard of paradoxical feats by descending into Hades, and calming the wild dogs and the vicious Erinyes. The guardians of Hades are dogs with massive jaws and would tear anyone to pieces, yet he manages to calm them. A miracle!

What makes the influence of the lyre of Orpheus so strong? The singer of the Most High knew the secret which was revealed to the *anointed* one of the Divine Bosom (the eternal bosom, like chronos or the dwelling place of the Supreme Being, is one of the basic principles of Orphism). The evil in the world has arisen out of a lack of love which, in turn, has come from a fatal mistake on the part of the first man: his rejection of the cross, the Tree of Life. It was in Adam's nature to fall, as his refusal to partake of the cross (the Tree of Life) reflected his inability to experience holy passion due to his coldness of heart.

Orpheus does the opposite. Like all the prophets from Hesiod to Bahá'u'lláh he takes the cross as the universe of Divine Wisdom. He enters the state of holy passion and burns with love. Then, with the help of the burning candle, he enters Hell's caves of precepts.

The evil dogs, oh how they suffer! They do not know supreme love. The terrifying Erinyes (even the demons from the lowest spheres of the underworld shun them) pacified the heavenly love as if they had once been deprived of it. Hell is set in motion. The reflected sphere of Adam's fall is man's universal renunciation of the cross and therefore of the Altar of Union and supreme love. With it, Orpheus conquered the underworld. So, having essentially abolished hell, i.e. put an end to the torments of hell and led Christ into the world of the Greek Hades, the singer has achieved the impossible. Like Christ, he has led Eurydice out of the underworld.

Not one mortal has ever returned from there. It is unheard of! He was let in as a messenger, and not as a convicted slave. They received him as an envoy from Heaven. Nobody objected even though the Olympian deities and the angels of the Most High had forbidden anyone to go down into the realms of the underworld. He succeeded in doing what no other mortal had done: to pacify the evil of hell. He had established peace in the universe.

This meant little to Orpheus, though. He was interested in the heights of supreme love and conquering not only death or fear and sickness, but also hell itself, the ultimate enemy. It could be conquered by taming the malicious evil of hell's pincers, jaws, braziers and other tools of torture. So Orpheus sought to bring Eurydice out of hell, he was in profound, abundant love, leading her with this love.

He was stopped. His heart ceased beating. He was tempted. Orpheus fought with only his profound love. It surpassed all norms, judgements, laws, balance of fate, and preordained destiny. It triumphed over the material world and would return him to the house of the Most High on one condition: he must agree not to look back, meaning he must forget about original sin.

Eurydice rushed after Orpheus, but the shadows of hell pursued her. They played on her conscience. Hell has a terrifyingly strong attraction. Those who dwell there would like to leave that rotten egg and foetid pool full of soul-devouring bacteria. Here, too is the mystery of Orphism, which is always very similar to Christianity: souls go to Hell of their own free will. Eurydice was won over by the lyre of Orpheus, just like the Erinyes. Greater than the other inhabitants or the sentries of the underworld, she was able to hearken to her husband's music. She had grown accustomed to his divine harmonies. But even she was somehow attracted by the darkness of sin. Eurydice began to be afraid. She was tormented by doubts. She was uncomfortable with the thought of seeing the Light and world of the Most High again. The inmates of the underworld remained in Hell only because they themselves wanted to. In their own evil way they had adapted to the bad egg of the cosmos.

Eurydice began to resist. She pulled her husband back. She appealed to his conscience. She did not understand why and where he was taking her. She was afraid she would perish. Now she was being torn apart by the sharp teeth of the evil old hags. The Mother of Persephone wept for her.

'What are you doing with me? Look at me. Talk with me. Where is your love?' cried Eurydice to Orpheus. 'You love everyone except me. Where are you dragging me off to? Why are you disobeying the will of the Most High? Didn't the Divinity you sing about allow me to be bitten by a venomous snake in the forest and descend into the kingdom of shadows? Leave me alone, you lawbreaker, you betrayer of the faith of your fathers!'

Orpheus was forbidden to enter into a dialogue with his wife. This was one of the conditions imposed on him by Hades, the lord of the underworld. He must not turn around and enter into conversation with Eurydice. Again and again Orpheus tried to entice his beloved away, and his heart was filled with the most supreme love. The flame of holy passion had never burned in such a way before. Orpheus was not simply in the fires of Hell. He was in the deepest bowels of the underworld. His beloved was driving him into the very depths of hell. She tormented his heart, dealing him fatal blows and reproaching him for his coldness, indifference, betrayal and treachery. Orpheus could go on no longer. He was exhausted, all his strength was gone, he had lost his reason, and so he turned round to show Eurydice his torment and his face which was covered with blood from his suffering. Eurydice would understand when she saw him!

But, as soon as Orpheus turned, the shadows carried Eurydice into the abyss forever.

Oh, Orpheus! Even eternal death could not separate him from his beloved. Therefore, that is what his Mistress, profound Heavenly Love, wants. Only those who are full of lust need intercourse, foreplay etc. Virginal love knows no bounds. Death has no power over it.

Orpheus remained with his beloved. He continued to roam the earth, singing of his Eurydice wherever he went, no matter which countries he visited. His singing caught the attention of the travelling Argonauts.

However, Orpheus could not find peace anywhere. His demise was full of suffering. Orpheus returned to Thrace, the place which was dear to him, as it reminded him of Eurydice and of his youth. Here he encountered a crowd of wild bacchantes. Respectable mothers, honourable plump wives, and maidens, all intoxicated with heavenly wine, were engaging in frenzied dancing. Orpheus preached among them. He took out his lyre and sang a bacchic song of Divine Love, which made their dionysian frenzy ever more boundless. These bacchantes were searching for the same thing as the evil dogs of the underworld and the snake-haired Erinyes – supreme love. Upon hearing its voice, the bacchantes literally lost their senses and, with their frenzied dancing, having fallen in love with the Divine Orpheus, they tore him to pieces as they each wanted all of him – the king, the messenger from Heaven.

Legend says that the head of Orpheus prophesied and sang for many more years. He sang the sweetest songs of the love of the Most High.

***

Another deity of the Roman pantheon was Dionysus (in Christian terms, the personification of holy passion). The heart is the essential focus of Dionysianism. Through holy passion a person develops a divine aspect to their existence – the dionysian origin.

Dionysus (born without sin, and as the powers of fertility of the Most High), enters into a union with Demeter (earthly virginity), from whence the human world is born. Both Dionysus and Demeter dwell in the other-worldly, eternal bosom of the Divine Mother, which appears from time to time as either bright ether or the shadows of the underworld – universal chaos. According to Orphism, a person has a dual nature: a Divine Nature and that of Ben-Elohims[7], a titanic nature. In him can be found particles of burned out ash. Releasing of the Divine Origin (falling in virginal love) can occur by means of a struggle with the titanic, Ben-Elohimism (sin, lawlessness etc.). An Orphic must tirelessly struggle with the Ben-Elohimism (titanism) in his heart. His whole being must be pure. Clothing in robes of virginity is a token of the dionysian origin within him.

There is no essential difference between the peaceful Apollo and the devout Dionysus, however much European thinkers set them apart. Apollo and Dionysus are two hypostases of the same thing. Dionysus is manifest profound love, and the holy passion of falling in Divine Love beyond all realms. Apollo is the peace gained after the Deposition; higher peace. Orpheus, the son of Apollo, drinks his portion from the cup of Dionysian holy passion.

In essence, the peaceful singer found himself in a state of eternal holy passion. He had to fight monsters, visit hell, drag a mortal soul out of there, and break all the laws of the universe. Finally, that last mystery, which surpasses all Hellenic mysteries, is the unprecedented dance of life and death. The Bacchantes, hungry for Supreme Love, met him and found perpetual consolation. The fire of being in heavenly love enabled them to be freed from themselves in ecstasy and they tore Orpheus to pieces. His immortal bodies were transformed into a sun. Orpheus the sun emerges from his tomb like a bridegroom singing the next Greek love songs and ballads to the Heavenly Olympus.

17-19.06.2005 Deris Island

---

[7] Ancient Hebrew: 'sons of God' – dark spirits (archons) who rebelled against the Heavenly Father of Pure Love (Genesis 6: 1-2,4).

The Flying Dutchman,

or the Truth about Catholics

The 'Flying Dutchman' is one of the allegories of the medieval Grail. It tells the terrible truth about a female raider, thief, murderess and bandit.

Cut-throats and scoundrels. There is no place for them on earth. Who are they? They are the work of satanic humanity: young snakes hatching from their eggs. Clouds of vampires swarm over their churches. The Canterbury Ghosts fly over their cathedrals and over ever wide open crypt doors.

The allegories of the Grail cite a sealed, profound meaning. On interpreting them, like the parables from the Gospel of Christ, you discover the great mysteries of the Heavenly Kingdom and, at the same time, those who disgrace and slander these inner mysteries.

***

This is a sorry caricature of the Kingdom... It is a gang of cut-throats, hypocrites and mummies. Is it worth counting the curses directed at the Roman hag – this whore, who sat on a 2000-dollar seat, sponsored by American millionaires, until the third millennium?

What is this? This truth can drive you mad!

The Grail spoke of her allegorically, not out of fear. The Templars were not afraid of anything. They could annihilate the Roman Church by direct confrontation one to ten thousand. The keepers of the Grail, armed with the sword of David and the Holy Lance, and with the army of the Archangel Michael behind them, were indefatigable and well protected. The Queen of Heaven called them up to join the army of the Immaculate, Unblemished one, which means that they cannot be defeated by the devil. However evil or deep the wailing of Beelzebub may be, he has not fired a shot or threatened inquisitorial punishment or annihilation. He could not do anything without the tragic face of the Grail and the spots of the blood of the Lamb upon it.

Two great Knights, who received communion from the Chalice after a three hundred year quest, died of bliss...

The Grail, the Chalice of Christ, proposes a responsive Grail. The communicant dies for Christ. The Last Drop of the Blood of Christ, which is hottest after his words, 'Father, it is consummated!', is enriched by the dying drops shed by the Knights Hospitaller, the Knights Templar, the Waldensians, the Albigensians, the Knights of Malta, the holy saints and those who were simply tortured and killed, burned or quartered.

When drops of blood appear on the canvas of the Grail the virginal lambs and warrior maidens are called up to take part in the atonement (in the language of the Grail it is the reparation; the return of the responsive Eucharist). Within the Grail, the fifty-year-old vampires, who come to church on Sundays to partake in the Eucharist but then return to their former way of life, are said to be on a 'childish' level, or suffering from a sickness. The Saviour generously feeds people with his own Flesh and Blood, thus enriching the composition of the inner person and triggering metanoic changes and the deepest metamorphosis of our inner being, for the express purpose of enabling Christ to be born within us and realise His plans. He sacrificed Himself out of love for humankind.

The Templars, fulfilled by that same responsive Eucharist of the dual Grail, became indefatigable in battle and brought terror to bear on the Saracens, the heathens and the enemies of the temple of Jerusalem. They went into battle and were victorious, fighting a hundred to one, with the familiar countenance of the holy Archangel Michael, and with rapt, heavenly expressions on their faces. In their hands an ordinary sword was transformed into the sword of the Grail.

The Grail, similar to an ordinary silver goblet, was filled with the Myrrh Blood of Christ at the round table during the mystical meal of the anointed brethren. It came like a king to Solovki and anointed the last Russian Tsar, *Mikhail Romanov II*, as keeper of the Grail. The transformed, radiant Russian Grail held the blood of the five million virginal lambs of the Solovki archipelago.

Oh, holy Chalice, lifted up by the priests of Melchizedek! Oh, immortal wine of resurrection! Through His Flesh and Blood Christ is multiplied and has made His mark on the now completed Divine Civilization.

***

Like the other Grail legends, this one, too, is concealed from the outside. Imagine the reaction of the owner of an original Reubens, Da Vinci or Matisse upon encountering a forgery: 'cheap rubbish!'

This is precisely the attitude of the Royal Dynasty of the Grail towards the Roman Curia. In Rome, Christ is crucified every day. These are duplicates of a carefully concealed original. It is a counterfeit Christ. They are false apostles. It amounts to a defamation of the holy ones. It is a feigned succession.

In the castles of the Grail is the Holy Being and its sweetest of music. With the Roman vandals, all is pretence. They believe that the Blood of Christ was spilled onto the sand and not collected in the Grail. They have kept the Cross of Golgotha which disappeared and was recovered in the 4th century. However, the Blood was collected and is preserved to this day, with the mysterious power of the transubstantiation in the silver goblets of the Knights of the holy army. From that time onwards faith, prayer, icons, and the souls which they had misled, deluded and intercepted, spilled onto the sand. They were washed from the face of the earth. They were covered up with sand and stagnant mould. Their memory was erased over the generations...

***

Oh, Henri Herrmacher (lit. 'Churchmaker'), victim of St. Bartholomew's night (August 1572)! He was the maker of the Church. The mystery of the Church.

After witnessing the murder of his family who were stabbed to death over a period of several minutes during the St. Bartholomew's day massacre, Henri, his young daughter and a servant miraculously managed to escape within the castle of the French king, Henri Navarre. Like Seraphim the Tender the traumatised Herrmacher received the Solovki gift of hearing: he could hear the death cries of his wife and blood-covered children. 'Mo!.. (ther of the Most High) Fa!..(ther).' These cries of anguish of the cross were imprinted forever on his heart. For weeks afterwards he could not hold the protestant Bible in his hand. Its pages appeared to be stained with blood. There were spots of blood in Deuteronomy, Isaiah, and Mark and each spot seemed to bear the faces of his martyred family. His dear wife, his precious children... They had not gone away. They remained with the zealous Huguenot.

Herrmacher locked himself away in his castle and cursed Roman Catholicism day and night.

His prayers were heard. The Most High always hears the prayers of anonymous lambs, like dumb fish on land who can only silently open and close their gills...

Marie, the Huguenot's daughter, was brought up in the protestant tradition. Over the years, though, the Huguenots themselves developed hatred towards the Catholics. The unfortunate man's daughter fell in love with a Dutchman called Peter (the church of Peter).

When he saw the young man, the father, without uttering a word, seized him by the collar and threw him out of his castle. But their love turned out to be stronger than that. Marie married Peter the Catholic in secret. The grief-stricken Henri cursed her together with the whole of the Catholic Church.

'From now on all her members will be cursed! My daughter, her husband, their fate and their destiny shall be cursed forever until they are forgiven by my martyred wife and children in Heaven. Most High One, I summon your retribution!' Henri continued to pray during his all-night vigils. It did show itself to him: at midnight, newly murdered martyrs came to him. In the same way, during the time of the red GULAG Seraphim the Tender was surrounded by thousands of murdered, downtrodden, enraged souls. The Solovki Tsar blessed them with a different destiny and then these potential demons were transformed into peaceful angels who blessed the world and were honoured as martyrs.

According to the legend, the couple found themselves on a Dutch vessel. There is nothing more to understand beyond this. The ship hit a reef. One of the crew members survived and constantly repeated one phrase, 'The cursed couple! The cursed couple!.. The father put his curse on them and it is all their fault. The disaster is on their consciences. We tried to set them down on the shore. The sailors insisted that we should throw them overboard when the storm came. It was no good. It was too late!..'

Henri was horrified by the news of the Dutch shipwreck and set out in search of his daughter. He was prepared to remove his curse and forgive her husband, Peter.

It was in vain. The Breton Henri Herrmacher saw how, at the moment the ship was lost during the storm with menacing clouds, bolts of lightning, a terrible howling wind, and crashing waves, it disappeared in the dark sky somewhere into the abyss. Afterwards it was seen ascending into Heaven and once more fading into the distance.

From that time onwards the 'Flying Dutchman' had an infamous reputation. Its passengers came to the Breton and froze to the spot as they were subjected to his magic curse. Ocean traders and passenger vessels were terror-struck when they encountered this vessel being carried along the waves, as they understood that disaster was imminent. Henri himself eventually died in mysterious circumstances.

***

The parable was never completed. The 'Flying Dutchman' is the Catholic Church (the Roman harlot), as seen by the True Church. This is the ultimate truth in this regard before the court of Heaven. There are no other instances. Judgement will be made from monks to Popes by this inexorable, supreme and ultimate instance – the ultimate truth of Divine judgement.

Hired hypnotists and Aristotelian scholars have shaped the Roman image for centuries: 'immaculate', 'holy bride', 'holy church', and so on... Belonging to it 'secures a heavenly destiny'. An indulgence (absolution of sins) 'cleanses'. It is 'directly descended from Christ, Peter the apostle, and his vicars'. The 'Eucharistic Christ' lives in priests. The 'angels walk' with Catholics...

Now, it is true, judgement is upon them. The Rabaim (ancient Hebrew) are those who hate the Most High.

'For I am the Lord thy God, a jealous God, visiting the iniquity of the fathers upon their children unto the third and fourth generation, to them that hate me.' The Protocols of the Elders of Zion prophesy that the Church will be split between those who love (the havaim, those who love Him, the *anointed* ones, saints, those who are joined with Him and those who have come down from on high) and those who are evil (the rabaim, those who hate).

Do not consider those who churn out curses like the commandments in the Torah of the rabbis ('anyone who spits on the ground whilst pronouncing the name of the Most High or utters an abusive word will be sentenced to death')! It is well known that the serpent is the most cunning of all beings under heaven (wild animals). It is two-faced. On the outside, of course, they are 'for': they intercede, they perform rites and they appear to be upright people. In secret, they are full of hatred, but the intensity of their hatred surpasses the envy of Satan and the scores of the *Ben-Elohims** against the Most High.

In the thousand or so years of its existence, the Inquisition succeeded in generating so much evil, and creating such a feeling of the underworld in the Catholic Church, that the demons from deep within the fires of hell marvelled at it: how was it possible for their ways and means of torturing unfortunate sinners to infiltrate the surface of the earth, and for it to be allowed by the Most High for the sake of their repentance?

Their religious painting of Christ 'Tendresse', sweetness itself and 'saccharin', the lamb in white clothing with rays shining from the Heart, as depicted in the painting produced from the words of the saints and visionaries, Faustina Kowalska and Luisa Piccarreta, are not blessed but cursed by the Most High. The true Christ of the Holy Being will hold them to account for each of the messengers which were sent to Him, saying to them, 'cursed murderers!' Just as aborted babies will hold their mothers and doctors to account, so too will the saints in Heaven hold the Roman doctors of theology and creators of institutional philosophy to account.

These scores to be settled are endless and terrible. The Heavenly judgement of the Catholic and Orthodox churches will last for centuries. The accounts of everyone would have to be heard, and there are billions of them, like grains of sand on the sea shore and stars in the sky...

But this will be in heaven, where there is a different kind of existence and a different kind of time. So the judgement will be cast in an instant.

What was Christ like? Erase the latest news of Him being alive! The Inquisition knows what it is doing. The slightest hint of the Holy Spirit in Christ of the Parusia is classified by them as heresy and is subject to defamation, persecution, 'liquidation' by German shepherds, batons and other cunning methods.

The more they persecute the living Christ ('The Lord is alive!' exclaimed the Jews in the time of the Most Holy Virgin Mary, and our Queen loved this exclamation, replying, 'Indeed it is so! The Saviour is among us', and smiling a smile full of wisdom, sorrow, silence and mystery), the more their Christ became unbearably sickly, worldly, false and banal after the persecution of the *Anointed* King in the face of His messengers and followers. Attractive to ignorant people. A cheap second kind of indulgence and a pathetic excuse for the sinner.

***

My Lord, my Lord! There are so many scores to settle! From those of the millions of Indians, slaughtered by the Spanish Conquistadors with the blessing of the Roman powers that be, to the Marranos (baptised Jews) and the Muslim Saracens at the hands of the crusaders. Millions of cries of anguish. Half a million Huguenots, slaughtered in just a few hours on the eve of St. Bartholomew. The fires of the Inquisition.

Those whom they have tortured will present their accounts to be settled for every day of the nearly 2000 year existence of the Roman Curia. There are accounts to be settled for the misled and the deceived, for the billions of Catholics who were promised a heavenly destiny simply for regularly receiving the host, lighting candles and kneeling with their hands clasped to their breast as they chant the rosary: 'Ave Maria Gratia Plena.' There are billions who have been deceived. Pure hearted Ethiopians, Japanese, those moved by the heroism of the 26 martyrs in Nagasaki, and Italians who have turned to the Church. The Waldensians and the Albigensians will bring their accounts to be settled. They are cursed, just as Henri Herrmacher cursed his own daughter in the legend of the Flying Dutchman.

In its true state, the Catholic Church is that very ship, full of vampires and ghosts, bringing death in its wake and sailing through the waves. It inhabits a distorting mirror looking out onto the Holy Being of the Grail: it is a fanciful being. Having rejected the authority of wisdom and a clear perception of the Most High, and having scorned the testimony of the witnesses to the revelations of the Holy Spirit throughout the history of Christianity, they have put themselves in the hands of ghosts and have become Canterbury ghosts and evil vampires.

Anyone who has any connection with them is cursed: anyone who harbours them and anyone who marries one of them like the daughter of the Huguenot with her 'Peter the Dutchman' – the church of Peter, the Catholic Church. All the misfortune of this world comes from that couple. They opened the gates of hell and a crowd of vampires massed behind them, having presented their endless scores to be settled.

One day they will all be entered on the roll call and presented to the court. When the Holy Spirit comes, He will begin the judgement over the Church. What will the Roman Harlot say then?

In the eyes of the True Church of the secret catacombs, the Roman Curia is the 'Flying Dutchman', a bewitched vessel, which, instead of sailing into the harbour of the Kingdom, drifts instead into the port of the diabolical civilization and into the Abyss. How will the 2000 year crusade against the followers of the Grail end? It will end with the triumph of the Holy Grail.

The 1000 year reign and the triumph of Christ, the King of Heaven, will begin with the carrying out of the Chalice. The Lord, having exposed the Roman Harlot, will emerge, surrounded by His glorious retinue of true saints. Thus the Universal Church will be revealed, and indeed it has already been revealed. There is a scattering of the wisdom of Melchizedek. Priests anointed with myrrh have come down from Heaven each carrying in their hands a staff of resurrection and eternal life.

***

Cursed by the whole of creation, the Roman Inquisition is heading in disgrace towards the abyss. Thus, the saints in Heaven await the time when the 'Flying Dutchman' will cease, and the Bermuda Triangle will no longer swallow up ships as they sail towards bright harbours.

23.06.2005 Deris Island

❧

The Royal Genealogy of Christ

The Mystery of the Messianic Dynasty

The Royal Genealogy of Christ

The Messianic Dynasty of the Grail

This is the most delicate and yet the most important subject. It is the Achilles heel of the Roman Marauder. This is the end of the line – there is no way out and no justification for the office of the Great Inquisitor. It is the end of the road for the Dominican order, for the portly pseudo-Franciscans, rational rats wallowing in fat, for members of the consistory, and others who pass themselves off as 'heirs', 'successors', 'vicars', or 'instruments'. They claim that 'the Holy Spirit is at work' and 'Christ is present' etc. in their sacraments (religious rites) and masses (religious services). There is nothing there except obvious deception and the raving of provincial vampires, invading crypts at night like vicious bats...

Mary Magdalene. The Slavonic version of her name from Byzantium is Magdalina: it sounds musical, like 'mandolin'. Who is she; this petite, headstrong, red-haired courtesan from Magdala, with a tendency towards violent outbursts, known for her salon and her orgies, condemned by the Pharisees and saved by Christ? 'The other Mary'; Mary filled with holy passion. She went to the Lord's tomb and, not recognising Him, thought Him to be a gardener. Beyond this lies the Grail.

Who is she?

In the legends told by the Minnesingers such as Wolfram von Eschenbach and others, she is assigned the role of the 'secret woman'. The 'Desposins' came from her. Was the virginal Christ 'romantically involved'?..

Of course, the Vatican strongly denies this, insisting on the fundamental virginity and the purity of the Saviour. Mary Magdalene remained for them a red-haired, raving harlot similar to Lady Macbeth, hiding in the shadows and going to the Lord's tomb at midnight, in a trance, to look for him.

Tibet preaches the version about normal marriage. The cosmists favour the legend of the Desposins (Royal Messianic Dynasty), the special 'Family heirs' and the Dynasty of glorious, invincible Knights, including Galahad, Perceval and Lohengrin.

The two versions are not at all compatible and indeed contradict one another. On the one hand, Christ is a normal father of a family, engaging in Adam-style relationships, and, with His seed, the dynasty of Christ, the Desposins, is conceived (the esoteric version). On the other hand, the Saviour has no connection at all with Mary Magdalene and He is a pure Virgin. The Dominicans base their monasticism on the virginity of Mary, the virginity of the Divine Mother, and their inquisitorial 'perpetual virginity', in the manner of a harlot. (According to their bewildering version, it is possible to be an executioner and a judge, hand out death sentences, inflict torture, take the world's spirit and the glaive of Caesar, and yet still remain virginal. The virginity of these soulless Minotaurs and behemoths is purely physical).

Let us talk rather of Mary Magdalene! Who is she in the legends of the Grail? It is said that she is the other Mary. What the Orthodox people say of the Most Pure Virgin (that she was born in a state of sin and then purified for her mission as the Divine Mother) also applies to Mary Magdalene. Mary was 'conceived in a state of sin'. She belonged to Adam's branch and was susceptible to corruption, but it says in the Gospel that she sought the Lord.

When forgiven by the Saviour, Mary achieved complete holiness. As well as seeking Him, she also loved Him to distraction with a holy passion and her love for Him was virginal.

Mary of Magdala prostrated herself before Him, saw Him as no-one else saw Him, and perceived his Divine Wisdom. She was the first of the Seraphites, the fragrant rose of the *Divine Union*, the great saint and anointed one who is admired in Heaven, and who dwells in the Holy Being. She has been crowned with the golden garland of music.

In the Kingdom, her place is alongside St. John the Divine (the favourite). However it is said that the Bride, the one who loves forever, and the Mother of the generation of Seraphites, was the first to partake of the Altar of Union.

The Divine Mother, like Christ, was eternally immaculate and without sin. So it is taught in the Russian Grail which existed before the mentality of the Russian inquisition came about (Joseph Volotsky, and the theologians at the time of 'the most quiet' Alexei Mikhailovich and the tempestuous Peter I). Mary of Magdala was miraculously cleansed of original sin by Christ and prepared for the spiritual union.

What is this? The great mystery! Surely, He Who brought Lazarus back from the dead after ten days is the All Powerful Divinity, as perceived by Christianity? Is He not the celebrated Only Son of the Most High? Has He not been given the rod of resurrection, one of the mysterious attributes on the Grail's altars of the Holy Being, and treated as the rod of Aaron in the Ark of the Old Testament?

So what about the Lord 'falling in love and being intimate' and conceiving? Heaven forbid. Both versions are ridiculous, vulgar, insulting and awful. The last truth, though, the truth which has changed the course of world history and leads to the path of the True Church, lies in the fact that Mary really did conceive of Christ and gave birth to a wonderful, innocent boy, who was the very image of the Christ child in Bethlehem. In her own way she copied the Virgin Mary with the Christ child in her arms.

From this point the mystery becomes much more profound

than simply that Mary was born immaculate of Joachim and Anna: without stain of sin. It is much more hidden and incomprehensible, and therefore much more persecuted and surpasses all understanding – it is within the Holy Being.

*

As Christian agapes and communities began to emerge, the apostles spread the faith and gathered together the first parishioners and sponsors (the work was continued by the former candidate for Rabbi, Saul, who became the apostle Paul, and then by deacons, priests and bishops).

The Grail responds to this dreadful mistake (the introduction of the heathen, priestly hierarchy to the Virginal Bride of Christ, the True Church) with the catacombs.

The Grail goes into the caves – into the Holy Being.

Nothing is known about Mary of Magdala. Nor is anything known about Joseph the Younger, Joseph the Blessed, the wondrous, radiant, divine child, the invincible Knight who took the Chalice from the hands of Joseph of Arimathea and became the first great Keeper of the Grail after Joseph.

*

How did Mary Magdalene conceive?

...Her healing was almost instantaneous. The wisdom of the Lord, which had exposed the Pharisees, 'Whichever one of you has committed no sin may throw the first stone at her', moved her. Mary loved the Lord with all her heart. She fervently assumed the wisdom of virginity and the Saviour revealed Himself to her as the King of the Grail.

After many heated conversations, the crowned King of wisdom shared with Mary of Magdala secrets which He had only ever revealed to His immaculate Mother. He, the Saviour, called Mary Magdalene 'The other Mary'. Mary was in a state of shock, ecstatic with delight, transfigured and her body was immortal. The Saviour awakened hot springs within her. Mary was revealed in the vision of the glory which accompanied Him. Mary partook of His words: received them and consumed them. Then, in silent rapture, she fell at His feet, wiped them with her hair and kissed them. Just like the wives of Jerusalem, she wrung her hands, not knowing what she could do for Him.

He did not simply change her life and rescue her from the hands of those hypocrites who had accused her of a sin of which they themselves were guilty. He revealed to her a new universe and a new religion. The Law of Moses is an insignificant diversion for 'these little ones' and for the Adamites. There are such Immaculate Royal treasures and divine mysteries out there!

'Oh my true King! My beloved Divine Spouse! I searched for You with my whole being. I searched for You among the wealthy people, the merchants, the rabbis, those near me and the wise.'

His supreme love was open to Mary of Magdala as it had never been to anyone else. He explained to her the reasons behind many of His actions which were not fathomable to those followers who were uninitiated in the higher mysteries. Mary Magdalene was not party to the abomination of the Pharisees: awaiting the Messiah who would be the saviour of Israel, the day of judgement and so on. Mary hated the Pharisees from the outset. These malicious people declared her to be their enemy and hated her all the more after the seemingly defenceless Saviour showed His Royal, Heavenly power; He stood up for her and put that fatal, shaming question to them. They could do nothing and went away helpless.

Mary was the only person whom He could trust with the truth and to whom He could talk earnestly. It was to her that He entrusted something intimate, unique and exclusive. Their conversations reminded Him of the divine conversation (a Grail term) and the letters of love which fell from Heaven for the 'Suffering Bride' – the Divine Mother.

Mary saw Him in the light of Mount Tabor, radiant and

transfigured, full of rapture in Heaven and surrounded by cherubim. Mary contemplated the mystery of the inner sun and constantly drank from the inexhaustible chalice of blessings from His abundant spiritual stream flowing from His Royal Heart, and the rays of Divine Light radiating blindingly from Him, the King of Glory and the Messenger of the Most High...

Mary gave birth out of her holy passion – out of her sufferings and her love. She gave birth without blemish. The Saviour bestowed on her His Christly origin – the transfigured and immaculate composition of a divine person.

A ray of glory burned in her heart and in all of her being. There was a pillar of fire within her, and she was enveloped in a cloud of cherubim, the radiant host and the army of the Lady of the Grail's retinue, and the eternal sun of the Most High.

Mary ascended to Heaven. She was raised above the earth and, when she came to her senses, she understood that she was carrying the mysterious divine fruit of the Lord.

What is this? It is impossible to explain. Mary was carrying in her immaculate womb another god-man, the conception of the *divine humanity* and the heir of Christ.

*

The Grail has revealed this secret, which was distorted by the 'ladies' knights', the minnesingers and even more so by their admirers. A romantic version was enough to satisfy the fanciful notions of certain ladies.

The Grail, though, is a pure realm of ecstatic virginity. Mary was not only made pure, but also a delighted and enraptured Virgin. Christ's parable applies to her: 'Who loves more; the one who owed 500 denarii or the one who owed 50?' She has been much forgiven. Thus she loved Him in a passionate and elated fashion (way), with a holy passion. Like John, the beloved apostle, she followed Him and, what is more, she conceived. Joseph the Blessed could be called the myrrh scroll of the Divine Word which she swallowed (just as the prophet Ezekiel swallowed the white scroll in the desert). She immaculately and mysteriously conceived through the Divine Word. She is the first Mother of the radiant god-man and the protectress of the True Church; the other Divine Mother.

Within the Grail, she is the yurodivy Theogamy, like the maiden Cundry. The maiden Cundry, the 'Yurodivy ugly one' (i.e. divine beauty which is locked away forever) makes Perceval ashamed for understanding little and not treasuring the Grail.

Shortly after the First Coming of Christ, the 'Other Mary' completed that which the Most Pure Divine Mother had peacefully brought into being within her life-giving bosom: she gave birth to a divine child. To the Knights of the Grail, she is a small, radiant woman, who holds in her hands the Chalice containing the Blood of her Teacher. With the Lord's blessing, Joseph of Arimathea was his guardian and assumed the responsibility for the upbringing of the wonderful boy, the second young Christ who, from birth, displayed the wonders of his wisdom.

Here was the first progeny of the Saviour! A prototype of the mysteries which were completed by Him in Solovki; mysteries of the portrayal and multiplying of Himself in the molten pearl of intense sorrow, in a crowd of one hundred thousand rapturous young Christs: martyrs and anointed ones from Solovki (mortal prisoners whose bonds of death have been exchanged for bonds of Divine Union).

*

The care of the young Joseph was handed over to Joseph of Arimathea. A glorious line of Knights did indeed originate from him. The Saviour left behind on earth his Divine self or the priceless origin of Christ – the source of *divine humanity*. A Royal Dynasty really did spring from Him. They are known as the Desposins. The Grail teaches earnestly about them, but the romantic version must be omitted as well as the original sin and Adamite relations or 'physical union' between Christ and the former Jerusalem courtisan, whom he had saved.

She thought He was a gardener in the garden of paradise. The Gospels recorded her divinely passionate 'Rabbi!' There, the voice of Mary from the Grail is heard for the first and last time. Mary was His second mysterious loved one after the Divine Mother, eternally loved by Him.

Joseph of Arimathea became for the second time a 'Joseph the Betrothed' for his adopted son, Joseph the Younger. Another 'Holy Family' was formed: Mary (the sorrowful other Divine Mother), Joseph of Arimathea (a wonderful husband and guardian of the Holy Family of Joseph the Betrothed) and the wonderful boy himself.

Apart from the abilities which had been bestowed on him and which Christ had already revealed to the world during his lifetime, Joseph displayed amazing bravery from childhood. Whoever saw him would recognise Christ in him and say, 'A finer boy has never walked the face of the earth. What a Knight! What a soldier!' He killed a snake at the age of three. Never letting go of his sword, he fought with monsters, giants and dragons, overcoming them all with the strength of his Father.

His knowledge of the Most High was faultless. This Divine Child, the new child of Heaven, the second Christ, belonged to the future of humanity. His mother was miraculously purified and disconnected from her origins. His Father was the Divinity Incarnate, the Mysterious Emissary from the Kingdom, greater than Orpheus, greater than Moses, and greater than Zarathustra, Abraham, Isaac or Jacob.

As a youth, the heir, Joseph, was introduced to the mystery of the Chalice and served in the liturgy with Joseph of Arimathea. In his hands, the Chalice was able to transform the wine of the Knights into the Blood of the Lord for the first time.

Joseph knew about his messianic calling as founder of Christ's humanity. He knew how much his Father had endured, and what cross he had borne, openly exposing the Pharisees. He knew how he had been alone, not understood by some and persecuted and cursed by others.

The wisdom of the Most High and of the Saviour Himself, which came regularly to Joseph, had chosen a different, hidden and mysterious destiny for him. Otherwise the malicious vipers from Jerusalem would sense his existence. Their bloodhounds would seek him out. A rescript of Jerusalem's 'Third department' would ensue in order to deal with the slaughter of the innocents from Bethlehem who were sacrificed...

No. Joseph, the son of Christ, was assigned a different destiny than that of becoming the 14 001st martyr for Christ.

One of the miracles he performed was dematerialising, disappearing and avoiding danger. He was afraid of nothing. Having made himself invisible, he was carried along by the wind. Our Saviour loved him dearly and Joseph was the first to be honoured by the wonder of His unfailing presence. Our Lord, essentially, did not leave him and showed him the wonders of a father's love, in the same way that the Father did not leave Him, the Divine Son, in his burning, holy passion, at the age of 33.

Christ bestowed a powerful strength and many great gifts and graces on His heir. Much of that, which could not take place during the Saviour's days on earth, was passed down to Joseph the Younger, the radiant and glorious successor. The Grail has dozens of other names for him, including, 'Radiant Father of the Church', 'Keeper of the Grail' or 'King of the Messianic Dynasty'.

Just like Nikolai II of the Romanovs, the new Russian martyr, head of the New Martyrs, and inseparable from Tsesarevich Alexei (his son) for all eternity, the Saviour came to Seraphim the Tender in Solovki, together with Joseph the Blessed, who had inherited the wisdom and beauty of Joseph the Beautiful, the kind, gentle and wise character of Joseph the Betrothed, and the mysterious sceptre of courage against the religious hypocrites and many other qualities from his guardian, Joseph of Arimathea.

In the Grail Joseph the Blessed is referred to as Joseph IV

(King of Israel), after the son of Jacob, the Egyptian steward, Joseph the Betrothed and Joseph of Arimathea.

The name of Joseph was given to him by Mary Magdalene with the Saviour's blessing and it was, of course, taken from the eternal book, the Book of the Oracle.

The Saviour passed on to His son the miraculous power to defeat the red dragon, the devil, a fierce beast, and to shame the Pharisees. The most blessed Joseph became the father of the new Messianic Dynasty of earthly heroes and the new sons of the Divinity.

It was indeed from Joseph the Blessed that the Church of Christ came; made up of the true heirs of the origin of the Lord Himself as God-Man, which had been bestowed upon Him by the Holy Spirit and the Heart of the Most Pure Virgin Mother (Joseph particularly honoured Her, his immaculate and beloved Grandmother). Together with the Holy Spirit, whose procession I had the honour of witnessing on the Throne of the Holy Spirit in the holy mountain which lies by the sea at Kemer, walked the Royal Heir, Joseph, the anointed one.

*

The German Minnesingers and the French medieval mystic poets faithfully recounted the wisdom of the Grail: the inherited signs and the Myrrh-anointed Dynasty. The True Church came out of this hidden, locked away personality – the second Christ, born of the second Divine Mother, Bethlehem multiplied, and reproduced the Gospel. Thus, while the superficial Church was being spread by the apostles and the first communities were being set up, the other, Mysterious Church dwelt in the catacombs of the Holy Being and was hardly visible to the world. It was becoming stronger in seclusion, and the young boy was growing in Divine Wisdom and the Spirit.

The birth and the spreading of the superficial Church was a source of great sorrow to the Lord. He foresaw the glaive of Caesar and of the new Rabbis in the guise of the Christian teachers, preaching the new law. The artful one was capable of mimicry and adaptation to any of the circumstances dictated by the Most High.

The Saviour literally begged Joseph to remain hidden from the world and assigned him to his destiny in the Holy Being. Joseph was enshrouded in the cloud of the Holy Being and was declared king of the true Church of Christ and of the castles of the Grail.

He was received with such royal treasures! What springs he drank from! How the Lord crowned him! How well they were united! The Saviour delighted His heir with the Counsel of the Holy Trinity and set him at the feet of the Most Pure Divine Mother to receive Her blessing. In him, He saw the direct continuation of Himself and bestowed upon him the fullness, strength, essence and glory of the Holy Spirit. He never tired of calling him the Royal Boy and His only heir.

From him there came many heirs. The Saviour would come and bless each one of them with His great retinue.

These persecuted, pure, virginal Desposins, the 'Royal Dynasty of Christ', were not alone. Behind them were the gentle Divine Parents (Joachim and Anna), Joseph the Betrothed, Joseph of Arimathea and his sons, and the Most Pure Virgin, the eternally young protectress and Mother of the saints of the Grail.

The Saviour personally instructed Joseph on many mysteries and promised that Joseph would accomplish what He, the Lord, had been unable to accomplish. Joseph continued the work of Christ and completed His mission. Without sin, entrusted with Original Immaculacy, King Joseph of the Seraphites, crowned by Christ Himself who was tortured by the wickedness of the Pharisees and who is the Only Son of the Divinity, Joseph, who was accompanied by the Glory of the Most High, the heir to indescribable Royal Graces – this fourth Joseph revealed the gates of the Divine Civilization to the world.

His earthly mother, Mary of Magdala, the Holy Theogamy, was the first to be honoured with the mystery of union with the Divinity. Christ became her Immaculate Spouse and brought about an Immaculate Conception.

Wise theologians of the Grail have explained this by saying that Christ, who was born of the Holy Spirit, is the Son of the Most High. Joseph, His son, is the Holy Spirit, born of Christ. Joseph was clothed in the Holy Spirit, like no other mortal besides the Divine Mother.

What a protective shield Joseph had! The evil of the devil and the Pharisees could not touch him. Joseph was unassailable and invincible. The wonderful prayer of the Grail speaks of him:

> Immaculate, unblemished, unassailable,
> Led, perceptive, invincible
> Son of the Most Pure Virgin Mary
> King of Israel, anointed king,
> Son of Christ.

'Sons and daughters of the Bridal Chamber' is a Grail term, introduced by the Lord and barely fathomable to Christians (the Gospel says, 'Can the children of the marriage fast, as long as the bridegroom is with them? As long as they have the bridegroom with them, they cannot fast.'), which applies to Joseph more than anyone else. He is indeed the son of Christ, the personification of the Bridal Chamber. Together with the Lord he is the radiant first priest of the Temple of Peace in Divine Civilization III, and the wise holy messenger of the blessed union and the Immaculate Conception as a rule, rather than an 'exception to the rule', and as the Gospel for those born from on High.

The Church of Christ has spread through the Holy Being, and its posterity is not limited to family members. The scattering of the treasure of the Grail was carried out by the chosen ones and was controlled by the mysteries of the divine intent. It is difficult to say whether Seraphim Sarovsky, *Innocent Baltski* or Blessed Eufrosinia were direct descendants of Joseph of Arimathea, on the Grail branch. However, they were filled with the Glory of the Most High and they were true heirs.

*

It is not difficult to imagine how the Roman Harlot objected to this secret which was revealed to the world. According to the Grail version, she was assigned the mission of the Jewish 'bad counsel' (the Sanhedrin): to persecute, hate, envy, curse and slander.

The Roman villains, who had a political advantage, annihilated the Templars, who had been ready to declare their full independence from the Pope. The keepers of the Grail knew who they were and the marvellous glory of the two Josephs, Arimathea and the son of Christ, gave them the courage to defeat the arch enemy who was a hundred times stronger. Like their father, Joseph, radiant and blessed, the Knights of the Eternal Virgin held the indestructible sword of David in their hands.

After the declaration of Russia as the 'Third Rome' the Russian Grail was shut fast until it was warmed by the fiery glow of Solovki, the *Second Golgotha.* The glory of the soldiers Ilya and Enoch, Knights of the Grail, has appeared to me many times. Virginal Desposins, on fiery white horses, with swords in their hands: this is the knighthood of the Archangel Michael, leader of the heavenly soldiers of the high King.

Oh True Church! Reveal yourself to the suffering world, Oh yearning bride, saviour, comforter, bestower of blessings, mother, heavenly keeper of mysteries, gifts and mercies, much awaited by humanity and all of creation!

The version of the writings of the Grail on the Stuarts, the Merovingians etc. that the medieval monarchs were born of the Grail, is true. The Grail has ruled the world from the beginning. The Grail has power over all creation and the fate and destiny of all are in the hands of Its keepers.

*

Anyone who drinks from the Chalice of the Grail will become a true son of the Divinity and, like the Egyptian Pharaoh-reformer Akhenaton, will be given a Revelation about the Divinity and about the Father of supreme love. Not about the private god of Assyria, Israel or Egypt, but about the One who adores, 'Abba Father', the Jealous God (the Laws of Moses), El Kanna, who loves intensely, who is greater than Himself, who loves his Sons and Daughters enormously, as well as about Him Who concealed his love for centuries as it cannot be grasped by an Adamite.

'Children of the Most Pure Divine Mother!' exclaim the angels at the procession of the heirs of Christ. 'Wonderful! Glorious! Indescribable! Blessed! Alleluia!' Their ancestors Joachim and Anna applaud. 'Peace be with you.'

How wonderful is the procession of the True Church of Christ! It is clear now; it is not some kind of breakaway sect, or worshippers of some great saint, Patriarch or miracle-worker such as John of Kronstadt (more than a few of them came. The Saviour generously shared His treasures with us, with those who love Him and are anointed by Him from the beginning)... No, the other sense is to be found in the understanding of 'the true Church of Christ'! His origin is contained within it – the immediate offspring of the woman. It was indeed conceived of Christ.

Christ is not only the Son of the Divinity, but also the Father of the Church. He is not only its 'Head' in the sense described by bookish scholars, but also the Head of a Dynasty, the New Adam, the Forefather... We are like his followers and sons, in the context of the Bridegroom from the Bridal Chamber.

It is impossible to comprehend this concept of 'sons and daughters of the Bridal Chamber' without the inheritance of His origin and the immaculate seed. The Bridegroom is always with them. The Bridegroom will never be taken away again. The time of fasting is over.

Blessed are those to whom the Grail reveals Its mysteries! This means that the Grail has taken them and will generously present them with a mysterious 'white screen' on which they will be able, when they have grasped it, to read the Book of destinies, dates, characters, churches, the history of treachery, betrayal, resurrection, rods and arks. Divine Wisdom will give them strength and the sword of a Knight of the Grail. Then they will be given the title of invincible. Thus the Roman Harlot and the Byzantine Monster will not be able to do anything to them.

The one who is seated on the throne, imagining herself to be the eternal heir, the apocalyptic whore of Babylon, is capable of much. She fears only one thing – the Grail Chalice. An angel will come to her and knock at the door which will open slightly, as if blown by the wind. In his hands he will be holding a chalice of fire.

He will say, 'Drink!' and she will be unable to object. Her hands trembling, she will ask, 'What is it?' 'DRINK!' So, she will take the chalice. When she has drunk from it she will understand: she thought that it was a chalice of blessings but it is really the chalice of the wrath of the Most High, which has turned into a chalice full of curses. Then she will disappear forever.

*

Oh Mary of Magdala, 'the other Mary'! How you are needed today, bringer of myrrh, for today's potential sons and daughters of the Bridal Chamber who have not yet been converted! Come and reveal the secret of your instant transfiguration and purification! Give them the rod of *metanoia* from the Grail. May they receive from you the origin of Christ for Immaculate Conception and birth from on High!

As King of the Grail, the Saviour said to Nicodemus, 'Did you really not know about the mystery of Holy Israel? Did you not come into the world for this, in order to be born from on High? The law cannot help with this.' Then He, born from on high of the Holy Spirit, became the Father of the new humanity, having been conceived without sin by the Holy Spirit, with the power of supreme love and its ray of sun, Christ II, Joseph the Divine Child, and thereby laying the foundation of the Church of Christ. Alleluia! Praise to the Most High Father!

25.06.2005 Deris Island

The Second Immaculate Conception

Oh Holy Mary Magdalene! Myrrh Mother of the Grail filled with holy passion, and second Divine Mother. The Queen of Heaven had the honour of conceiving of the Son of the Most High of the Holy Spirit. But Mary Magdalene, who was chosen out of all mortal women, conceived, not of the flesh, but immaculately from Christ.

Her conception was filled with such holy passion, such torment and such blessings! Mary of Magdala is united through the Grail on the highest level. Her fervent, utterly devoted nature is preserved as the model of a myrrh-bearing woman. She is a queen among them. She partook of the Myrrh blood of Christ in a different Eucharist of the future through Immaculate Conception.

It was predetermined that the Divine Mother would originate a new kind of humanity of the Holy Spirit, and Mary of Magdala, although in a different way and 2000 years before her time, conceived the second Divine Child, Joseph, out of a mortal yearning for the Lord and out of her absolute love for Him. In doing this, Mary acquired Christ's Heavenly and God-Human substance fashioned by Supreme Divine Wisdom from the essence of the Grail, the substance of the New transformed Adam. Apart from the Divine Mother, Mary of Magdala is the second, within the Grail, to be called Mother of the new generation of sons of the Most High or life-giver of the Messianic Dynasty of *anointed* ones.

Many earthly kings and European monarchs became renowned for worshipping Mary of Magdala.

Her character is very close to the saints of the Holy Grail. The Grail does not know of the concept of ataraxia: insensitivity, lack of emotion, indifference, and destruction. The purpose of the seclusion of the Grail is to drink from the Chalice, leaving behind the world order. This seclusion is not reached through ascetic practices and 'inner works' so much as through keeping the candle of the heart burning and preparing the Bride.

The two main themes of the Grail are virginity and supreme love. It is about Christ as He is and not distorted through 'bad lenses or distorting mirrors'.

Mary Magdalene loved the Saviour to distraction and selflessly. As His first Bride, after the Divine Mother, she literally absorbed his being and conceived from His essence, carrying it from the very moment when He delivered her from death. She owed her life to Him (for saving her from the punishment of the Pharisees). She also owed another life to him; that of the son of our Saviour.

What Mary must have gone through, conceiving a child of Christ and giving birth to a son, essentially without a father! It is impossible to convey.

The Pharisees rejoiced: He had disappeared without trace! His memory had been erased! People would only remember Him as a law-breaker, a rebel and an imposter!..

The Saviour did leave something of Himself behind. The Lord carried on living through Mary Magdalene. Like the Most Pure Virgin, carrying the fruit of the Holy Spirit and therefore 'full of grace', Mary Magdalene was filled with grace, given to Christ by the Father, which she obtained from His essence and assimilated in a special way (through the Immaculate Conception, which is greater even than the Eucharistic Blood of blood and Flesh of flesh), and which Christ would not have been able to give in any other way.

It is this essence which is present in the Messianic Dynasty of Christ, placed there by its parents, Christ and Mary Magdalene, and by their son Joseph the Great, prototype King, Messiah and Prince – Christ of the Holy Spirit.

Did the Roman Harlot (the superficial Church) or the apostles know about the child who had been conceived by the Saviour? If they did know, they concealed it. Even the followers of Christ would have found it hard to comprehend an Immaculate Conception.

Adam's race was miraculously enriched through this conception. A being came into the world who had not been conceived by God, like Christ, the God-Man, but by Christ and the Holy Spirit through Mary, the former harlot, Adamite and sinner. Mary's flesh was transfigured, purified, united with the branch of the Seraphites, divinised and raised up to the Bridal Chamber.

The Seraphite generation will only appear through the worship of Mary Magdalene as she is presented in the Grail.

The birth of Joseph the Magnificent (Joseph the Younger) radically changes the history of the Church and gives a true picture of Christ's mission. Because of the foresight of Supreme Wisdom, it was determined that the Saviour should come into the world through Immaculate Conception and continue Adam's race immaculately; by founding a Royal Dynasty destined to rule in the third millennium.

Many tsars and kings of European and world powers were part of this dynasty including the last emperor *Mikhail Romanov II* in Russia. The religion and wisdom of the Grail would have been a source of particular interest for the august martyred couple, Nikolai II and Aleksandra Fedorovna, if only these righteous monarchs had been aware of other saints of the Grail apart from Grigori Rasputin.

Mary Magdalene immaculately conceived and this is a part of the Gospel of the Grail. It is no less important than the

Annunciation. Without it, there is no fullness to the story of the Gospel and Christ's actions are not complete. Deprived of Christ in the flesh and His inheritance, the Church would preach about no-one but a sterile eunuch; a 'theoretician', a 'teacher' and nothing more.

Those who accuse Christianity of 'lacking in substance' (Merezhkovski and Rozanov) would have 'lapped up' the wonder and beauty of this virginal Holy union resulting in conception out of the holy passion of supreme love.

In truth, the profound passion and devoted love which vanquishes death, mortal yearning and all earthly circumstances, produces the eternal fruit of the Most High.

26.06.2005 Deris Island

The Madness of Supreme Wisdom

Driven-mad-with-love – the name of Mary Magdalene within the Grail

Only the King of Heaven and the King of the Grail can create the Gospel of a love-which-is-not-of-this-world whilst experiencing convulsions, being pierced with nails three times, being beaten black and blue, having nowhere to live and covered in blood!

The ringing of the heavenly bell for the liturgy

Today I came down from Heaven, avoiding the underworld. What a marvel! The Orthodox underworld is difficult to avoid on the way down from Heaven. But the beast has not woken up yet. So, while the brute is still sleeping in its synagogue-lair, we will sing and praise God. Then, when he wakes up, we will gladly run away so that he can bite the dust more quickly.

It is too early to go into battle. The battle lies ahead...

The sword of the Grail, the sword of the Grail is in my hand! To battle! The time has come! Why is it 'too early'? On earth we have a saying – there is wedded peace on earth, and then into battle. We can only dream about peace.

*

Heaven revealed the Eucharist of the Grail. After this, we can take a damp cloth and, as if we were wiping chalk scribbles off a blackboard, we can wipe away everything that used to be known as the Eucharist.

Some professor wrote a lot of nonsense like algebraic formulae... His followers looked at it and said, 'Ah! The absolute truth; an axiom!' It is empty.

During the night, the Grail dictated some wonderful poetry of the Kingdom to me. This poetry, which is very complex, with a rhythmic, conceptual content, in general would have needed a draft and editing, but it is perfectly written (dozens of pages). No such draft exists. In the Grail, we only find purity and the white scrolls. The spots of blood are made white by the Blood of the Lamb. White is the colour of the Kingdom and of the Grail.

The Grail has its own music. Look into the Chalice and understand it like Joseph the Sweetest, son of Mary Magdalene. Joseph the Great, the Heir, heard the perpetual music of the Chalice. Inside it is the indescribable music of the Kingdom!

The heart of a person is a chalice ever full of the drink of the love-which-is-not-of-this-world. The temple (a ridiculous hut with decorated walls) is the resounding chalice of the Grail.

Leonid Bely heard it!.. He left his equivalent of 'The Beatles' ('Vyesyolye Rebyata' was a well-known group at that time) and became a Grail composer. Amazing!

*

The madness of Divine Wisdom! In truth, the third Gospel in the annals of Heaven should be called, 'The Madness of Divine Wisdom.'

Mary waited for Him in ecstasy. In ecstasy she hung on His every word. In ecstasy she poured the precious myrrh from the alabaster jar, inciting the wrath of Simon (and those followers who supported him); 'Why are you wasting such precious myrrh on His head?' In response, Christ prophesied, 'You have plenty of time to give myrrh to the poor, but I will not always be here. She has prepared My Body for its burial and anointed me for resurrection and eternal life. Thus, wherever the Gospel is preached, her name will be remembered.'

*

She literally went mad out of love for Him. Insane Love and Driven-mad-with-love are names given to Mary Magdalene in the Grail. 'How is it possible not to be driven mad with love upon seeing Him and hearing His voice?' she said to another

Myrrh-bearing Virgin who had been purified by Him. She really was almost driven insane upon hearing of the terrible sentence. She had been sure that He would simply brush them aside and march through like a victorious king. How could God be sentenced to death?

However, she would come to realise that it was not His intent to do this because of the love-which-is-not-of-this-world. 'Ah. He purified me, a harlot. He made me a Virgin and a Myrrh-bearer... Now he wants to do the same to the whole of Israel and the whole of humanity! Ah.'

During the Lord's Crucifixion, she could be said to have been in a state of extreme holy passion, which the world did not understand. The world cannot comprehend this at all. This is Gospel III, the Gospel of the love-which-is-not-of-this-world.

Mary has become a semi-conscious wanderer. Her hair is dishevelled. The holy one who has lost her mind through love, is in a state described by the Grail as a mortal, yearning for the Heavenly Beloved.

Mary is literally dying; she is fading away. Her strength is almost gone. She has given it all to Him. She has been crucified with Him. She is tormented by a mortal and exhausting yearning...

This mortal yearning is the height of holy passion. Through this mortal yearning, and together with the two crucified robbers and the myrrh-bearing women, she experiences His Jerusalem Golgotha.

*

He comes to her in the night in the guise of an Archangel (Mary is so bereft of her senses that she does not recognise Him), and pierces her heart with a lance of fire (the Divine Wisdom of the Caduceus). Mary Magdalene is rendered unconscious. And in the morning ('early' according to John's Gospel), she was the first one to hasten to the tomb first, so that she can embrace Him, to kiss Him, and shed her tears of myrrh over Him.

She is the living alabaster jar. Oh, wherever the Gospel is proclaimed, she will be remembered!

She is ready to enter the tomb when she sees the angel.

'What are you doing here? He is not here. He is risen.'

She does not understand. Mary has been driven insane with love. Where is her Beloved?

'Where is the Lord? What have you done with Him? Where have you put Him? Give Him to me! He belongs to me.'

At that, He comes to her.

John says, 'She did not recognise Him.' When He came to her, the holy one driven mad with love saw Him as a gardener dressed in white. 'Ah! Rabbi,' she said, 'My Bridegroom!' And so she was carried away above the earth in rapture, finally at peace.

Mary did not recognise Him because He came to her as the Bridegroom. Sweet, Myrrh Blood poured from His heart.

Mary wanted to touch Him... If only she could touch him! But He said to her, 'Do not touch Me. That is how it should be.' A heavenly cloud enveloped Mary. She was raised a metre above the earth...

The love which is not of this world brings the gift of new life! Mary Magdalene conceived immaculately of the Lord: from His messianic, Myrrh Blood of Golgotha. The humanity of Christ was conceived out of the messianic, divine seed.

*

'My Beloved, I can no longer see You. What have You done? Why am I without You? You will live for a thousand years. Is it true that you will not go away? You are with me!' repeated Mary Magdalene as if in a dream, like Shakespeare's Juliet persecuted by the Montagues and the Capulets. So He comforted her, more real than ever, Christ of the Holy Being, from the Kingdom where this Immaculate Conception had taken place.

'Mary, I am more than just your Bridegroom. I am the Husband of Glory. I will do more than just be with you – I will be within you, My daughter. You will conceive a second Christ from Me; a second Divinity incarnate. You will become the new Divine Mother and parent of a new nation. I will give you an Immaculate Origin, like nothing on earth.

I spent the Last Supper with My followers in Jerusalem, when I said, 'This is my Blood and My Flesh', and gave them the Chalice to drink from. With you I will realise the Eucharist of the third Gospel; we shall call it the messianic Eucharist. My Blood will be within you like a seed. My Flesh will become your flesh. Then, from our *Divine Union*, My Daughter and my Bride, a fine son will be born.

Call him Joseph the Great; the fourth after Joseph the Wonderful of Egypt, Joseph the Betrothed and Joseph of Arimathea. Call him this name in honour of Joseph the Betrothed, whom I will always love the most.'

*

It is said, 'Wherever the Gospel is proclaimed she will be remembered.' I will say that even 2000 years after the Gospel of the Kingdom has been proclaimed, in the 3rd and 4th millennia, the greatest minds of humanity will continue to contemplate the events which unfolded at the Lord's tomb.

The Bridegroom left the tomb, like the sun of suns!

The holy fathers came to a realisation: did the Bridegroom leave the tomb and become the Spouse of the Glory of Heaven, the Husband of the Most High? He enveloped the former harlot in a heavenly cloud and conceives through a simple, mortal woman; He, the God-Man! When He ascended into Heaven (He was still a Man; as He said, He had 'not yet gone up to the Heavenly Father') he left behind on earth a copy of himself; a perfect likeness, the very image of Himself!

*

'Ah, My Lord, Eloi! Will I never see You again?'

'No. Emmanuel! I am always with you.'

'Ah... I will not see you again, but, to console me, you have left me a boy. I will call him Joseph in honour of Joseph the

Betrothed. I will look after him just as Mary looked after Her Divine Child, and I will be consoled. I will see You in him. Is that not so?'

The Saviour smiled.

'Yes, Mary. But it will not be long. I will perform another miracle with you; the greatest miracle.'

'What is that, my Lord?'

'Our son will not replace Me. A day ago I promised the robber that I would take him to Heaven. I will take you to the Bridal Chamber. I will take you there before Mary the Divine Mother. Then you will know the love which...'

'Which is not to be found on earth? Is that it, my Lord?'

'No, Mary. You will know the love which is not to be found in Heaven.'

*

Mary Magdalene of Solovki! Was it not you who came into the through-huts, anointed with the oil of myrrh and said, 'In this frozen Siberian wilderness known as the GULAG Archipelago, you will know the love which is not of Heaven...'.

*

And so, nine months after His crucifixion and his apparition at the tomb, Mary Magdalene gave birth to a fine boy and named him Joseph.

She died soon after. The Lord took her body and soul up to Heaven. Nothing remained of Mary Magdalene, save her son, Joseph, an orphan. His mother had entrusted her son to Joseph of Arimathea.

Joseph took the boy into his family. In the ancient English esoteric chronicles, *Joseph the Heir* features as the twelfth son of Joseph, Joseph the Younger. At the age of seven, Joseph introduced him to the Chalice. He revealed to him the Grail, which he had never revealed to anyone before.

'This is your Father,' he said to him. And so, the young Joseph, gazing at the reflective surface of the Grail, saw Heaven in it and said,

'Yes, this is my heavenly Father! Abba, Abba, Abba!'

The 'Abba Father' of St. Paul and his epistles and the ancient Jewish Adonai, Elohim etc., cannot be compared to Joseph's exclamation, 'This is my Heavenly Father! Abba Father!'

He was a boy of unearthly beauty. His was a beauty which is not of this world. He was also full of unearthly love; a love which is not of this world. The Lord came to Joseph when he was one year old and said,

'My child! My Father crowned Me Lord of Heaven and earth. You will become my successor; father of the Messianic Dynasty. Your children will become powerful monarchs of Europe. As My Blood and My essence, they will inherit the Royal Crowns of the Heavenly Israel. As perfect prophets they will see the Most High with their own eyes. As perfect kings, anointed from on High, they will rule according to the laws of Divine Wisdom. And as perfect priests they will perform the ceremony of anointing with myrrh and will anoint the brides for the Bridal Chamber.'

Many of the descendants of Joseph the Sweetest will later become Merovingians, Stuarts, Romanovs (Nikolai II and Mikhail, Seraphim the Tender) – keepers of the Grail Chalice.

Joseph the Sweetest was the new Abraham. The Heavenly Father said to Abraham, 'From you will come a new people. You will become the father of many new nations. They shall be impossible to count, like grains of sand on the sea shore and stars in the Heavens.'

Our Lord and Christ told His son, Joseph the Younger, 'I will give you all the kingdoms on earth and in heaven. And your Dynasty will rule on earth for thousands of years, but they will rule in a different way to that of the heathen kings before them: through their anointing with holy passion on the Cross until Our Messianic Dynasty prevails and triumphs over all the earth.' This was the Holy Union; the climax of the Gospel. Everything that He did up to this point was simply an introduction. The barren will give birth and the barren will conceive.

The heavens applauded. A gold inscription was made in the Book of Life: 'Gospel III'.

*

15 years later, He hurried to *Nightingale Mountain* to the Most Pure Mother, His Divine Bride. He came and was united even more closely with Her than with Mary Magdalene. This was the double Grail and the double Holy Union.

Ah. Everyone who visits the mountain of the Assumption near Ephesus experiences this rapturous, ecstatic, holy passion of the Bride. The atmosphere from when the Sun of Suns, the Bridegroom, came down to His Bride remains to this day. This mountain, the 'cloudy, damp mountain' is in the Holy Being. To this day, it stands on the earth like a cloud of the Glory of the Most High. It is His true Ark.

Meanwhile, somewhere in the centre of Ephesus, St. John the Divine, and then the apostle Paul, preached until a strong apostolic community was established, which would eventually succeed the superficial church. Then the Saviour left them. He came to the Ephesus agape at *Nightingale Mountain*, where Gospel IV was being realised: His Holy Union, not with Mary Magdalene (Gospel III), but with the Most Pure Virgin. It was an even more beautiful and perfect Gospel. Then, when the Most Pure One collapsed from exhaustion, dying of the love which is not to be found on earth or in heaven (!), He said to Her, 'You will become the Mother of a new people. In your Immaculate Womb, the Civilization of Christ will be conceived.'

Then came Gospel V – Solovki. Gospel VI is the Blazing Solovki giving birth to the divine civilization! A Wedding celebration the size of the universe! The last Armageddon, rising from the tomb is the releasing through prayer of the prisoners of the spheres of the underworld and the heavens.

So finally, Oh Lord, I will say that, with You, this last, passionate Gospel VII is completed: Your eternal Glory, Your eternal Kingdom, Your eternal triumph and Your eternal rejoicing.

*

– Father, I want to do as you do. Can I do as you do?

– Will you come with me to the hut at Solovki for 25 years: from the conversion to Orthodoxy to *Nightingale Mountain?*

– I will come, father! I will come!

– Then follow me and I will take you to sanctuaries which are not of this world.

*

At 6 o'clock in the morning, at 6 o'clock in the morning
The Chamber of the Eucharist is full of Light
My gentle ones, my beloved ones
Hurry earnestly to light the altars.

The liturgy lasts from 6 o'clock in the morning until 6 o'clock in the morning (of the following day)
A burning letter without pen and ink.
Christ comes and multiplies Himself
In the Knights of the Round Table.

At 12 o'clock midnight the huts are filled
With a heavenly fragrance.
Processing with Her Church is the Virgin Daughter,
Our Lady the Holy Theogamy.

Before Her soars the white dove, its wings fluttering
The Holy Spirit is known by sight and by name
With a golden incense burner in its beak it leads the Wedding procession
The Boy-King is the Christ of the Second Coming.

Two maidens carry the embroidered amice
And two silver patens bearing bread for the Seraphites.

Father full of holy passion, be calm and take comfort
Your children are living Arks

The guardians of supreme love and the caskets of pearls
Were wakened by You from their deep sleep
The music of the Kingdom rings out in their clear hearts
The liturgy is performed by the light of candles which never go out.

*

The Eucharist is a mystery of the Grail. There is no Eucharist without the second Gospel – the Saviour-on-the-Blood. His wine becomes Blood, and then... His Blood becomes wine! It is not only wine which becomes Blood through transubstantiation, but in the Chalice, the Blood of Golgotha becomes an inexhaustible wine. There is no Eucharist, wine turned into Blood, without the *Second Golgotha;* without the Blood which becomes wine.

Nor can there be any Eucharist without the third Gospel: Mary Magdalene. His Blood is only active when the 'responsive Grail' is present, or, as the Divine Mother said in Fatima, when there is a Eucharist of reparation ('reparation' means participation, i.e. offering up the Holy Gifts).

What kind of madness is this? How can the Holy Gifts be retrieved? By throwing up? By throwing them out?

'Offering up the Holy Gifts' means to become a Eucharistic lamb oneself.

'He that hath the bride is the bridegroom', said John the Baptist about himself and the Lord. A bridegroom must have a bride; otherwise he is not a bridegroom. The bridegroom feeds his bride with the blood. A bride offers up her blood and her life to her bridegroom.

In Christianity as it evolved, Christ was forbidden to be a Bridegroom and the Church was forbidden to be a Bride! In Christianity, there was no bridegroom and no bride – only the evil inquisitor and the Roman villain.

However, this is how the other Christianity was born.

*

Lesson №1 of the Grail is the mystery of the Eucharist of the Grail. As the Blood of Christ 'spilled onto the sand' according to the theology of Rome, so, too, will the Flesh and Blood of Christ 'spill onto the sand' if they do not, in essence, become part of a different composition and a different inner blood? Our composition is not yet ready and the Blood cannot be accepted – it will vanish into nothingness. As John Chrysostum said, 'not to judgement and condemnation' turns out to be, 'to judgement and condemnation!'

Who, though, can say that he is of one composition and one blood with Christ? Only His Blood heir, in whom is His origin.

So, apart from the Last Supper with the Jews in Jerusalem, He held a Nuptial Supper with Mary Magdalene. No-one knew that it was taking place. The Nuptial supper exceeded the Last Supper. It was a Nuptial Supper full of Mystery. At the Last Supper He gave of his Blood and Flesh to be partaken externally, through the mouth. At the Nuptial Supper He entered Eucharistically into the entire being, into all twelve immortal bodies and, in Holy Union, the Altar of Union, He completely divinized a simple mortal; saint Mary of Magdala, filled with holy passion.

She became of one composition with Him. From Him she received His origin, which she could not have received any other way.

This is the highest of the high, the greatest of the great and the most mysterious mystery of the Grail and its 150 Heavenly Castles. In order to come to know it, one must be united with Heaven. This is the mystery of the Eucharist of the Grail and the true Messianic Eucharist.

In the new Church, they understood it. It was understood in the other Church. There were twelve pure ones, twelve new generations, followers and heirs of Christ. They spread out and were honoured by humankind as invincible noble Knights, Monarchs, Kings and Tsars, until, on the mountain of the fifth Gospel, in Solovki, the Grail was handed to our father, Seraphim. It was handed to him as the last Russian Monarch with the words, 'You will be crowned in the name of all the saints for a thousand years of Christianity in Rus.'

*

The Gospel is not about the fact that Christ was conceived immaculately by the Virgin Mary two thousand years ago. Even the Muslims have no doubt about that. They accept that 'the prophet Isa was conceived immaculately by Mariam'. It must also be understood, though, that He who was conceived immaculately, conceives.

This is why, a hundred and fifty years ago, in answer to the question posed by Bernadette Soubirous in Lourdes, 'What is your name, beautiful Lady?' the Most Pure Virgin, tense and full of holy passion, looked towards Heaven and seemed to read Her response from the screen of the Grail.

'I am the Immaculate Conception', She said in French.

What was She looking at and what was She reading from?

This is the name of Christ within the Grail.

He, Who is known as the Immaculate Conception, offers up his Blood of holy passion. Therefore, only after having experienced the second Gospel (the Gospel of Christ-on-the-Blood; the three hours of His crucifixion and the seven last words), and after Gospel III (that of Mary Magdalene) and Gospel IV (Nightingale Mountain) it is possible to understand Christ's mission. Then, to us, He will be more than the Judeo-Roman 'Saviour', 'Liberator', 'Redeemer', and all the other labels given to Him by the inquisitors, and He will become the true Bridegroom and the King of the Bridal Chamber.

*

...During the Divine Mother's Revelation on the Mystic Throne (burning hot rocks 5 metres above sea level) I saw, full of rapture, the solar Triumphal arc. Millions enter through it. This is the arc of the Eucharist of the Grail, the arc leading to the Holy Union, to the true Christianity of the Kingdom.

09.07.2005 Moscow

The Mysterious Procession

The Mysteries of the Elders of the Grail

Virginity remained the sealed mystery of the knights of the Grail. There were no ascetic, inheritance or 'training' keys to it. The charisma of a virgin is passed down through dynastic succession: it is the inheritance of Christ's origin of primordial purity.

The Roman version of the 'bishops who followed on from the apostles' and any others claiming rights of succession is a dreadful parody of the supreme anointings of the Grail. In the majority of Orthodox monasteries, there is rarely even one in a hundred monks who have reached the same level as the wise maiden i.e. taking on their virginity as a privilege over the world and drawing from its inexhaustible source. Most tolerated this fiasco; they turned into mindless robots, neurotics or pathological types with a sublime or fluctuating libido. Amongst the monks were many schizophrenics, sodomites, or butchers with sadistic tendencies.

The Grail's battle with the Inquisition, which lasted for many centuries, was, essentially, a battle between wise and foolish virgins. For the Grail virgins, Divine Wisdom was given (inherited) through the breath of two eternal virgins, Christ and Mary. The wisdom was given to the official, 'permitted', institutional and barefoot Carmelites, the Franciscans and the Gregorians, by paying with their incredible efforts, and under the condition of the presence of an Elder, who miraculously kept himself safely in the monastery.

Thanks to the zealously guarded virginal origin, the knights were victorious in battle and achieved superiority in the sciences and the arts. They were fuelled by their virginity. The other world seemed to be senseless desert, full of the emptiness of profligate lust: such were the heights they had reached by acquiring the robes of virginity and the immaculate essence of their Divine Mother. The idea of the Most Pure Divine Mother and Her mystery as a 'Casting Mould' and a perfect 'role model' was borrowed by Louis de Montfort from the knights of the Grail.

The superficial church, the 'Roman villain', seemed to be unbearable and impossible to them. What right do these imposters have to pretend to be heirs of Christ? Who are they if they do not have immaculate origins? Who are they if Christ did not give them His breath? How can they partake of His Flesh and Blood if they have a different composition and they are not His children?

Christ is the King and He has many heirs. Like a wise King, He made sure that His heir, the virginal Joseph, completely mastered all earthly knowledge. Christ passed on to him the blessing of the Most High, anointing and the mark of a king. He also entrusted His Own Body to Joseph of Arimathea and Joseph the Sweetest, who was named in honour of the Saviour's stepfather, Joseph the Betrothed. What other line could exist?

Their mass deception is sheer mystification. The Popes falsify the Gospels! There is nothing in them but lies. Their evident fiasco is the absence of Christ, no knowledge of the will of the Most High, the receding of the Most Pure Virgin and the Holy Spirit: they exchange them for dogma, compulsory rules, churches, hierarchy and an obligatory set of beliefs.

How worthless! How little it means to the Lord what people think about Him and how they understand Him! Something else is important to Him: whether they can see Him, whether they know Him from within and whether they feel Him within them.

The Lord left behind His son. However, as the Father was one with the Son in the Trinity, so Christ, the only-begotten, remained as one with His direct descendant, Joseph. From the second keeper of the Chalice after Joseph of Arimathea, came the tradition of the multiplied origin of Christ and Christ present in the inner.

*

The myth about the early Christian agapes, as if they were awaiting the Second Coming, and 'Come, Lord! Yes, Come soon!' cannot even come close to the mystery of the presence of Christ, once one with Joseph; one with His son and their descendants.

The Heavenly Father left His only son (Christ was essentially alone on earth) but He never abandoned Him and was one with Him. In court, when the Jews asked Him, 'Where are the two witnesses?' the Saviour responded, 'The Father is my witness. And I am one with the Father. If you knew the Father, you would realise that the Father lives in me.'

And so, united in flesh, the Son of the Most High experienced the presence of His Father in their holy union! Such was His unprecedented love for the Father. With the Church of His messianic dynasty Christ shared the same perfect relationship as the Father-Son relationship within the Trinity. He was literally united with every one of His followers. He was bound to them with innermost cords so that they would recognise Him from nearby and marvel.

*

How many wonderful parables and how many sacred gifts the Holy Spirit gave them! Years have passed by. The knights of the Grail were enraptured and delighted by the miracles which the Saviour performed again and again, each time exceeding the last. His abundant presence seemed so elevated that even the pages of the Gospel story seemed to fade. 'The God is Who He is', said the *anointed* ones of the Grail.

Through this divine, meditative introduction to the Grail, I would like to take a look at the blasphemous, slanderous church through the eyes of the heavenly Grail, in order to make a sober analysis of it and to see it for what it is. From way back this 'fornicatress living in luxury' has used her hypnotic charms as if there was no-one else but her: she is the 'only judge' and she has been granted the 'full authority and the presence of the Divinity'. Now the reader has the opportunity to take a sober look at the situation and to be released from the Roman charms which have led the world into such a sorry state and made it completely void of faith.

*

The first meal around the mystical Round table is thought to have been endowed with holy passion with the exclamation, 'Oh!' The knights of the Messianic dynasty and their fellow warriors, the radiant virgins, were called to drink from the inner chalice; from the origin of Christ, present in their blood. As they did this they repeated, 'My heart is ready! My heart is ready!'

Following the ecstasy of the Holy Being, the page of the Grail, dressed in noble robes, brought out the lance. A Drop of Blood flowed from the point and down the shaft. It dripped onto the hand of the page and literally set it alight, penetrating his whole being.

This was the Holy Lance with which the Roman soldier, Longinus, pierced the Lord's Body, and which is known as the invincible lance of the Grail.

The Mystery of the Last Drop

The Mystery of the Last Drop has been preserved by followers with holiness and trepidation. Supreme love in its entirety is concentrated in the Last Drop. The Lord entered holy passion at Golgotha in Jerusalem and, for three hours, an incredible divine light poured out, leaving a message in Blood. This was the Ultimate Gospel which cannot be expressed in words. The Last Drop exceeded even these three hours of the indescribable bliss of the sunshine of Supreme Love and the birth of the sun of the new Divine Civilization. The Last Drop took His followers to the mysteries of the 3rd, 4th and 5th millennia; the mysteries of the future.

This is why the Last Drop is always connected with the Lance. The Blood in the Chalice was never used up.

Through contemplation and drinking of the Last Drop, the knights entered an even higher state of ecstasy. Their minds were enraptured in holiness. After this, began the mystical meal in the Holy Being.

Behind the page a young maiden carried two silver patens (plates) in her hands. Each of these bore the image of the vault of the heavens and the mysterious mark of Christ, the enraptured Bridegroom from the Royal Dynasty of Christ. In Byzantine theology, the foundation, known as the paten, entered the sanctuary and the place where the Chalice was kept, and represented the whole of the universe which is blessed in the Chalice of the Right Hand of the Most High.

They also carried two clean towels like the white cloths which Veronica had for collecting the Blood which multiplies and is spilled. The Last Drop crystallised like myrrh; it became transparent and was imbued with heavenly fragrances. They alone were enough to delight the heavens.

After the young maiden in the white and blue with the silver plates and the two white towels, at the Grail celebrations, came three young men with crowns on their heads, blue ribbons around their waists and carrying a white stole in their hands.

Behind them the page carried the miraculous Grail.

Its attraction was unlike anything else. Anyone contemplating the Chalice finds himself in the Holy of Holies, in the immediate presence of the Divinity. Christ dwells in the Chalice. Here is His Blood and His being (His Flesh closely connected with His Blood). The presence of the Eucharistic Christ of the Sacred Vessel was even greater than His immediate presence.

*

The theological schools of the Grail teach thus:

'Children, if the Lord came visibly and preached to you, you would remain as fast asleep and as ignorant as His followers. The Saviour foresees you, wise maidens, and wants to give you His Inner Self, and for this He does not need to appear in His superficial form. So, the time of the Last Supper and the raising of the Old Testament Chalice are over. The Eucharist is being realised and has been set alight from within. Particles of the same composition allow you to enter into blissful union with the Divine Beloved.

Pay heed to His sermon for today and His Good News for today! The Gospel of Christ continues. That which He wanted to say today, he will pass to you in the mystery of His Last Drop, the flame of which is so strong that it alone is sufficient to set alight all the oceans of the world.'

*

There can be no future for the brothers and sisters of Medjugorje or for the self-discrediting Niepokalanóws or Carmelites.

The Brethren of the Knights of the Grail are a model for the brethren of the whole of humanity. Alas for us, the masons, who were hated by the hunters of the Roman Curia, took more away from this brilliant, pure and sincere brethren than the well-fed abbots and so on, whose pockets were filled with money from the 'symphonist purses'.

*

The Grail did have its own spiritual leaders. However, the majority of these were hidden from the world and were generally in Christ's royal dimension, the Holy Being. Receiving the breath, and the mark, rather like fingerprints, is considered to be the highest level of training.

There is no need, my friend, to see Christ from the sidelines, or to hear His voice. No, my child! The Saviour gave us something greater than the never-ending and ubiquitous psalm-sounding voice of the Most High. And it is greater than discerning the voice of the Bridegroom.

My child, the Bridegroom does not limit Himself to just

talking to or healing the Bride: He invites her to the *Divine Union* and binds Himself to Her with mysterious bonds which are so sweet and blessed that no marriage bed can compare to them. This, my child, (the mysterious elders of the Grail set it up) is why the Divine Wisdom of Christ is handed down through secret channels, the origins and the marks.

Be attentive, open your heart and tighten your bonds! If you want the Lord to give you more than you know, you must burn with love. Love Him even more.

Know that all the wisdom of the world comes from Him. Know that all blessings come from Him. Know that He is the King who reigns in heaven and on earth. Life comes from Him. From Him come endless mercy and a treasury of gifts.

'Endless' means that you will receive all you had hoped for and more besides. How much you receive, though, will depend on your readiness to devote your life to Him and to favour Him above all the fleeting things of this world.

My child, – the elder continued, – why do you complain that the Lord does not appear to you except through texts, mysteries and the invisible work of the Holy Spirit? The Chalice! My son, do not forget the Chalice of the Grail! It is greater than any apparition of Christ. It is the greatest mystery of the Most High. The Lord is among us! The Lord is and always has been in the Chalice. May His Blood serve to enlighten you? It is a sign of the unprecedented love which is poured out and which surpasses everything, including the greatest human understanding. Go beyond your own boundaries. Become greater than yourself.

God, my child, became greater than Himself in order to become human. You too must become greater than yourself in order to receive the Gospel of Christ.

*

Unfortunately humanity becomes intoxicated on substitutes and imitations. The Chalices and hosts of the institutions are just one continuous swindle. The receivers do not understand that the sacred trophy they stole from the saints whom they murdered is not for them. In their hands it is a cursed object. All their actions are cursed and everything they have acquired by dishonest means also bears the mark of the curse.

If their pathetic imitations and stolen treasures were put on a ship, it would doubtless be doomed and sink to the bottom of the ocean. In the desert the owner of this treasury would be bitten by a deadly snake and, in the world, it would be attacked by robbers and stripped of everything.

The same fiasco is to be found in theology. Lying teachers have fed their unfortunate, misled followers on a diet of works by heathen philosophers such as Aristotle, Plato, the intellectual works of Thomas Aquinas and the ascetic treatises of their hermits as part of the work of an institution which purports to exist to serve a holy purpose... Nonsense! If they have achieved anything holy, they have only done so with the help of the Grail. The hazy light of the Grail, received at second or third-hand i.e. through external sources, seemed to have broken out and to reach them.

Look, my son, – continued the elder – millions of people receive the Flesh and Blood of the Lord. How many of them are sorcerers, serpents, dragons in human form, atheists, swindlers and so on? Such impurity! What is going on? The heavens are completely bewildered! My son, this is an absolute abomination!

From the point of view of their catechesis, it is sufficient for a newly converted person to know the fundamentals of the faith and to be baptised by a priest... It is essential to receive Christ's composition, to be of the same essence through spiritual purification, and for the heart to burn to a temperature high enough to melt a pearl, so that the Blood of Christ is set alight invoking the responsive Grail – Christ's age-old desire is to give His life out of love – kindling a fire of love and the constant ecstasy of holy passion day and night!

Did not Mother Eufrosinia whisper the prayer of Christ during those two hours which she devoted to restoring strength? She remained within the Holy Passion of the Eucharist from ten o'clock until midnight...

The Chalice did not abandon her. The Grail stood over blessed Eufrosinia, while she rested, half sitting on an old, black leather couch which was faded and worn.

*

My child, child of the Grail! Do we, the heirs of Christ, not want the royal power of the Divine Son to be spread throughout the whole world?

Oh Grail! Listen to what I have to tell you. The entrance to the Grail is via the holy anointed one, Mary Magdalene.

Even John's Gospel, the finest one, hardly mentions her. How theologians have racked their brains trying to understand the Virgin Mary as the Divine Mother, the Mother of God, the Eternal Virgin and Co-redeemer!.. The memory of Mary Magdalene has been erased. She is still the 'former harlot', wandering aimlessly, wringing her hands in despair at the Lord's tomb.

One Divine Mother is not enough, my child. The Gospels mention the 'other Mary'. John chapter 20 confirms what I have said: on the Sunday, Magdalene was the first to go to the tomb. She was the first to have the honour of seeing Him risen. He appeared to her straight away. He cared for her. In her he saw his posterity, holy union, and divine nuptials.

My child, without the mystery of mysteries, Mary Magdalene, Christ remains somewhat ethereal, in the mind and abstract.

The 'other' Mary was endowed with almost as much Divine Wisdom as the first Divine Mother. The Most Pure Virgin is to be divinized above all. After Her is Mary Magdalene. After Mary Magdalene is John, the favourite apostle. Then comes

Joseph the Sweetest, the royal heir and the most venerable prince of the dynasty of the Most High.

As an *anointed* one, Joseph was superior to the greatest and most revered monarchs in the world, such as Nebuchadnezzar, Caesar, Alexander the Great or Napoleon.

Mary Magdalene conceived by the Lord. This means that never before had He had such a close union with anyone, never before had he entrusted Himself to anyone, and the fire of divine love had never burned so brightly in anyone before. How seldom people appeal to Mary Magdalene! Meanwhile, after the Divine Mother, the second Mary became a 'role model' for the knights and maidens of the Grail. By imitating the Most Pure Virgin, she wanted to be like Her. Thus, she loved Him ecstatically and to the point of madness.

How many times Mary repented of her sins, recognising them with sorrow: her love affairs had happened whilst deeply deluded!

'Oh, if only I had known about You, Divine Beloved! My Divinity, my God, my Life! You are so fine! Why does no-one see you? If only I could give my life for you! If only I could give ten lives for you! If only, like the apostles, I could spread the news about You! But I am only a simple woman, and a sinner who has been made whole by You. You only needed to say, 'Go and sin no more', and the sin had been completely erased from my memory. You only needed to look right into my heart and You had ignited the flame of heavenly love within me. A bush was set alight within it, and I saw the bush where Moses had heard the voice of the Most High.'

Mary went to the tomb early in the morning. It was still dark. These two words 'early' and 'dark' say a lot.

It is too early for humanity to comprehend the mystery of Christ. It is understood within the Grail. The time has not yet come.

It is still dark. It is midnight, my child. How can you think about the king at night when all the kings are sleeping? 'Watchman, what of the night?' It is still midnight but dawn is approaching.

The soul of humanity is still dark, and the shadows of the underworld wander in the obscurity of unconsciousness. An unenlightened person, in the shadow of the ancestral curse that comes from original sin, is not ready to accept the light of Christ and become a child of the light.

Meanwhile, during His time on earth, the Saviour taught people as though they could have become His heirs. He taught for all eternity and He taught about the Holy Being, knowing that all the worlds that are seen and unseen could hear Him. 'Become sons of the light, while you have the Light, lest the darkness overtake you.'

It is early and it is dark...

Mary sees that the stone has been rolled away from the tomb. She runs away in confusion and in a trance. She understands nothing and remembers nothing. Where is her divine Beloved? How could He have abandoned her?

If He loved her, why did He not come down from the cross and get rid of those cursed Pharisees? Mary knew that, at Golgotha, stood those who had sentenced the Son to death; the same people he had made ashamed earlier, when he said to them, 'He that is without sin among you, let him first cast a stone.'

Oh, she does not believe anything! She does not believe that He was crucified, that He was dead. He is alive! He is the Divinity! He cannot die. He worked a miracle for her. He is risen.

She is the second, after the Most Pure One, to know that He is risen and will come to her with even greater power. He raised her from the dead. Thus, He told His followers that, if anyone drinks from the Chalice of the Grail and then dies, they will rise again.

Racking her brains, Mary ran to Peter and John. It was important to her to touch His flesh, to kiss His forehead, and to wash His wounds in her tears. To be driven mad with love, to hold Him and to remain with Him. Could she really not allow herself to do this?

'They have taken the Lord out of the tomb and no-one knows where they have laid Him!'

Mary's confusion spreads to the disciples. Peter and John are consumed by a holy passion. 'They ran together, but he who loved the greatest ran the fastest.' This was John, the spiritual stepbrother of Mary Magdalene.

The disciple who loved and the bride who was loved. Mary Magdalene and the friend of the Bridegroom.

What the disciples did not know (that Scripture said He would rise again), Mary knew with her feminine intuition. This is why she 'stood weeping outside the tomb' (Jn. 20:11).

Oh, she could not get enough of Him! What a miracle it was when suddenly, stooping over the grave, She saw two angels dressed in white, one sitting at the head and the other at the feet, where the Saviour's body had clearly lain. She was surprised by the angels' words, 'Woman, why are you weeping?', as if the angels did not understand why she was crying!

The angels of the Grail were amazed by the outpouring of so much holy passion and called Mary 'woman, wife.'

'I don't know where they have put Him, my Beloved.'

'Saying this, she turned round and saw Christ standing, but she did not know that it was Him.'

He did not go anywhere! He is here!

'Do you not know that He is not here?'

For the others, he is not. For her, though, He is here, omnipresent and belonging only to her.

She is the heart of the Gospel III (after the passion on Golgotha II). This is the Gospel of Mary Magdalene and His messianic branch.

Having heard His voice, she thinks He is a gardener. She senses the fragrance of heavenly flowers. She recognises His voice, but she dare not believe.

'Oh Sir! You must have been sent by God. Tell me where you have laid Him and I will take Him away', she says, again using her feminine intuition, not doubting for a moment that she has been given the right to find, bury and embrace Him. Only those connected with Him in a special way can say this. She attempts to touch Him and look at Him as before with her loving gaze.

'Sweetest Rabboni! My teacher, my Life, my Divinity!'

But He said to her:

'That is enough. Do not hold me, for I have not yet ascended to the Father. I have done everything that was needed. Now go to my brethren and say, 'As the Father sent me, so I am sending you.''

Commentators have only understood these words superficially as the apostles being sent out to spread the news. However, His Father sent Him by means of His birth from on high and by Immaculate Conception, and so He is sending them, the Knights of the Grail, into the world in the same way.

*

The theology of the Second Immaculate Conception is kept in the libraries of the Heavenly Grail. It is infinitely rich. There are thousands of volumes. There has never been a theologian who did not devote at least a few years to the heavenly contemplation of the Second Immaculate Conception.

What did Christ give His son of His own God-humanity? Can Joseph, born without blemish and royal son of God, be called the divinity himself? If he is an exact copy of Christ, is he not God, too? If so, then Mary Magdalene is the Divine Mother.

Divine Wisdom has brought about a new mystery of the Holy Trinity!

No, the Grail does not want to 'expose' this mysterious occurrence; the birth of the dynasty through Christ. It will remain a mystery and will not be the subject of theological debate, 'ecumenical councils', and all that led to the deadlock of the Antichrist by the 'glaive of Caesar', vanquished a thousand times over by the sword of the Grail and the sword of David.

Even from the little that has been said, though, it is clear that Mary Magdalene played a special role in the Gospel of Christ.

*

And so it is she, Mary Magdalene, filled with holy passion, in the house of Simon the leper who had been cured by Him, who brought an alabaster jar full of expensive myrrh and poured it on the head of the Myrrh King. She honoured Him in a way that no-one else had done.

This was a sign of heavenly divine love. Even the disciples objected: 'Why all this waste? This myrrh could have been sold for a large amount of money!' But He replied, 'Wherever My Gospel is preached all over the world, what she has done will be told in memory of her.'

This means that the Gospel cannot exist without this other mystery of the anointing in preparation for burial and resurrection and therefore without remembering the other Mary!

The myrrh of resurrection is a symbol of fulfilment through the Holy Spirit and worshipping of the whole of humanity through the person of Mary. She was to become the mother of a new, divine nation.

01.07.2005 Deris Island

The Way to the Castle of the Love-which-is-not-of-this-world

The Final Mystery of the Grail – Living in Supreme Love

What is the Grail? Where is the Grail? The Grail is the kingdom of the most virginal, most blessed state of being in love which cannot be found on earth, in its debased Adamite state. In order to receive the origin of this pure, heavenly existence in the kingdom of the Holy Being, it is essential to obtain the red rose and the white lily of the Grail, an olive branch and the ivory Horn of Plenty.

Can the Grail exist on earth? What exactly causes the vibration or the condition of the heart, known as virginal, which is continually growing in Love or the 'eternal flame', as it is called by the king of the Grail, the last Russian Emperor, *Mikhail Romanov* (Seraphim the Tender)?

To those who have fallen in virginal love and have been renewed (those renewed in Christ, the neo-adamites, or the Seraphites), this virginal love reveals a wonderful state of perpetual ecstasy. It is a love which never fades, which surpasses the spectrum of human (Adamite) experiences, and which conquers an individual's personal enemies (sin, flesh, the world, sickness, hell or death). It also conquers a person's 'objective' enemy – the devil.

The enemy uses all kinds of intrigues against the Grail, but can achieve nothing. He stares, but does not see. He breathes fire from his mouth, but burns nothing. He bites with venomous fangs, but his poison is benign. He makes threats and flashes his weapons like a powerful giant, but nothing happens.

*

'Tristan and Isolde' is the greatest of the legends of the Grail and perfectly expresses the nature of the perpetual ecstasy of being in virginal love. It is a state which surpasses that of the Adamites and their kinds of love. It even surpasses itself i.e. it is constantly increasing, and it surpasses that of the angels (surpassing that which surpasses).

Tristan (keeper of the Grail) is Joseph the Radiant, the glorious son of Christ, the second divine child, heir, boy-king of the Divine Civilization, the Saviour's successor, and one with the Holy Spirit, immaculately conceived by Mary Magdalene and existing in three persons (Tri (three) -stan). Isolde (Elizabeth) gives birth without blemish just as the Church of the Grail does, and she is the Queen of the Seraphites.

Tristan and Isolde undergo incredible suffering and torment. Isolde is imprisoned without trial by the 'black barons' (in the Grail the Inquisition takes the form of lords of gloomy castles) and is sentenced to burning at the stake. They give her to the lepers. Tristan is tortured, dies and then rises from the dead. Isolde anoints him with healing oils following a fatal blow from the knight Morholt. In keeping with the laws of the Grail, Tristan defends a small and persecuted power from the threat of the Rephaim. As king of Loonois (Lyonesse) and son of the king, Tristan begs, goes around in rags, covers himself in filth, poisons himself, and makes himself so ugly that he is unrecognisable...

The whole world is engulfed in the passion, the ecstasy and the unbelievable phenomenon that is the wedding of Tristan – Christ of the Parousia (the Second Coming) in the Grail and his royal dynasty – and the golden-haired Isolde – the Perfect Church, giving birth from on high to the new sons of God.

The Queen is perpetually filled with holy passion. Her heart has been wounded. Tristan does not come out of his consuming holy passion. The knights of the Grail are so overcome with grief that they cannot even think of making themselves comfortable. But the mystery of the Grail takes over and no intrigues, grief, threats, death sentences, executions, dragons or warriors can do anything with the ecstatic love, which is kept warm by the eternal flame and melted pearls. The Divine Wisdom of the Grail teaches the one thing that helps a person in their striving to know God, to do good and to live in a perfect society: love works miracles.

Starved of true, heavenly, virginal, unearthly love, tormented by rationalism, and caught in the clutches of the devil, cold, confused, 'frozen' humanity will yearn to drink from the springs of the Grail. Humankind yearns to drink the Love Potion which was given to Tristan and Isolde by the maid, Brangäne.

The divine potion was intended for King Mark but it was given by mistake (through the foresight of Divine Wisdom) to the mystic King Tristan. The Love Potion, which he drank on board the ship, was the Chalice of the Grail, the true Eucharist which sets the soul on fire.

So, this is the sun of the new humanity! This is the light of new life! The Grail is in the hands of the Glorious Branch of Melchizedek: the Grail which has come from the Second Solovki: the Grail is the never-empty chalice. The Grail, (a simple bottle of cheap wine drunk in the square in front of the grocer's shop in Buzuluk!) works miracles far greater than the thousands of ornate gold and silver chalices of the Inquisition institutions all put together.

One of the Kings of the Grail, *Innocent Baltski*, had three silver chalices made in preparation for a heavenly revelation. The first held one litre, the second held two and the third held three litres. The three-litre chalice was inexhaustible. It was possible to drink from it time and time again and all of humanity could drink its fill.

The last mystery of the Grail, the gift granted to humanity, is to live in supreme love. Its unique advantage is that it grants a state of rapturous ecstasy by igniting the candle of the heart. It soars above the world and works miracles. A person remains happy, no matter how many sorrows he is burdened with by God. He conquers them triumphantly and gloriously. Finally, as he passes through the gates of death with the strength of this rapturous, ecstatic, eternally virginal love, he is crowned in the Chambers of Eternal Love.

Thus, the elders of Solovki want to tell this mystery of the Grail to the world. The mystery has been granted at the cost of the Last Drop of the five million soldiers of Elijah and Enoch: five million last drops shed as they let out their final cry of anguish, before stepping over into eternity.

The blessed tomb is a miraculous revelation of the Grail. Those who have passed away yearn to drink just one drop from this vessel. They come to the liturgies of the priests of Melchizedek and are not interested in the fine Sofrinsk and other ornate vessels. These are not particularly difficult to produce but they do not contain the sacred Love Potion which has such power, even over the underworld. Orpheus once drank it and, with his love songs, he overcame the dog, Cerberus, and the twelve vicious hyenas which surrounded it. Snakes were calmed and the evil Erinyes ceased their raving and presenting their scores to those who had stepped over in to the darkness of Hades.

*

The Saviour has concentrated His Kingdom of Supreme Love, the lamp of the soul, and the inner sun within the Grail and nowhere else. He has named the Grail His Church. He has made a burning repentance (just as with the power of the staff of the Grail) dependent on putting on the robes of virginity and igniting the flame of the heart. Thus He has given this wonderful, rapturous, indescribable, incomparable, holiest state of being in ecstatic love as a key to deification (Theosis) and a key to the fulfilment of one's earthly purpose.

This is why, without the Grail, a person cannot reach the supreme mystery of their existence. This is why, when faced with the general crisis of the old churches, those in Tibet claiming to have found the new 'gardens of Moriah', and new religions, Divine Wisdom responds with the Grail Chalice. Humanity then takes an interest in it, like nothing seen before, and yearns to learn as much as possible about the Grail.

Now the Grail is selecting new disciples of Him who was Crucified and Risen, through the power of this ecstatic myrrh-anointed love. They are striving to enter through the heavenly gates of the Holy Being into this wondrous castle of the true sons of God: the sons and daughters of the Wedding Chamber. Then, when the Keepers of the Grail, together with the young maidens and the myrrh-bearing women, light the eternal flame of Jerusalem in their heart, their soul is blessed. It no longer wants to be separated from this wonderful experience of ecstatic love. With this love, it can work miracles, it can rise from the dead, it can overcome enemies and it can convert the cold-blooded, the hard-hearted and the weary. Eventually, with this love, the soul can cling to the Most High like a bride and be crowned in eternity.

25.06.2005 Deris Island

The Art of Training the Order of the Knights Templar

At the beginning of the story of Tristan (meaning 'sorrowful' or 'weeping elder') the greatest mystery of the Grail is revealed – that of the immaculate birth of the 'glorious divine child', conceived blamelessly out of the love of Mary Magdalene for Christ. This is a story of unprecedented love! The unfathomable victory over death is almost a Wedding Chamber, like the Assumption. The only ones resting in the family tomb are Joachim and Anna, the grandparents of the founder of the immaculate dynasty on earth.

Like Isolde, Mary Magdalene (the first Queen of the Grail) loved the Lord! He released within her, the former harlot, such potential for virginal love! Mary climbed a metanoic ladder of unprecedented turmoil, connected with the former harlot's ability to give herself entirely to the virginal happiness of chaste love.

Mary was amazed by her transformation. It seemed as though there could be no greater miracle. What could have been greater than the comforts of love, sensual pleasure, rich clients, smiles, parties, society and feasting? Mary loved sincerely, had affairs, sacrificed herself and wept. She loved selflessly and unconventionally. She broke the laws of the Pharisees which was why the Sanhedrin sentenced her to death by stoning. The Saviour protected her (although He knew that she was guilty). If it were not for the protection of the Most High, they would have stoned Him, too, and torn Him to pieces.

She loved Him, as no wife has ever loved her husband. He

was a Husband filled with the radiant Glory of the Divinity, which surpassed the beauty of the immortal angels. He was the first to come down to earth. She gave Him the love of all the virtuous wives in the world. She cared for Him second of all after the Most Pure Virgin Mary. Her love was filled with all her sensuality and all her willingness to sacrifice herself, to serve Him out of love and to die for Him. How Mary loved the Lord! She loved Him second of all after the Most Pure Virgin!

*

Meanwhile, Mark (the symphonist monarch, or Herod) reigned as king in Cornwall (the world church) alongside the barons (the religious authorities). However, Rivalin (Christ), king of Loonois: (loo = lap; nois = nous (Greek) divine mind; meaning 'heavenly lap' or 'heavenly bosom') waged war on Mark. Rivalin (the Lord) was deeply in love with Blancheflor (Mary Magdalene, the White Flower of eternal virginity). Out of the love between Rivalin/Christ and the beautiful Blancheflor (the fragrant white flower of the Grail), Tristan was born (Joseph the Younger, Joseph IV, the adopted 12th son of Joseph of Arimathea).

The King (Christ) went to war against the devil and the 'Synagogue of Satan', leaving Mary Magdalene in the care of Joseph of Arimathea (Marshal Ruald, also known as 'Firm Word', who was faithful to the last and the keeper of the last mysteries).

Blancheflor waited for Rivalin for a long time (Mary searched for the Lord, 'Where have they taken my Beloved. Where is He?'). He would never return, though. Then, one day, she learned that Rivalin had been killed in battle (the Lord was crucified). Blancheflor (Mary Magdalene) began to languish. Then, in unbearable sorrow and racked with grief, she gave birth to his son.

Taking him in her arms, Blancheflor said:

'I am dying of grief; because I waited for my Christ (Rivalin) and He did not come. My son, you were born out of great sadness and so I am naming you Tristan or the Sorrowful One of the human world, the Weeping One of the magnificent Grail, the Crystal Vessel.'

After these words, Blancheflor (Mary Magdalene) kissed her son warmly with a heavenly kiss and, having passed on to him his inheritance from Christ and her love, as well as promising eternal maternal care from heaven, she passed away.

Ruald Firm Word (Joseph of Arimathea) took Tristan away and brought him up (the son of the Saviour, immaculately conceived). Then, when the royal boy turned seven years he entrusted him to his wise mentor, the groom Governal (an officer of the Grail).

From this point onwards, the story describes the art of educating the knights Templar and reveals the internal details of the birth of the invincible warriors. Here the legend of the Grail is almost the same, verbatim, as the revelation of Askold-Nikolai, founder and messiah of the Russian Grail, who was true long before Vladimir the Baptist of Rus'.

Tristan was trained in the following arts, as befitted him heir of the royal dynasty of the *divine humanity*. It is destined to reign on earth for a thousand years and, until that time, it is to be kept away from the world in the Holy Being. He mastered the lance. Joseph gave him the Holy Lance and revealed to him the mystery of the Last Drop as well as the filling and multiplying of the Chalice. He gave him the sword of the Grail (the blade of eternal virginity), the shield (immaculate origin) and the bow (the art of unblemished virginity to defeat enemies). He learned to despise lies and treachery (the superficial church) In the Grail, this inheritance of deception and treacherous deeds is given grave consideration. He learned to help the weak (serving others selflessly) and to keep his word (promise of faithfulness and the warm-heartedness of brotherhood). He studied singing (a silent prayer of the Parousia in the presence of the Divinity), the harp (the inexhaustible Psalter and the mysterious entrance to the Wedding Chamber) and hunting (spiritual warfare).

The lance, sword, shield and bow are accessories from the treasury of Divine Wisdom. Worshipping Her is at the heart of the school of the Grail.

From the True Church, the young Joseph (Tristan) obtained the gifts and graces of the Holy Spirit, immortality, the pearls released through fire (the Grail, released into the heart through communion), and the ability to form a union with the Most High, with his fellow men, with verse, with the animal kingdom and with the sea. When Tristan rode on horseback it seemed as though his horse, visor, armour, sword and shield were all inseparable parts of one indestructible whole.

Everyone praised the fine youth who was steadfast and strong. From the earliest days of his childhood, the boy showed signs of the wonders of Wisdom. Like the Lord, he could speak from birth. He shed tears and asked Ruald the Firm Word (Joseph of Arimathea) about his father (he wanted to know every detail), and about his mother who loved him immensely. This mysterious disciple of Christ and father of the royal messianic dynasty succeeded in his studies like no-one else.

Through its allegorical symbolism, the story of 'Tristan and Isolde' also shows how the Grail sent the immaculately conceived son of Christ into the world.

Some Norwegian merchants (the Pharisees) lured him onto their ship, exploiting his straightforward nature, purity of heart and his indescribable beauty and intellect, just like Joseph of Egypt.

'But the sea does not like treacherous ships (the Pharisees' churches) and does not come to the aid of kidnappers and betrayers.' The saints of the Kingdom are enemies of the Roman Villain and the Byzantine Rogue. Luring the holy ones into their camp, they invoked a storm at sea.

Because of the robbery committed by the merchants and

swindlers (the vendors in the temple, or Mammon in the Mafia church) the ship seemed to be on the verge of disaster, and the sailors (simple believers) understood what must be done. 'We must put Tristan ashore!' The *anointed* one could no longer remain in the protection of the old church.

They 'set ashore' the son of Christ. Joseph the Blessed spent a long time in seclusion. There was no place for him on earth. The Pharisees, with their German Shepherds, could sniff him out anywhere, in any country. The Saviour set aside the small *Nightingale Mountain* for him, for his assumption, on the Altar of Union, into the Holy Being. Here, the enemies are powerless. They cannot reach the throne of the Most High in the fifth dimension. Not one of them can walk before the Most High, heed His voice, walk about both on earth and in heaven, or follow the mysterious commandment of 'Shema Yisrael' ('Hear, Oh Israel, what I say to you today. Follow it and carry it out'), 'Love Me with your whole being' etc.

'The heavens shone and the boat set Tristan down on a sandy beach.' Thus began the road to the Castle of the Grail and to the True Church.

The young Joseph struggled to comprehend Christianity with its dogma, the theological arguments among the first Christians, the endless definitions of the truth from the different schools, 'heretics' and 'orthodox' Christians, and so on. This rift was unfathomable to him. He knew Christ from within, on a spiritual level, better than anyone else. Christ lived in him, just as the Father lived in His Only-begotten Son.

'Beyond the deserted hills (the loneliness of the chosen one in the world), he discovered an endless forest (spiritual knowledge).' Tristan (Joseph) realised how Judeo-Christianity had only a limited understanding of Christ's mission. The endless forest symbolises the hidden Divine Wisdom of the mission which is not yet accomplished. In the world, Tristan grieves over Governal (his first mentor for the True Blood), who had opened his eyes to the Lord, to the Blood which had been collected on Golgotha, to the fate of the Chalice, and to the miraculous Immaculate Conception out of love, out of mortal yearning and out of his mother's death from untold happiness (Mary Magdalene / Blancheflor). Doing penance in the superficial church, the future King of the Grail also grieves for Ruald (Joseph of Arimathea) and for the land of Loonois (the Chalice of the Grail).

'Suddenly in the distance, he heard the call of a hunting horn (the Horn of Plenty or Cor Benic which proclaims the wondrous, supreme gifts of Christ manifest in him). A fine stag appeared on the edge of the forest (Joseph found the gift of instant ecstasy in the Kingdom as well as first-hand knowledge of his father, Christ). Hunters and a pack of dogs (in Grail terms, the true image of the church as 'dogs hunting down the saints') were following hot on the trail of the stag. The hunters plunged their spears into the stag (the mystery of the Holy Lance at Golgotha and the Lord's heart, pierced by the Roman soldier), and were about to cut off its head with a knife (the terrible punishment which the Pharisees had planned for the dead Lord).'

Tristan stopped them and taught them a different hunting custom. The precious hide which Tristan took from the stag is a sign of the inheritance of the mysterious robes of the divinity incarnate and the essence of Christ.

'Let me hunt with you (those who seek the mysteries of the Most High)! I will show you hunting pleasures which you have never known', Tristan said to his new friends. The horsemen led him to the court of King Mark (an heir of the Grail related to the royal dynasties of the Stuarts, the Merovingians and many other European royal families). The beautiful castle of Tintagel (meaning 'Crystal Palace of the Immaculate Conception') arose before them. According to the legends of the Grail, it was here that Christ was mysteriously united with Mary Magdalene. Here, in the Holiest of Holies, the Immaculate Conception took place. Tristan (Joseph, the 12th adopted son of Joseph of Arimathea) did not know of this.

King Mark (the European monarchies) was moved by the beauty, intellect and knowledge of the royal boy, the true ruler of Loonois (the Kingdom of Christ on earth), and took him into his service. 'During the day Tristan accompanied Mark in the court room (the Inquisition) and on hunting parties (spiritual struggles), and at night he kept vigil, playing his harp in the royal quarters (composing a silent prayer).'

Ruald the Firm Word (Joseph of Arimathea) spent many years searching for Rivalin's (Christ's) son. Eventually, he found him in the Grail and realised that the time had come to reveal to Joseph the mystery of the Keeper of the Chalice. Having been raised to the rank of a knight by his uncle (Joseph of Arimathea serves the Eucharist together with Joseph the Blessed, the son of Christ), Tristan goes to sea in Cornwall's ships and challenges Duke Morgan to a battle (in the Grail, the image of this rogue, who illegally seized the kingdom of Loonois, represents Caiaphas, the spirit of the world's Pharisees and the murderer of his father, Rivalin (Christ), to a battle.

Having killed him in fair combat, the young heir takes the reins of the Kingdom of Christ.

But what is this? The time has not yet come. Tristan calls the faithful Ruald (Joseph of Arimathea) and says to him, 'My father!' As Christ called the Betrothed One 'father', so Joseph the younger calls his adoptive father, Joseph of Arimathea, 'father', seeing Christ in him. He knows that, as Joseph suffered for his Father, so, too, Joseph of Arimathea guards the greatest of all mysteries, the ineffable treasure – the Saviour's Blood, from which come the future of humanity and the transfiguration of the present.

'My Father! The Most High determined today that the world should be ruled by You. So I will leave this land (the Grail, the Kingdom of Heaven on earth), although I love it infinitely. My place now is in the world. I will go to Cornwall and serve King Mark.'

*

The Grail remains in the shadows, in the catacombs and in the Holy Being. It is completely inaccessible but can always be seen. It is possible to see it today, here and now. No-one can distinguish it from under the veil, though, without Divine Wisdom to open their eyes.

25.06.2005 Deris Island

❧

The Story of the True Church

Tristan and Isolde. This is the story of two devoted lovers from England...

What will people say? 'The elder[8] is mad! He has exchanged leadership for the monastic life of Ignatius Brianchaninov, Barsanufius the Great, John the Prophet and Abba Dorotheus, cutting himself off in the wilderness and engrossed in the legends of the medieval minnesingers which are like children's stories!'

Tristan and Isolde are greater than these learned and aged leaders. The latter have not experienced ecstatic love. If they had it would have been sealed off and effectively forbidden. The majority of it would have been 'lost' in the royal censor. It was not considered appropriate to indulge in the likes of holy passion and ecstasy.

Those who experience human passion should go to confession and rid themselves of human passions. On the other hand, a person experiencing holy passion is lifted up so high before the Most High that the priests come to him to make their confession.

There is another reason. The Saviour did not leave any ascetic or spiritual treatises and He Himself spoke in parables. 'Tristan' is a great and wise parable of Christ, in a long adventure novel. But what a joy it is to use the Grail's hermeneutic key to reveal the mysteries of supreme love and to see what lies behind these allegorical tales! What a marvellous world is

[8] *Elder* – here, the author of the book.

revealed behind them! So many priceless pearls can be found in something which resembles a fairy tale for five-year-olds.

I have found more in the legends of the Grail, which are aimed at children, than in the learned monks' 'guides to perfect holiness'. It is a different world. This is the story of the True Church.

'All that you are saying is madness, isn't it? What about the textbooks of Znamensky, a doctor of theology, or the catechetical tomes of Grigory Dyachenko? What about everything that Professors Golubovsky and Glubokovsky, or church history authorities have to say about the mystery of Christ's work and His mystical body (the church)?'

Alas for us. The true history of the Church is sealed and encrypted. Possibly the only way to access it is through allegory and mysticism. From beginning to end it has been subject to injustice, torture, passion and repression. It spread everywhere, but this went virtually unnoticed. All of this can be seen in the story of Tristan and Isolde, a story of the superhuman love of two people who love with profound, spiritual passion, driven out of their minds with love, who drank the fiery Love Potion (the Grail) and literally took leave of their senses because of that love.

If only humanity would follow the example of the beautiful love of Tristan and Isolde, and not Sergiev Posad or the Vatican!

The Byzantine Rogue demonstrated its approach to church history. It 'wiped away' the second Solovki Golgotha without trace. The hundred million dying groans, the hundred thousand filled with divine rapture, the power of the Kingdom, the Lamb transfigured on Sekirnaya hill, 150 apparitions of the Divine Mother, and the birth of the burning hierarchy, are as nothing to it. Worse still, it is something hostile and the number one threat. The Patriarchy created the impression that nothing had happened. As far as they were concerned Seraphim the Tender was a 'fraud', an 'imposter' and a pretender to the Romanov throne. The True Orthodox Church 'never existed', the catacombs were 'dreamed up' and so on. The *Solovetsky Archipelago* is only the history of Zosima and Savvaty and there are now some 5-star Intourist hotels on the site of the martyrdom of the *Second Golgotha,* which was heralded by the Most Pure Virgin during the time of Peter the Great.

This approach, initiated by the Patriarchy, has always been an inherent part of the rogue church. It is guided by its madness and self-deception, bordering on clinical idiocy.

In order to identify the true history of the Church it is necessary to don a pilgrim's robes and to assume the image of a wandering preacher. Then, instead of visiting the shrine of St. Sergius (the traditional saint of the Orthodox symphonists, the 'Black Hundred' and necromancers), one should go to the unheralded cell of the last Russian Tsar, Seraphim Romanov, on Frunze Street in Buzuluk. Perhaps one should also venerate the myrrh-weeping cross on his anonymous grave which is now unknown to anyone except two or three of his surviving fellow 'pains in the neck'.

So did the treasury of Solovki leave without a trace? Never! The Virgin of Solovki weeps myrrh. The victims of Solovki are beginning to speak! Their story is allegorical, though, and it is continued through something unique – the Divine Civilization and the Immaculate Conception.

The true story of the Church is not just hidden; it does not want to reveal itself. It deliberately conceals itself from the uninitiated because, in the Grail, it is known that Christianity is intended for the people of a future generation. But we preach Christ crucified; unto the Jews indeed a stumbling block, and unto the Gentiles foolishness.

The way to access the mysteries of Christ is not only through an elder (*starets*), but also through the Grail.

Paul experienced the burning conversion of the church.

'You cannot be saved through the law. You can be saved by Christ, the redeemer.'

What did Paul experience during this conversion (not a personal one, but church-wide) which broadened his vision to encompass the whole universe? God is not only the God of the Jews, but also of the Greeks and the whole of humanity. Christ came to save everyone.

Is it possible to be saved by Christ today? Not by the 'old' Christ from two thousand years ago, and not by the grey-haired 'Ancient of Days' and the Heavenly Host, but rather by a thirty-year-old Lamb, bearing the sins of the world on His shoulders.

If Christ had fulfilled His mission (deification) maybe it would not be possible to be saved by Him today. However, the Saviour created the other Church; the anointed one and the bride, which is hidden from the world. He has made a place for it in the Holy Being. Now he has decided to tell the world about the birth of the Civilization of Christ.

You cannot be saved now by the 'holy fathers' or through repentance. Like Paul's laws, they are for children. You cannot now be saved by the Jerusalem Golgotha, but only by the Second Solovki Golgotha. Only by drinking from the Chalice of the Grail and climbing the holy stairs of deification to the place of the Assumption on Nightingale Mountain, can you be saved. Declare and confirm the throne of the *Divine Union* and the wisdom of Holy Theogamy.

The disciples of the Most High are called now to reject Christianity. After having undergone Paul's church-wide *metanoia,* understand that Christ, as a grey-haired old man of two thousand years, cannot save you. You can be saved, however, by the Boy King; the young Paraclete, the Holy Spirit, radiantly magnificent, immaculate, perfect, the crowned conqueror and as beautiful as the civilization of eternally young virgins which He proclaims.

25.06.2005 Deris Island

The Sword of David versus the Sword of Tibet

Paul dared to teach about the 'mind of Christ'. The mind of Christ really is granted by Divine Wisdom. The origin of Christ, though, is greater than his 'mind'.

As the Holy Spirit gave His whole being to Christ, the betrothed Divinity Incarnate, through the Virgin Mary, so Christ was destined to pass on, in the most intimate way, His essence, composition, mysteries, holy pollen, and the image and likeness of the God-Human. This He did, by means of the most mysterious method known to the Grail – Immaculate Conception.

From Christ, Joseph the Brilliant received that which no other disciples were able to obtain; not just His spirit, but His soul and His flesh as well. The boy was so like his divine Father, that people said, 'He is the very image of the Lord!' He truly was one with Christ. It can be said that the Lord's life on earth was being continued in His only son.

Joseph passed the origin of Christ on further (in the same immaculate way as the Lord had done previously). This is the most important element of the existence of the god-human in order to enable the deification and transfiguration of an Adamite created for Christ by Divine Wisdom.

The mystery of Joseph reveals a new aspect of the church. The Roman Harlot, with her magnificent celebrations, her carefully thought-out and logically structured (more for the benefit of the institution) dogma, council decrees etc., pales into insignificance.

The greatest mystery is that the Lord was with the other Church!

*

...In his youth Joseph has a victory similar to that of David. This is mentioned in 'Tristan and Isolde.'

A giant Irish knight by the name of Morholt (the enchanted origin of Eternal Death), flexing his muscles, demands tribute from King Mark. No-one could fight Morholt, who was known for his physical strength and his magical powers. His sword was enchanted and his lance and arrows were poisoned. With him, anything could happen.

Morholt is a symbol of the heathen strength and the magical powers of Tibet. A knight of the Grail cannot become firmly convinced of the strength of the invincible sword of David unless he can be victorious in a similar way; by defeating the glaive of Caesar. Morholt is the personification of the proud strength of Caesar. He is proud, conceited, arrogant and, like Goliath, confident of his own victory.

That which happened in Israel is repeated: David was the only one who volunteered to defeat Goliath, indignant at the insults of the Most High. Tristan was not afraid of Morholt and threw down the gauntlet.

The fighting took place on the distant St. Samson's Isle. Just as with the fight between David and Goliath, the fate of the country was decided by the clash of two warriors.

The physical combat was preceded by spiritual sparring in which the nature of the fight was decided. Goliath attempted to intimidate David, 'why are you coming at me as if I were a dog?' David, though, retorted with an outburst of righteous anger, like a lightning bolt, saying, 'I come to you with the power of the Most High.'

Morholt sailed to St. Samson's Isle in a boat with a rich, purple sail. He was the first to arrive and set about making vital preparations. He found his opponent surprising. The heathen

Rephaim was overwhelmed by the fact that, in the realm of King Mark, there was someone who was not afraid of him. Humble Tristan arrived soon after him in a simple boat. Having disembarked, he kicked his boat back out to sea.

Morholt could not help asking:

'What are you doing? Why have you not tied up your boat?'

'What is the point?' replied Tristan. 'Only one of us will be leaving here alive. Is one boat not enough?'

The outcome of the fight was a forgone conclusion. Tristan had the powers of heaven on his side. Thus Tristan prevailed.

The dialogue which took place shows Tristan's unprecedented belief in his own victory. The same was true of Joseph the Brilliant and Great. He was a 'Desposynos', king of the dynasty of Christ, and the second divine human after Christ, his Father on heaven and on earth.

After several hours of fighting, Tristan split the skull of the proud Morholt with his sword, and then returned to the mainland in his enemy's opulent vessel. The people were shocked. Shouts of terror rang out, 'Morholt!'

Soon, though, as the boat approached, they saw Tristan. In his hands he held two swords.

The return of this knight of the Grail in the boat is not only a sign of victory, but also of a spiritual conquest. The sword of the Grail had been put to the test.

Joseph the Brilliant, the greatest of the kings of the dynasty of the Most High, demonstrated a miracle of bravery: the sword of Eternal Virginity, the sword of the Grail, turned out to be more powerful than the sharpened blade of Tibet. The fallen angels' magic did not work.

The Mystery of the Grail is that It continuously battles with 'the rulers of the darkness of this world' (Paul) in human form – giants, titans, and feigned sons of the Most High – and defeats them. The sword of David is kept in an ivory casket and passed down from Christ to His son with His blessing.

During the fight, Morholt managed to wound Tristan with his poisoned lance. The hero's blood was contaminated: he drank from the cursed cup before drinking from the goblet of hot wine. The Holy Lance and the Last Drop were fighting against the poisoned and bewitched magic lance. The sword of the Grail fights against the glaive of Caesar and the sword of Tibet.

A warrior of the Grail is familiar with spiritual adversity. He also has the keys to victory. His is the war cry:

Led, perceptive, invincible
Pure, spotless, untouchable
Son of the Most Pure Virgin.

Not one of the heirs of Christ has ever suffered a single defeat at the hands of their enemy. The dynastic branch believes that the Saviour brought about redemption for the whole of humanity, but He passed His power on to His posterity, as a Father to His children, the spiritual and mystical dynasty. We are particularly talking about a spiritual dynasty (in spite of the fact that many of the heirs of Christ through Joseph married and had children) as the mark of the Grail is passed on primarily through spiritual inheritance and often by immaculate means.

Joseph resembled his Father... His body was becoming frail and his blood was slowly drawing to a standstill. Tristan asked King Mark to take him away in a boat without oars or sails. Why would he need a sword and oars? He only needed a harp (the Psalms of David). That was all he needed to restore his spirit. For the rest he would rely on the Most High and on his Father, Whose presence was always with him. The Lord frequently appeared to Joseph. Their love was boundless.

Morholt's niece, the fair-haired Isolde, was the only one who knew about healing medicines...

The woman bore such hatred for her uncle's murderer. Although she wanted him to die more than any other woman in the world, she was also the only one who was able to save him.

Such is the wisdom of the Grail. Medicinal ointments and herbs are intended to be used in oils for anointing.

So, in his youth, Joseph experienced holy passion, death, and the great battle with evil spirits. He received his training, though, from true teachers (Governal, the groom and friend of the simple and pure hearted Joseph).

***

The love between Tristan and Isolde was chaste and filled with holy passion. They had no carnal relationship.

Banished by King Mark (the symphonist monarch surrounded by four aristocratic bishops), Tristan and Isolde fled to the forest of Moriah (to the enclosure of the Holy Being in the fifth dimension; the garden of Wisdom). A woodcutter spotted them and informed the king. The unfortunate Mark swore he would kill Tristan and Isolde or die himself.

He saddled his horse and galloped into the forest, followed by his retinue. There, he held his sword over Tristan and...

What is this? 'The lips of Tristan and Isolde had not touched. The sword's sharp blade separated their bodies.'

In the Celtic tradition the sharpened blade which separated the two sleeping bodies is a symbol of the lovers' chastity. The sword of the Grail, the sharpened blade of supreme love, separated the two beautiful, chaste lovers and saved their lives.

'Dare I slay these living saints?' said King Mark. 'Their love is not of this world (it is of unearthly dispensation). To kill them would be an even greater sin than to have them die a martyr's death by burning at the stake.'

Mark removed his emerald ring and placed it on Isolde's finger.

This is a sign of the Grail: the symphonist king loses his connection with the True Church. A symphonist monarch can be kind, quiet like Alexis of Russia, possessed like Ivan the Terrible, a reformer like Peter the Great, or else like multiple incarnations of Caesar on the throne. However he appears in the eyes of the people – good or evil, great or weak – he remains outside the True Church and has been ensnared by Roman-Byzantine symphonism.

The wisdom of the Grail teaches that the glaive of Caesar is powerless against the sword of Eternal Virginity. Eternal Virginity illuminates the mind which unites with the Grail. This sword has defeated dragons. This sword has penetrated to the very bottom of the swamp. This sword has slain snakes in the cave at the bottom of the swamp.

The sword of David is the brilliant, sharpened sword of Eternal Virginity. Divine lovers place it between each other as they recline on their Altar of Union, so that the enemy can have no power over them. The glaive of Caesar cannot reach them as it has already been carried away above their heads.

*

Tristan and Isolde experience the endless temptations which are sent the virgin lovers by Holy Theogamy – the Divine Wisdom of the castles of the Grail.

They have no opportunity to receive communion. It is ordered that they be burned alive in front of everyone. The king gives his beautiful, beloved wife to a hundred repulsive lepers. Yvon promises the most disfigured of them that his wife would be subject to a disgrace worse than death. She will lead an unbearable existence. No woman on earth has ever ended her days in such a terrible way as to be handed over to a pack of lecherous lepers whose foul stench could be smelled from a mile away.

When they are in virginal love, the sword of this love (or the banner of supreme love) protects them. However much supernatural suffering they are called to bear, love always prevails.

*

The Second Solovki should only be read in the light of the Grail. Only through the light of the Grail is it possible to explain the superhuman suffering of Seraphim and his twelve *starets*[9]. However, their Holy Being, their return from the radiant heavens of the liturgy and their immortality are the revival,

[9] Wise followers.

in Holy Rus', of the fine orders of knights, especially the most perfect order of the virginal Knights Templar.

Ordinary lovers sleep holding each other closely. There is no dividing sword between them. This sword which separates flesh from flesh, though, also protects and preserves. The Grail teaches that there is no stronger shield than the unsheathed sword of eternal virginity. It gives strength to its glorious warriors.

From the depths of despair, obscurity, the interminable office of sin, eternal pursuit, and in anticipation of eternal torment, from an unexpected judgement, or the Antichrist, or being banished from a monastery, the knights of supreme love and their beautiful myrrh-bearing women never experience the states of grief, despair, hopelessness and abandonment which are inherent to the Adamites – they are happy because the strength of love which has been ignited within them conquers all hardships and troubles.

The forest of Moriah is an endless swamp full of snakes, obstacles and dragons' lairs, obstructing the way to the Grail. It is possible to pass through the fires of temptation within the forest in order to reach the fulfilment of Supreme Love. Happy is he to whom the Grail comes; he who is chosen by the Grail in its white ivory castles. Inside there are tables of onyx and rings of pure emerald. Happy is he who, having tasted the potion of divine love, no longer fears anything and easily overcomes all the obstacles on the way to the kingdom of supreme love.

*

It is important to understand that what is referred to in the Greek language as 'agape' (supreme love) is superior to human mutual affection and even the higher notion of romantic love. The secret of entering through its gates is known only to the dynasty of Christ and the Grail. Without being anointed by them it is impossible to pass through.

25-26.06.2005 Deris Island

Owain, the Divine Man,

or the Grail which has been returned to the suffering world

Oh my Templar brethren! Today you gallop on dun horses; golden-haired knights riding out to guard the new church of Solovki, the church of the eternal sun of the Most High, the church of Christ Multiplied, and the church of the inner sun.

The evil villain worked hard to erase the memory of the knights, the likes of which were not to be found on earth. The knights of the White Lion, the knights of the sword of the Grail, the knights of Supreme nobility. The knights whose Lady is the Eternal Virgin; knights of Eternal Virginity. The knights and invincible warriors in the spiritual fight. The knights whose chain mail, armour, visor, sword, lance, horse, shared meals, brotherhood and fellowship were shrouded in a mystery which was completely inaccessible and of unearthly origin.

Silver goblets, silver tables decorated in gold; sandalwood beds draped in crimson silk and cambric... Oh, how sweet these things are! How they caress the ears of the Bride! How fine her Bridegroom is! How great is the two hundred-year-old Song of Songs amongst the knights of the Grail and the keepers of the Chalice!

This is where the True Church is to be found! In an instant it can take control of all the castles in the world. Its army is stronger than that of the black thief, the bishop of Rome.

By coincidence, the treacherous villains managed to drive out the order of living saints – the order of the Holy Archangel Michael on earth. They were the embodiment of angels, having taken a vow of eternal virginity. They knew Christ in a special way: he was in their blood. They were His dynasty, the dynasty of the messianic Lamb. Thus the Grail gave them kingdoms, worlds, lands, clothes, castles, relations, admirers and happiness. This was completely indescribable. They loved allegories and were happy and contented. Their favourite occupation was inventing parables and fables and entertaining one another. They were filled with supreme light as they drank from the mysterious spring. Their poetry, odes and fables about the Lady of the Spring spread throughout France, Ireland, England and indeed the whole world. When they came to the attention of the Roman 'Highnesses' and 'Excellencies', the latter became sullen and plotted to destroy the Knights of the Immaculate Virgin.

What kind of spring was this which was guarded by a Black Knight on a black stallion?

'Using a silver goblet, draw water from the spring, pour it out onto a stone and you shall hear thunder and lightning. You will find yourself in a fine castle. Before doing so, though, you must first defeat the Black Knight.'

This is a miraculous spring (the Orthodox Church speaks of the Life-giving spring) – the Immaculate Conception. This is not the Most Pure Virgin as described in iconic *akathists,* portrayed on fonts etc. This is the Immaculate Conception, the origin of the other life and the Seraphitic Lady.

This spring not only cleanses, but also brings immortality, satisfies a person's inner hunger (his immortal composition). It does not just 'wash', but also brings about a new birth. This is a life-giving spring: it is the Heart of the Most Pure Virgin. It has not forsaken the sons of Christ. Mary stretched out over them and washed them, and they were reborn.

*

...The handsome, golden-haired Owain rode up to a marvellous, radiant castle surrounded on all sides by a moat filled with water (the Grail). The Owner of the Castle (the keeper of the Chalice) came to meet him with two golden-haired heirs. 'They took me by the hand and led me triumphantly into the great hall of this beautiful castle' (where the mystical meals are held and where Christ of the Grail came, talked and enraptured).

What did Owain, Knight of the White lion, see in that hall? There were twenty-four virgins, each one prettier than the rest, in golden robes decorated with a mysterious range of spiritual symbols (the hieroglyphs of Divine Wisdom) seated at tables and embroidering an atlas with gold thread. They were so beautiful! No woman in all of Britain and Ireland was more beautiful than them. These twenty-four maidens from the retinue of the Keeper of the Grail, these twenty-four wondrous saints of the True Church, shone with virginal beauty.

The virginal knights were surrounded by these beautiful myrrh-bearing women. The women waited on the knights who sat at a round table, just as the Most Pure Virgin waited on Christ and the apostles. They helped them out of their dusty armour, then washed it and polished it so that it glowed like a fire. They set the table and served wonderful dishes, expensive wines and salads with delicious herbs. Then others entered carrying trunks full of fine linen clothes scented with expensive perfumes and yellow silk scarves decorated with a border.

This is how the Grail describes the mystical meals, during which the Blood of Christ is multiplied. The likes of such meals have never before taken place on earth. Christ came and shared Himself with them. The wedding feast at Cana continued every day.

No-one can comprehend the life of the Templars. It was transported away to other castles – those of the Holy Being, or the Kingdom. The Grail, which was kept at Monsalvat (the Templars' castle), did not sleep and did not remain inert, but came, filled with holy passion, multiplied and fed people. Thus the Knights became the Progeny of Christ, sealed in Him as the living, messianic dynasty.

To call them angels would be too mild. They were much

more exalted than angels and more powerful than demons. They were full of mystery, in the image and likeness of the Most High Himself.

Before the meal the serving maidens brought out silver bowls and pitchers of water. They washed their feet and tenderly looked into their eyes. 'How else may I serve you, gracious knight?' said one of the beautiful maidens. The knight could not take his eyes off her because of her beauty, grace and elegance, as well as her extraordinary attire. He enquired, 'What does this hieroglyph mean? Why is this octagonal Burning Bush coloured orange? And what is the significance of this mysterious emerald framed in gold on your finger?' The table was covered with a transparent cloth made of a heavenly fabric. The dishes laid on it were pure silver and gold. The knights and maidens sat around the table in silence until they began the rapturous prayer, filled with holy passion, of the dynasty of Christ.

In them was the blood of Joseph the Brilliant, the Keeper of the Grail, the sweetest comforter, and the only son of the Lord. The Saviour multiplied Himself through His children. This Immaculate Conception was mentioned in the heavenly scrolls of the book of Genesis, 'Be fruitful and multiply.'

*

'Oh holy knights! How long is the hour of blessed communion?.. There is too much evil in the world!'

So, Owain, the blessed knight of the White Lion, having tasted the wine of the horn of plenty, bade farewell to his dear sisters, returned to them the yellow silk scarf with the border of blue lilies, and set off to answer the call of the Grail bell, in aid of an innocent person.

'Where is my Lord crucified?' asked the radiant knight who was not of this world, and who had bathed in the life-giving springs. He yearned to unleash his wondrous bravery. He was looking for a worthy opponent.

His opponent is the adversary, the enemy and the devil. Oh! Only the knights of the Grail, the holy Templars, can gallop bravely on white horses into the castles of this 'black baron', the 'bloody count' and the monster in whose power a beautiful wife languishes. The warriors of the Grail are not of this world and their opponents are the Ben Elohims, the 'black knights' and the feigned sons of God. They each hold swords in their hands. Who became an enemy of their Father through the flesh and blood of Christ? The 'Black Knights' of the Sanhedrin.

The people of Christ (the dynasty of the Most High on earth and the birth of the true sons of God, born of Christ and Mary Magdalene, and from the Holy Spirit in the waters of the Most Pure Divine Mother) only have one adversary – the one-eyed and one-legged Black Giant, the 'devil incarnate', or the Pope. This is precisely how he is seen in the castles of the Grail. This evil villain guards his dense, bewitched forest (this world which is under the power of the devil) and tends to his herd of wild beasts (those not versed in spirituality; a blind congregation).

Behind this black knight lurks another evil monster – the Black knight on his black horse. Only a one-eyed pirate can go to the place where the devil lives: Tibet.

The Grail and Tibet. Such absolute opposites! This is a clash between the two origins on the earth! Christ and Master Morya. The Tree of Life and the Tree of Knowledge. Saint Eufrosinia and Helena Roerich. Saint Seraphim the Tender and Madame Blavatskaya.

It is impossible to understand anything with only a simplistic approach towards the Grail! The 'Black Knight' is the name of the enemy. The black knight, on his black horse with a black cudgel in his hand, guards the Holy Spring.

Oh! How can this be? Has Lourdes been handed over to the Pope? Did the Divine Mother appear to one of the members of the Roman Curia, saying, 'I am the Immaculate Conception'? No. She came to Bernadette Soubirous, a semi-literate peasant girl whose health was failing (she later contracted tuberculosis of the bone).

Why was Bernadette dragged off to a catholic convent? Was it so that the local religious order could take out their jealous anger on her?

'How can this be? For a quarter of a century we have fasted, kept vigils and endured self-mortification and embarrassment yet the Most Pure Virgin has never come to us. Why did the Most Pure One Herself appear to you, a cursed, ugly, illiterate peasant girl? Why did she reveal to you the life-giving spring, where millions have been cleansed?'

This, though, is how Divine Wisdom ordered it should be. The Templars guard the Temple of the Most High – the temple of the eternal Jerusalem. The black knights guard the spring at Lourdes. It is only possible to enter into the miracle of the Immaculate Conception, the Immaculate Origin and Primordial Purity by drawing water from the spring in a silver chalice, which hangs on the tree of their theology, and pouring it onto a rock.

The entrance to the Holy Mountain is guarded by a dragon. The entrance to paradise is guarded not only by cherubim brandishing fiery swords, but also by a swarm of snakes. It is not possible to enter the exalted Castle of the Grail without defeating the devil.

'I came into the world to enter the union with the Most High...'

First of all you must break the bonds of union with the devil and defeat him who found his way inside you first, binding you with the bonds of love and using the unifying particles intended for the Most High to tie you to himself instead. You must defeat the branches of Adam and Eve, who committed a sin which I do not wish to be a part of.

'...To enter into a union with the Most High through suffering humanity.'

Having defeated the devil within myself and severing the ties which bound me to him, I now want the Knight of the White Lion and the Eternal Virgin. I want to protect humanity from the one-eyed, one-legged Black Giant!

As soon as the Eucharist of the Grail is complete and the water from the silver Chalice has been poured onto the hot stone (which makes it sizzle and evaporate, radiating bliss like that which comes from sacramental wine), there is a roll of thunder and a storm breaks which is so strong that not one leaf is left on the tree; hailstones pierce the skin to the very bone, and very few manage to escape.

Such is the rage which the bishop of Rome feels towards the army of the Grail! After the apparition at Garabandal, there was a clap of thunder and such a storm broke out that the leaves on a barren fig tree were blown off, one by one. Their knowledge turned out to be empty lies. Their courage, like the leaves on the tree, was blown away in the vortex.

*

Oh great Owain, you were not afraid of the black villain! As you were brave enough to witness the ultimate truth about the True God, you were not afraid of the Roman threats and the thunder which sounded in your soul!

You bravely saddled your horse, rode up to the castle, drew water from the Immaculate Spring and poured it onto the stone of the Grail. Then, a terrible knight in a black mask appeared before you. An evil dread emanated from him. Everything around quaked at the sight of him and the ground beneath him trembled.

The knights were sent flying, shattering their lances so that they had to draw their swords. The Sword of the Grail versus the glaive of Caesar. The Lance of the Last Drop versus the poisoned...

Oh, the symbolism in the legends of Lancelot, King Arthur, Robin Hood, Till Eulenspiegel and Tristan and Isolde is all the same! There is a mysterious sword, shield, lance and horse (the true faith). There are beautiful maidens in castles, mysterious ceremonial meals, hot wine, battles and so on...

The life of a warrior of Christ is a fine one! There is no need to go too far to find an example. Did I not find myself in the Castle of the exalted Grail when I met mother Eufrosinia on the threshold of the Pochaevski Monastery? This was still spiritually alive at that time thanks to her prayers, and I fell at her feet in her blessed cell – a straw hut about five times the size of a dog kennel, in the garden of some sodomite old woman who lived with her son.

*

What kind of a church is this? The leaves swirled around. The fig tree was dry and surrounded by beautiful birds in colourful plumage. They sat on the branches and began to sing the sweetest and most passionate of hymns...

'Such madness!' thought Owain and listened involuntarily until he could hear groans coming from the bottom of the valley and the black knight on his black horse came flying towards Owain, almost knocking him over. Owain struck the knight with a fatal blow, cutting through his helmet, hood and skull as far as the brain. The black knight galloped off, conscious of his imminent death, while Owain spurred on his horse and chased after him.

It is not easy to get into the castle of the Life-giving Spring! Across the path are iron railings and the gates of the fortress (the Dominican monks of the Inquisition).

What is this all about? Is the story of Bernadette Soubirous and the revelation at Lourdes about the Immaculate Conception not the greatest mystery of the Grail? Indeed it is, although the Templars existed long before the spring at Lourdes. Time does not exist, though, and events mingle with signs, destinies, banners and years.

The iron gate of the monastery fell on the horse (Owain's true faith), slicing it in two and even chopping off the ends of the knight's spurs and almost injuring him. At the same time, the inner gates of the castle shut tight and Owain was trapped in the narrow space between the inner and outer gates.

'Locked away in a monastery.' This was how the Knights of the Grail described the temptation of the ascetic life in a medieval monastery. They were like caged birds behind the iron gate forever.

Upon entering the 'American owls' convent (the convent of the mystic, semi-paralysed old mother Angelica), I said to the Abbess, Catherine, 'Oh caged birds! Is it not time for you to fly out in the open and spread the Gospel of the Kingdom? Is now really the time for being locked away in a convent and collecting taxes for red-haired impotent informers and Roman priests?'

'Who are you and where are you from?..'

'We are the Knights of the Solovki Grail! We have come down from heaven. We have come to set you free, young maidens. The Grail and the hundred and fifty fortresses of Christ are in need of magnificent clothing. Who will serve at our shared meals, help us out of our armour, clean it and bring the purple paschal garments, with the purple mantle embroidered with royal crowns in gold? Who else but you, caged birds? You are not allowed to fly beyond the confines of the convent. You are languishing here but do not know why. Inside you are captive canaries. Within your heart is a canary in a cage instead of an altar with the unifying particles – the priceless golden pollen of the Royal dynasty. Let us fly out of the cage, little birds (I called upon them to preach the Gospel of the Kingdom)! Inside the cage is the serpent who is your Bishop Bowdy, the Inquisitor and the Black Knight who is holding you under lock and key.'

I acted like Owain and stunned them. The Roman serpent had not managed to bare its venomous fangs and squeal to the bishop, before we had given communion to Mother Angelica's twenty-four sisters, the 'American owls', living mystic saints with the anointing oils of Solovki. They were bathed in a beautiful fragrance and said, 'We, the Brides of Christ, have never been anointed with such fine oils! Our lamps are burning and faith has been resurrected within us.' 'Tomorrow at ten o'clock in the evening,' we said, 'we will saddle the horses and be on our way. There will be two to every saddle – one knight and one maiden.'

*

...A beautiful golden-haired girl came running up to Owain.

'Oh knight, I want to set you free! How did you come to be here? How did you end up trapped in that cage behind the iron gates?.. I will try everything in my power. We are kindred spirits, my friend! I love you. Take this ring from my hand. It has an emerald in it. Clutch it and you will become invisible. This signet will take you to the Grail and transport you into the Holy Being. Hurry, my dear. The Dominican monks are on their way. They will open the castle gates, seize you and kill you. What a surprise they will have when they cannot see you!'

The Grail is opened up in the Holy Being. The knights disappear just as instantly as they appear.

The golden-haired maiden gave Owain the sign and then, inside her beautiful rooms, she set before him a silver table decorated with gold. Owain lay on the bed but could hear cries of anguish. The castle resounded with terrible screams, 'O-o-oh!' The master of the castle was dying.

Having defeated the Black Knight and entered the castle of the Life-Giving Spring, Owain met with his Lady.

Oh, how beautiful our Virgin is! Jacques de Molay, the last Keeper of the Grail and head of the order of the Knights Templar, who was tortured by the evil inquisitors, was burned at the stake without a blindfold: 'Let me not turn my gaze from the Most Pure Virgin! She will save me. Fire of the Holy Spirit, give me life!'

Oh fire which does not destroy; fire of true chivalry and the true Knights Templar! Turn the Roman straw into ashes! The established Roman machine will grind to a halt. Its cogs will cease to turn and its instruments of torture will no longer function. The Knights Templar, the army of Christ, will rise again and will bring back the Grail for the purpose for which it was intended. They will bring it to fifteen-year-old homeless youths and drug addicts.

The legends of the Grail are prophetic.

Oh most beautiful woman on earth! Owain falls in love with this woman, who is more beautiful than any other woman on earth. She, though, is devastated. Owain killed her husband and now offers her his hand. Eventually, having overcome fear and prejudice, she decides to entrust her heart and the spring to the handsome Knight of the Grail.

King Arthur rejoices when he reads of the victory on the glorious screen. The Great Spring, which can cleanse the sins of the whole world, is no longer guarded by the black knights of Rome, but by Owain (or O-N, the divine man!).

*

It is impossible to describe in words the mood of the Knights Templar. Outwardly, they followed a very strict regime. They received communion every day, stood for hours at a time, and devoted much time to their fighting skills. The true life of the Knights of the Temple, though, was hidden from view. It consisted of ceremonial meals around the Round Table, conversations with Christ and the mingling of His Blood with theirs.

The Chalice worked marvels. The mere presence of the Grail, which came transfigured in white light shining in the Great Hall, changed their existence. The spark of divinity entered their hearts and was ignited by the flame of love. The knights became full of ecstasy and bliss and were thus transfigured. They remained in this state even at the times of day devoted to the usual daily routine.

There were many such fraternities. Fighting skills, swordsmanship and riding could be learned from the Hospitallers, the Crusaders and many others. The Grail was kept at Monsalvat. Its guardians were fully aware who they were, from Whom they had come, and who the imposter was; the faithless whore and the 'Roman Villain' Its sacraments were not valid. It had usurped authority and crucified Christ.

These new rabbinic cults and their sickly-sweet chants are hateful to Our Lord. It is AS IF HE had never come, AS IF HE had not left behind His Blood, AS IF HE had not been transformed in the Blessed Sacrament, AS IF HE was not standing alongside us, AS IF HE had not promised us a place in the Kingdom, AS IF HE was not walking alongside us and showing us the will of the Most High, AS IF HE had not remained in the chalice of the heart and after communion... They are villains and liars!

The Knights Templar did not use allegories because they were afraid of Rome and could not speak openly. The Saviour did not speak in parables out of fear of the Jews. He was fearless. It was not fitting, though, to speak of the mysteries which were to remain closed to the Adamites.

Nor was it appropriate to reveal these to the Christians – those Adamites who strove to come to know their Lord, their messianic King, and their anointed Christ, within the limits of their unenlightened Adamism. Their church was only established to rule them with a rod of iron and specifically to prevent them from being transformed from Adamites into Seraphites. The Grail flourished in legends such as the chronicles of the great King Arthur, the ballads of the Minnesingers which tell of flying ships, the Lorelei, the knights of the swan and Sir Perceval and the quest for the Holy Grail.

Beautiful women, smiling as they watch the competitions of the Knights of the Round Table, only figured in distorted, popular versions of the legends. The knights of the Grail worshipped only one Lady – the Most Pure Virgin. They preserved virginity, seeing it as a sharpened sword to be used against the devil, and were fully aware that the Most Pure One is the token of their salvation. She is the perfect image. She is their 'role model' (Louis Grignion de Montfort, one of the greatest Marian saints and Knight of the Grail and of the Round Table).

The Knights Templars' veneration of the Most Pure Virgin was a secret, just like their school of chivalry. They could not preach about this openly without a special blessing. Worshipping the Queen of Heaven involved putting on Her robes of virginity, burning with love for Her, yearning to be like Her, and understanding the vision of Her mission. The knights kept sacred the revelations of the Queen of Heaven, this heavenly Gospel from the Divine Mother, and sought only one thing: to help their Lady to accomplish Her mission of giving birth to a new kind of person.

The plaintive Roman song about the 'Protector' and 'Intercessor' of sinful people ('Pray for us sinners') seemed comical and pathetic to them. She is not just a passive Protector, otherworldly, always 'on the other side', or 'behind a fence' and remaining aloof! No! She is the only One: She, like Her Son Christ, her sweetest Bridegroom at the Altar of Union, is much more than can possibly be imagined!

This is not 'I' and 'you' that have become 'we', but something indescribable and new. Putting on the robes of virginity changes one's existence. Something else is born which is neither God nor human, neither angel nor demon, but a god-human!

Nowhere and never before has there been such reverence for the Most Pure Divine Mother, as that of the order of servants of the Celestial Temple (the Vatican executioners and the crusaders spitefully dubbed them 'templars'). The Queen thanked them in return. She gave them something which she had never given to anyone else. She gave them Her virginity, Her shield and Her Invincible Power. The strength of the Templars came only from the protection of the Most Pure Virgin (just as soldiers always rely on help from on high – from Her – for their victories).

Such love! Such love between brothers, which is only possible through virginity and the Holy Being! The devil had no power over the Templars. The brothers lived within each other. 'He who is closest to me is closer than myself, just as the Most High is closest of all to me. I am a part of the Most High and of my neighbour who is close to me' (one of the mottoes of the Knights Templar, the Keepers of the Grail). How much more can humanity learn from this perfect brotherhood of all time, which was destroyed by the diplomatic intrigues of the French King and the Roman authorities!

Oh knights of the Immaculate One,
Guardians of the true faith – Templars!
Blue and white scarves with red crosses,
Swords of damask steel,
Army of invincible,
    spotless and inviolable,
Seraphites, loving in ecstasy.

The scarlet rose and the white lily
Are their distinctive signs.
On a white stallion. The White Lion
And the mark of the Heavenly Father on the forehead.

Twelve wise maidens
Serve them at the Round Table
In King Arthur's castle.

The Templars in rapturous ecstasy
Are anointed with expensive ointment –
They are preparing themselves for the heavenly meal
The knights, the brides of Christ.

*

Who did the warriors of the Grail fight with their swords? Witches and sorcerers. The 'offended' people they defended were the unfortunate victims, the accursed and those bewitched by black magic that can always be found around the world. The knights were aided by the sword of Eternal Virginity, the sword of the veneration of the Most Pure Virgin, and the inheritance of the Blood and the dynasty of Christ. The armies of heaven fought on their side as they had the Immaculate Origin in their blood which was transferred from one warrior to another on the battlefield, through the Eucharist, serving their neighbour and sharing the cross.

They proclaimed the Origin of Christ secretly and spread it by means of commands which are scarcely related to the history of the superficial church. The idiocy and the falseness of the Roman mass (the religion of the accursed, where there is neither the Blood of Christ, nor His presence, nor His posterity, nor His origin) was all too apparent to them. The true Royal ceremonial meal was the absolute opposite of the witches and weavers of spells; those treacherous conspirators. During the Eucharist of the Grail, the castles of Christ unlocked the treasures of Holy Being and the bliss of the communicants knew no bounds.

25.06.2005 Deris Island

The Messianic Era

It is 12 o'clock midnight, judging by the white screen of the Grail. Around the clock, in my short-sighted 'holy forgetfulness', I know, with scrupulous attention to detail, what is happening and where.

There is no need to deliberate over 'somewhere out there' or to ask anything... The gaze drifts softly and gently into sleepy bed chambers.

It is midnight. They are sleeping...

Until the sleeping ones clothe themselves in the robes of virginity, just as the medieval soldiers donned their chain mail and armour, the Mother of Supreme love cannot embrace them and make them whole.

Take a look at a thirteen-year-old prostitute from Perm, though, full of profound holy passion, on Tverskaya Street in Moscow, and a fifty-year-old businessman from San Francisco... Eternal orphans. They need only to be comforted by love.

Neuroses, complexes and sins cannot be exchanged for candles. They are caused by a lack of supreme love. If someone hurts someone else, there is not enough love. You, my friend, must be accountable and take the consequences. They have not been given enough love. It should not be given grudgingly but generously. In order to serve wholeheartedly and selflessly you must give of yourself without fear.

You will also need ecstasy with a slight hint of madness. It helps the wanderer on his way when faced with loneliness, meaninglessness, harmful thoughts and so on.

*

Beautiful Mary Magdalene, holy maiden of the Grail! How glad I am that you were 'purged' by censorship and that you were not 'recorded in scripture'. How good it is that the red-haired courtesan, the whore who associated 'with tax collectors', was the entranced 'other Mary'! If there is a holy whore in the Grail, then the 'Holy Roman' church is a whore.

I will sing you a song, Mary Magdalene, as you are second only to the Divine Mother. You are worthy of honour just as the Magi and the shepherds of Jerusalem, contemplating the radiant divine child, Joseph the Great, in the other Bethlehem, born of you out of a mortal yearning for your eternally beloved Christ...

Could I but follow the fate of Joseph, the heir and founder of the messianic dynasty? The messianic era began with Mary Magdalene's Immaculate Conception of Joseph, the first king and keeper of the Grail of Christ. Then, from him, came the messianic line: twelve immaculate kings and invincible monarchs of Europe.

Merovingians and Stuarts...
The cards have been shuffled.

Mary Magdalene is a molten pearl. Christ came to her first after His Resurrection and pierced her heart with his sharp, burning lance.

Oh, Divine Wisdom of the caduceus! It was granted this right. This was all he could use during His time on earth.

'Wake up Mary! Do not cry.'

'Lord, Lord!' she wrung her hands in despair and pulled her hair. 'Immortal God, why did You die? I was ready to die for You, but you were supposed to live for more than a thousand years. Oh, immortal God!'

'I will remain in your heart for a thousand years and I will remain on earth forever in the form of this wonderful boy. He is a copy of Me. Take Him.'

Mary fainted and remained still for a while; the pale, beautiful, sacred mother. She carried the immaculately conceived second divine child, Christ the younger (the copy, 'copio') and died shortly after his birth.

Her death out of mortal grief for her dear Beloved was the most exalted assumption! This was the highest form of holy passion. The two Marys were honoured with it – His Divine Mother and Mary Magdalene, the Unwedded Bride. He would have sung His song to her, accompanied on the sublime lyre which Tristan, dying on the island, requested instead of a boat, sword and oars.

*

People fabricate stories about Christ, as if He worked miracles all day, like some kind of idol: He turns up somewhere and prophesies and the crowd applaud or sentence or crucify Him... There is no peace or calm of any kind. It is a prayer of the night, filled with holy passion, and with a bloody ending...

They turned Him into an idol. Eufrosinia did not make up any stories about triumphs. She was a gentle saint and she has been rewarded with more than a crown in the Heavenly Kingdom. The fragrance of the Solovki Myrrh relics spread across the whole of the Siberian Archipelago, even reaching as far as Moscow.

If Christ were here today He would stay quietly hidden away while his disciples travelled the world as part of some new-age sect. By some turn of fate and through Providence, Christianity became the official religion in the 4th century. If it had not been for the conversion of the obstinate Byzantine emperor, Constantine, it would have remained the sect of the 'Nazarene' or the 'Galilean'.

Julian (the successor of Constantine who had given the order to execute not Christians but pagans who refused to be baptised) did not persecute as much as despise Christians for losing the mark of faith. 'If the Galilean is God, then why does He not come down, heal us or even speak? Where is His power?'

In the third century, at the time of the martyrdom of the Christians, this would have been impossible. His power was perfectly manifest. Christ was present in holy passion and in cries of anguish, always like the *yurodivy.* Just as everything had become 'fine', 'peaceful', 'just' or 'by the book', the renegade Julians came on the scene.

The best thing which could happen in Christianity is the voice of conscience.

'Where is Christ? Where is Your magic?' Like the first apostles, even a pagan or an Antichrist could ask, 'Where are you, Lord? Where do you live?'

'Come with Me and you will see.'

Just try going with Him! The Inquisition will follow you and you won't get very far.

Christ disappeared as soon as the Inquisition began within Christianity.

*

This holy family which consists of Mary Magdalene, Joseph of Arimathea and Joseph the Heir, is incredible. One version of the story says that Mary died straight away or soon after giving birth, and another says that she lived a little longer... Does it really matter?

It is something else which really matters: the fact that true Christianity was shut away in the catacombs. From the 4th century it went away into the Holy Being as it was opposed by the strictly regulated Byzantine model.

There was such sorrow in heaven that Holy Rus' had adopted the 'corrupt Byzantium' model (V. Solovev) and not the Grail! If only Prince Vladimir had chosen the Grail from all the religions on offer, such as the religions of the Khagans, the Greeks, the Muslims etc. Then, the throne of the True Church would have been in Holy Rus'. Christ would have fed His Bride, Holy Rus' from the Chalice which is never empty and thus protected her. Russia would not have adopted Byzantine Orthodoxy, but that of the Grail! However...

'My Son, the one thing which all world religions have in common is the Chalice. Everything else is superfluous' (The Lord).

Russia, Orthodoxy, Islam, Turkey... All former empires will be removed from the face of the earth. Only the Grail will remain; the Chalice in the right hand of the Most High, and the Host of Hosts who wants to drink the heavenly love potion from it. He tasted it once before, was driven insane and ended up in the Holy Being – a religious insanity filled with holy passion. He can no longer describe or explain anything, as in the Grail legend of Tristan and Isolde. It only remains to take a decisive leap out of the chapel (the old church).

...Tristan was sentenced to death because he had 'broken the law'.

He who was a national hero and had saved the land from the sabre-brandishing Rephaim, Morholt! He who was an invincible knight, a fearless saviour and a minor Christ, was sentenced 'by the letter of the law' to the death penalty.

No, this is not the subject of a new film, but a window of holy passion onto the Grail.

'Allow me, brothers, to pray to the Most High before I die', says Tristan, seeing a chapel on the top of a cliff.

Executioners are always very sentimental. When he arrived at the chapel, Tristan instantly opened the window and jumped off the precipice, praying to his Heavenly father – Christ. His prayers were answered straight away. His clothes ballooned out in the air and the 'Eternal mourner' (Tristan in translation) was safely set down on a rock in the sea. He left no trace.

A disciple of Christ is called to make this leap from the chapel: from the superficial to the True Church, from the church of the altar into the Mysterious one, or from the transient church into that of the Holy Being.

Once, the Most High opened our eyes to the mystery of the church and led us to the outer temple with candles, priests and other accoutrements. Now, he is opening our eyes to the True

Church, the Church within a church. Like Saul, who became Paul, we must pass through the 'conversion of the church' and 'take the leap from the chapel'. I did it. St. Eufrosinia did it. In her 75th and final year of life, having always been a zealous 'Orthodox of the catacombs', she said, 'I am from the Centre of the Divine Mother.' Thus, the writer of the Church Slavonic *akathist,* which was written over three thousand years ago, captured the Words of the Divine Mother which had only just been recorded by her descendant and follower.

Marvellous! The church has undergone such a transformation!

In Heaven they told me to renounce everything which yesterday I held dear. 'Have mercy!' pleads my heart. 'Renounce sin? Of course! Renounce evil and the inherent shadows... But how can I renounce holiness? How can I renounce the keys and the rods which were handed to me by the Most High for ever?'

Moses renounced the laws of Sinai when he saw Christ at His transfiguration on Mount Tabor, when he saw the radiant faces of the Grail.

Nothing can be understood without first being revealed by the Grail.

Mary Magdalene, the former whore and the greatest saint, stands as a *yurodivy* at the entrance to the True Church. Anyone knocking at the gate will not be met by the iconic prayers of St. John Chrysostum, forty days' prayers and other poetic frills (Joseph Volotski is not a long way from this, either), but rather by Joseph the Hermit, the universal mourner: Joseph IV, after Joseph of Egypt (son of Jacob), Joseph the Betrothed, and Joseph of Arimathea.

*

The life of Joseph and his posterity are preserved in the Grail.

The genealogy of the priests of Melchizedek... Is this possible? Yes, it is possible in the Holy Being and in the scrolls of the Grail.

Joseph became the twelfth, and adopted son of Joseph of Arimathea. He was an orphan and was scorned by the other sons. They married well, had children and then just like millions of others disappeared without record. This twelfth son, (Mary Magdalene's Immaculately born son) just like the young Christ teaching in the temple, recognised his Father in the Eucharistic Chalice as he shared the liturgy with Joseph of Arimathea, and was filled with an indescribable bliss. He said, 'I am a priest of the Chalice!'

Joseph the Younger, this twelfth son of Joseph of Arimathea, was called to be a virgin. How, then, was the baton of posterity passed on? There were twelve immaculate conceptions or, more accurately, infusions. The mystery of the Grail is the multiplication of Christ and His infusion within the font into the dynasty of His descendants. These descendants were the European monarchies – Charlemagne, the Stuarts and the Merovingians. Their heads were cut off and then they were crowned in glory and extolled by the people. They suffered shame and mortal torment but they did not abandon the rod of the dynasty which had been passed on to them. They guarded the Grail as the most precious treasure. It is not meant to be revealed until the decrepit old Vatican whore is swept away, consigned to oblivion and stripped of her former wealth and lost kingdoms.

*

Since entering the Grail, I have been unable to write properly, informatively or instructively, to disclose anything or comment on anything. I can only write in a *yurodivy* way about the 'impossible', the indescribable and that which is only transient. That 'impossible', though, is much more valuable than all the rule books, practical manuals on how to live the perfect monastic life and other old paraphernalia all collected together.

The saints were not fed by the 'instructions of elders' but by the Chalice of the Grail. 'Elders' was an invention on the part of the devious inquisitors to ensnare these holy people. No 'Orthodox Saints' have ever existed. Nikolai II fought with the Orthodox Church which betrayed him not once, not three, but a thousand times, eventually forsaking him and hunting him down.

Seraphim Sarovsky was from the other Orthodox Church – the Old Believers. When the sun shone in his heart, the Divine Mother came to him and he became 'born of Her': a heavenly elder, rather than an object of veneration for the crowds of the Black Hundred.

Seraphim Sarovsky went away into the Grail. He has no need of relics, veneration or memorabilia – he only needs disciples. So, Seraphim the Glorious, was there no-one to be found among those whom you welcomed into your hermitage, apart from the sisters in the convent? The Grail always has twelve *yurodivy* virgins in its retinue. Innocent the Immortal, another King of the Grail, wrote in his *yurodivy* writings about his 'Fyodors', 'Theclas', 'Prokhors' and more besides. It did not matter where he was exiled to – Anzer Island at Solovki! It did not matter how much he was tortured or what signs of torment he bore on his forehead! He just carried on writing, filled with bliss, having drunk from the Chalice of the Grail.

No blow inflicted on this office will be greater than saying that the Roman Villain has been exterminated! The True Church has always existed. Christ has continued His succession through the immaculate Seraphitic humanity, although this has hitherto remained concealed. So, at the site of the Assumption of the Most Pure One on *Nightingale Mountain*, is the Altar of Union. The True Church has been revealed and the time has come for settling scores with the Roman Villain.

It is brought to trial and the scores are laid out from all sides: from heaven, from the underworld, from the bottom of the sea, from the ash of the fires of the Inquisition, from those tortured alive, from those hidden divine mothers who were 'liquidated', christs who were suppressed, and so on.

The 'righteous' numbered in their thousands. They were princes of the world with bronze sceptres in the form of snakes and mitre-like crowns. One *yurodivy* came along and swept them all away with one word. No-one dared to contradict

Him. 'You do not know Him of Whom you speak.' 'How is this?!' – they retorted angrily. 'How can we not know Him when we sing His praises, confess to Him, glorify Him, suffer for Him, spread His faith and wholeheartedly await Him?..'

If they had known Him they would have remained silent. Whoever knows Him does not know Him. Whoever does not know Him, proclaims that he does.

The greatest fool and imposter is he
Who clothed himself in dogma.
We have no need of
A sergeant, an informer, a boy with no hair,
Or a sentimental Torquemada.

We are inmates of Solovki
Of the true Christ.
How can we recognise Him?
In His coming and staying
And setting our hearts aflame
And establishing peace.

At His apparitions
The soul contorts itself like that of a yurodivy.

How many more hours are there to go,
Until the ashes of their knowledge and prejudice
Dispel Christ Who is unprecedented and near?
Fear the Most High! One of His mysteries
Will always come in a form,
which no-one had expected of Him.

The Divine Mother appeared to a mystic in the 19th century (not a word about this ever appeared in Patericons or chronicles) as a village milkmaid in a simple peasant coat with a scarf of down. He recognised Her. She came to Solovki as 'Maria, a sister of mercy'. She did not conceal Her identity or disguise herself. It is only fools who believe in the white silhouette of Zeitoun, Our Lady of the Gate of Dawn in a blue mantle with gold stars and wearing a gold crown, Our Lady of Kazan or the Virgin of Vladimir... However, She comes as a kind of bride – a mystic Mourner of the Grail and the great Grieving

Mother. Today the heavenly icon is stuck in a pine tree somewhere, but tomorrow it will knock on the door to the image of the earthly Pilgrim, the wandering preacher.

It is the same with the Lord. Just as it is impossible to say how His Face will look, so it is with His apparitions. It is impossible to say anything definite 'once and for all' about Christ. Only those who cannot see Him from close up and do not know anything can confidently and arrogantly lie, as if under hypnosis. Thus all these fathers of the ecumenical councils and the emperors who presided over them, lied and acted as Antichrists. They explained aspects of philosophy, but they did not come to know Christ.

They did not recognise Him when He came as a *yurodivy*.

*

What a wonderful prayer is to be found in the Grail! It is a prayer filled with such holy passion!

It is given to us by Christ Himself. His prayer is that of Gethsemane and is about the whole world... It is instantaneous. It is not long or exhausting. It is direct, innocent and all-encompassing. What a wonderful prayer is to be found in the Grail! It is straight from the heart. It bears stigmata, it remembers millions simultaneously, it is an instant source of rapture in the Holy Being, it converts, it exalts those wishing to rise from their sleepy beds, and it is the 'joy of all who sorrow.'

What kind of joy is brought by the 'Joy of all who Sorrow'? The death bed is transformed into the Altar of Union.

27.06.2005 Deris Island

Playing on the Facets of the Grail

My soul was full of sorrow and turned to God. I said: 'Lord, I have always sought the last truth! For the sake of this truth I was ready to renounce everything. Then I understood that the last truth is You, and so I renounced everything worldly, all religions, both esoteric and searching. So, I turned to the Orthodox faith, which I thought was true. However, having spent over ten years in these two churches[10], I found nothing but witchcraft, hypocrisy, murdering of saints and crucifying You. Therefore, I am glad, Lord, that You have led me to the True Church.

I understood that the Grail is the Church which You have created. It is hard to find and hidden away in the catacombs of the Holy Being.'

To declare oneself to be of the 'true Orthodox' catacombs means very little. There are other catacombs – those of the Holy Being. The Chalice is hidden inside there.

I am grateful, Lord, that You left Your true Blood – your origin and your progeny – here on earth. You lived and worked among people who were worthy of You through their nobility, aristocracy, sacrifice, faith, beauty, virginity, disinterestedness and integrity.

I am glad, Lord, that You created a new superior people, persecuted by the Roman Harlot and the Byzantine Rogue. I

[10] The Russian Orthodox Church and the True (Russian) Orthodox Church; see details at the Glossary.

am grateful that You, having first given me the pearl of faith, have now revealed the pearl of the Church. I will stay with this Church forever. I have always belonged to this Church. Those saints whose lives I have described belonged to this Church. All the anointing, rods, marks, blessings, abundant mercy and gifts I have received from it, are really from the Grail. The Grail has remained hidden, though, until such time as it saw fit to reveal itself through me.

*

I can see the meaning of my life in the affirmation of the Church of the Holy Grail – the True Church which has existed from the creation of the world, through the Immaculate Conception of Jesus Christ by the Most Holy Virgin Mary, and then to His crucifixion and death. The Gospel then continued through another Immaculate Conception (like a second gospel cycle) by the most blessed and myrrh-giving golden-haired virgin of the Grail, the royal Mary Magdalene. This was the conception of the Messianic dynasty, the Son of Joseph the Younger and the Blessed, and, through him, the continuation of the blessed branch of immaculate Seraphites, which have spread throughout the world.

The blasphemy and the crime of the Roman Harlot lie in the fact that it has done everything in its power to wipe the memory of the True Church from the face of the earth. Just as the Byzantine Rogue turns a blind eye to Solovki, pretending that nothing happened there, so the Roman Harlot has attempted to wipe all trace of the Church of the Grail from the face of the earth. However, the mystery is becoming clear and that which they fear most of all is being revealed.

The Grail began a 'silent protest' in the catacombs and, throughout the twentieth century and through the last martyrs of the Solovki, the *Second Golgotha,* it prepared the civilization of Christ. It was so well hidden from the rest of humanity, just as the Saviour was hidden in Israel away from the Hellenists and others. Such was the will of God, until such time as the way had been prepared for His Second Coming and His triumph. As the Second Coming is so near, the Grail reveals itself through the triumph of Its saints. The True Church of the Holy Being is being revealed.

The Grail is spread and multiplied among the saints of Its spirit, Christ, Who leads the battle with the arch-enemy. For two thousand years the Grail itself has led the battle with the Roman Harlot – with those 'bloody barons', 'black thugs', dragons, monsters, snakes, thieves and robbers, as they are known within the Grail.

*

I heard a deep moan and understood that this is the moaning of the Grail. I understood how the saints of the Grail moan and how this is a tortured and crucified Church.

I felt the pain of the Grail. I had been told that the Grail has left this world. It is sought after by many who have not been called and are not able to enter virginal purity, always remaining worldly people. The Grail is hidden from this world so that no-one can look for and find it.

The Grail is not just a vessel, though. It has many facets (the inner Grail, for example). Now it is working through three *anointed* ones. They are manifest in this world. I am that King, anointed one and Keeper of the Grail, in whose flesh lie the bones of the Grail.

Like the priests of Melchizedek, I came down from heaven. The gifts are given to our fathers through the Knights of the Grail. The grace which is found in our liturgies comes from the Chalice of the Grail. It is present but unseen. I saw a white vessel being transformed imperceptibly. It is present in any of the liturgies served by myself and my children, the sons of the Wedding Feast. I only need to touch the chalice (this small wooden vessel) for it to be filled with the grace of the Holy Grail.

The Grail is thankful that this great truth about the True Church could be confirmed. It is thankful that I had the courage to renounce Orthodoxy and Catholicism and everything about these religions which was dear to me, and to bring these sacrifices with me into the Grail. I underwent the most difficult tests – poisoning with deadly venom, cursing, poisoned arrows, paralysis and the blazing fire from the jaws of a dragon.

It is said that this Church is the true one and that I should not leave it. I am a child of the Grail. I have been anointed and bear the spirit of the Grail. I must forget the accursed values of the Roman Harlot.

Their affairs are so terrible and blasphemous that, as soon as the scores to be settled are presented, the sky will be covered with ominous clouds and they will be struck by lightning (including the innocent who have been seduced by them and even those who have not been seduced but found themselves in the wrong place at the wrong time and were caught by the lightning bolt).

There is no need to search. There is no other kind of Grail. The Grail is the myrrh-anointed Church of the saints. It is Christ, working through His vessels. Through the last Russian emperor, *Mikhail Romanov II,* the whole of the Messianic dynasty entered Solovki, the *Second Golgotha,* and proclaimed him the greatest Keeper of the Chalice of the Wedding of Fire. Then Seraphim gave this chalice to me.

I looked for God and found Him in Orthodoxy. Now I am disappointed by Orthodoxy and Catholicism. There is no God there. They are evil sects of the Antichrist where there is nothing but hypnosis, lies, filth, guile, commercialism and that most fundamental of falsehoods upon which their whole administration is founded.

I did not turn to the faith and leave the world behind in order to serve in their administration. It was of no concern to me what their authorities had written or whether the spider's web was functioning and catching mice. I turned to the Radiant Church. I had always believed that the Church came from Heaven and, at my baptism, I was enveloped in the cloud of the Holy Being.

I am grateful that Heaven has given me this supreme and eternal identity in the castles of the Grail. Let the grace of the Grail be upon all my children for a thousand years.

*

From this holy garden which is the new Eden (Deris Island), I now proclaim the triumph of a thousand years of Christ and the Kingdom of the Holy Grail, i.e. the abundant Chalice.

How is it possible to build a divine civilization and a thousand year reign of Christ? With the Grail. The Grail is the Architect, Builder and Sculptor of all civilizations to come. It is that Chalice of blessings, the source of all blessings and grace, which will be miraculously multiplied several thousand times. Then, from these several thousand Grails, after the outpouring of the seven bowls of wrath in the 84th civilization, the thousand-year reign of Christ and the kingdom of the Holy Grail will become widespread.

I can see the 150 castles of the Grail with white lions, marvellous swans, golden boats, swords of David, countless silver ark-like goblets, banners, distinguished knights and suits of armour. The Knights of the Grail will come down to earth as the warriors of Elijah and Enoch.

Many times, following the revelation of the Divine Mother, I have seen visions of the warriors of Elijah and Enoch on white horses and of the glory of the Holy Virgin. This is the church of the Holy Grail, the True Church, which has nothing in common with the Roman Harlot.

The Grail tells me to be content and fear nothing. The Grail will win this battle. It is invincible.

The invincibility of the Eternal Virgin was revealed to me as a General who had never been defeated in battle. The Grail, though, is the general of the church. The true temple of Christ is the Grail. The Templars guarded the Grail, not the temple of Jerusalem.

Part of my task is to affirm the Kingdom of the Holy Grail and to erase the Roman witchcraft and Byzantine barbarity from it. All the enemies of the Grail will be confounded and will disappear from the face of the earth. The Grail will pronounce its judgement over the whole world and the true Blood of Christ will be poured over the whole of the divine civilization, when the Wedding of Fire, with a hundred thousand molten pearls, will be proclaimed throughout the world. Then the revelation of Solovki, the *Second Golgotha,* will begin.

I have found the True Church and will never leave it. This True Church is the Grail.

Christ left His Chalice behind. The Pharisees lie, saying that His Blood spilled out onto the cross and onto the sand. Christ left behind His Messianic Church. Although seemingly eradicated from the face of the earth, it will rise from the dead and challenge the red dragon.

*

Oh Holy Grail, how I have loved you! How attached to you I have become! I can see the sacrifices you have made. You, Christ, have been crucified twice! You are the same peaceful, crucified Lord, Whose Blood flowed into the Chalice.

I was drawn to the true orthodoxy of the Holy Grail by the blessed Maria Orlovskaya. I was moved by her vision of the liturgy (which kept me in the church). It is not a liturgy of 'reminiscence', but He is crucified and supramundane now, and the Blood flows into the chalice.

The only mysteries which attract me are life-giving, true mysteries. God cannot act in the past. There is no recollection.

*

Holy Grail, you embrace all worlds! You have so many names! The Church of Mystery, the Priesthood of Melchizedek... What is all this? This plays on the facets of the Grail.

*

The Roman rats dreamed up the 'theory of atonement' just to follow on from the finalising of the superficial Gospel through

Pentecost. They are completely ignorant of the real side of Christian history – the Messianic dynasty – which has led to their false dogma. The Grail does not teach that the Cross is a 'means of atonement', but, rather, the greatest law of the Kingdom and the key to the Wedding Chamber.

Holy passion is a category of the Grail. From the Grail comes the Universe of Divine Wisdom.

Ultimately, everything which was in Christ as the pioneer will also be given to all of His Messianic dynasty. It will repeat the actions of Christ. What has happened is that for two thousand years the Melchizedek Church of the Messianic Dynasty of Keepers of the Chalice was hidden from the world, just as Christ was hidden and, in fact, filled with the greatest holy passion.

Now the victory procession is taking place. It is magnificent. The Grail is radiant: its rays shine right around the world and it is crowned by twelve rainbows. The Heavenly Father Himself is holding the Chalice in His hands and passing it to His Son. His Son passes it to the Holy Spirit. Around them stand all the host of heaven and the councils of Joseph the Younger and Joseph of Arimathea.

The Josephs represent the three Testaments. Joseph of Arimathea and Joseph the Betrothed represent the Christian Testament. Joseph the Beautiful represents the Old Testament, and Joseph the Heir, the messianic king, represents the dynastic Testament of the Holy Spirit. Seraphim the Tender stands next to Joseph (the Heir) receiving the Chalice of the Grail from his hands and passing it on to our forefathers ready for the building of the divine civilization.

28.06.2005 Deris Island

MEMORIAL TO THE CASTLE MOAT

Once a glorious knight of the Grail rode to the castle of the Black Rogue.

Let us pause here. What is this? O-N is a Hidden man inside whom plays the reflection of the light from the facets of the Grail, just as sunlight is reflected on the surface of the sea. Owain is one of the twelve immaculate conceptions of the messianic dynasty and the branch of Christ.

Locked in mortal combat with the Roman Inquisition, those villains of the false church, the valiant and noble Owain would not have had a single victory without the white lion which he had once freed when it caught its paw in a rock and was just about to be bitten by a venomous snake. The white lion is the royal messianic dynasty: the Stuarts, the Merovingians and Seraphim Romanov. Owain is the knight of the White Lion, the White Swan and the White Font.

*

I cannot sleep at three o'clock in the morning in the Grail castles of the Holy Being. A bell has rung within me. What is this? Somewhere something is afoot!.. The glorious knight saddles his horse, dons the armour of courage and flies off to the castle of the Black rogue (the Roman Inquisition).

This knight whose rightful place is in the ivory castles, taking part in ceremonial meals where the tables are groaning with the weight of all the heavenly victuals, is treated as a 'misfit'. They do not even notice him:

> Prisoner with the burning flame and the oil of myrrh
> I am loved by no-one and a danger to no-one.

The screen of the Grail showed that same dark castle which was home to the evil villain. The gates were open, but Owain did not encounter anyone. 'Surprisingly inhospitable!' thought the courageous knight, filled with love's ecstasy. Undeterred, he proceeded into the hall. There he found twenty four beautiful noble women in fine dresses. They were seated at a table and burdened with a deep sorrow.

'Where are we? In the Holy Being? In the Kingdom? That would be something to remember, my dear', lamented one.

'Do not lose your courage', replied another. 'Everything is not lost. The Most High will hear our cries. There is the bell of the Grail. Our cries of holy passion and anguish will surely reach Him...'

'Who are you and what are you doing here?' the noble knight enquired of the beautiful women, each one more gentle, full of grace and pure than the last.

'The evil villain, who is master of this castle, drugged us with his sleeping potion (their black mass). He murdered our chaste menfolk (the male origin of the Church of Christ, which the 'Roman Villain' does not possess, but which the Templars and the Knights of the Chalice have in abundance). He took away their horses (strength), money and weapons... (This is how they always acted with the noble and true disciples of Christ, giving preference to those who grovelled, the corrupt Mafia, those with stuffed pockets, and the corpulent abbots with bulging eyes from the time of Robin Hood, the holy robber of Sherwood). They sacrificed our immaculate menfolk like lambs and threw their bodies into the castle moat, without saying anything to us. Now we are widows of Christ!'

Then they inconsolably burst into tears.

'Leave this place as soon as possible, noble knight Owain. Otherwise, you will succumb to the same fate and be thrown in the castle moat!'

*

The Memorial of the Castle Moat is so familiar! How many

skeletons of saints who were full of holy passion are buried at the bottom of moats around dark castles?

However, Owain, Knight of the Grail, was not afraid of Richelieu, known as the 'grey cardinal', or something of the sort. Incensed with anger, he ran out of the castle and saw a knight before him.

The devil gazed at him benignly, smiling an impish smile, like a bald devil from the dead planet Luna, or a person whose phantom has been directed on, as if he had never done anything evil in his life and was completely innocent. No, this dark villain believed it was his divine duty to slay these twenty-four noble men! If they happened to be saints then so much the better for them – they would be crowned in heaven.

The Inquisition has always been a master at justifying bloody acts, and is even worse than the godfathers of the Mafia or simple highwaymen. They, at least, prayed to the Most High, repented for their sins and brought bags of money to the priest at the altar in return for indulgences. The Roman Villains, however, those murderers of noble men and the elite of humankind, never repented. Their wicked faces always bore a hypocritical, false smile. These sentimental executioners loved the 'music of the Kingdom'. Most of all they loved to hold great processions with lighted candles, voluminous clothes and pious faces. Accompanied by the singing of 'Cherubim' or the 'Agnus Dei', they would parade past their flocks of several thousands, devouring them with their eyes: the embodiment of the Roman priests.

*

It is impossible to understand anything in a parable. Why did the twenty-four noble men and their beautiful women come to the Castle of the Black Rogue in the first place? What business did they have there? Why did these twenty-four counts all leave their own fine castles at the same time, with their tireless Psalter and rapturous prayers which were heard directly in Heaven, only to be murdered and thrown into the anonymous grave of the castle moat?

Their brides were arrested and held captive as they grieved for their beloveds. Who are these brides? These are the wise virgins. They are the holy people who were murdered by the Roman Inquisition and then promoted to the ranks of the 'Blessed' and the 'Saints' with the likes of Clare of Assisi, Teresa of Avila, Bridget of Sweden and so on (as long as they did not get in the way of the aims of their administration and their treasury remained healthy. For example, if the Vatican is to make a business presentation out of Padre Pio. All they need to do is bless this stigmatic heretic and 'pronounce him a saint'. Just from icons and small statues in his image, it would be possible to make over one and half billion US Dollars).

The logic of these villains is clear. How, though, did the Black Roman Rogue manage to attract twenty-four beautiful maidens and twenty-four apocalyptic elders, the keepers of the Chalice of the Grail, and intoxicate them with a sleeping potion (their dull, funereal, ritualistic liturgy, as it is described in the Grail)!

Listening to the sleeping devil

Listening to the sleeping devil, Owain was inflamed with anger. The Villain of the Moon smiled, though, and said, 'Ha! The spider has welcomed the fly into its web! And so here you are. You are not alone – there are more! I have tamed your righteous anger with my powerful gaze.'

In spite of the apparent cordial welcome, warmth, kindness, deep inner peace and self-confidence, the villain's deceit was to no avail. The Knight of the Holy Chalice was inflamed with a righteous anger. He understood that the Black Rogue was standing before him ('Thieves and robbers enter by another way. All that ever came before me will also come after me', is what Christ would have said about them today).

'No, I will not become your friend. We will not be friends, but will fight each other! Fight with your glaive of Caesar and fight against the sword of Christ. We will see who is who!'

'Very well... Let us fight', said the Villain of the Moon and the Black Rogue in the gentle voice of a eunuch. 'But you will not inherit my wealth' (the Vatican's countless treasure chambers and the key to the corrupt apparatus of the Black Rogue and the Yellow Devil).

'This is for Seraphim Sarovsky! And this is for *Innocent Baltski*! And this is for the Church of John! And this is for John of Kronstadt! And this is for our father, Seraphim the Most Tender! And this is for Mother Eufrosinia: the monks of Pochayev beat her in the stomach because she did not want to put on the priest's stole, which was embroidered with demons. She took it from the head of a woman who had just venerated the relics of Job of Pochayev! And this is for all those whom you have tormented and burned alive or sent to the torture chambers and caves! For Maximus the Greek! For the hundred thousand prisoners of Solovki!'

The Black Villain fought back to the best of his ability. The Roman Inquisition was on its last legs and the cardinals elected another anti-pope, which seemed ridiculous from the point of view of the Heavenly Church. They were the ones responsible for all the evils in the world, those who opened the forbidden gates, conformists, paedophiles, and serpents.

The hypnotic powers of the Roman Inquisition do not work within the Grail. Superior love is combined with superior sobriety, as is fitting in the world of Divine Wisdom. Love and Divine Wisdom are inseparable; otherwise there would be no way to avoid the serpents with their charms and temptations.

In his righteous anger, Owain knocked the Black Rogue to the ground with the sword of David.

'Do not kill me!' cried the languishing villain in a shrill voice. 'I promise that I will turn my castle into an almshouse where I will care for all those who are suffering!'

Of course! The banners of these executioners and serpents bear red crosses – they are the crusaders of charity. Few people know that these flags are painted on the reverse with black crosses and are put on the forehead of chosen saints.

*

The Roman Inquisition is unlucky: it is to be no longer. This host of shadows of the underworld, this 'church of Satan' and is to be challenged by the Supreme Church. This is not born 'of the apostles' and their 'successors' (vicars, priests etc.), but from the Lord Himself and the Myrrh Mary Magdalene – the 'former whore' who has become the greatest of the saints. You, the Roman Harlot, changed a saint into the Whore of Babylon and will be granted the destiny as described in the 18th chapter of the Revelation of John: you will be thrown into chaos with all your silver possessions, hypnosis, charms, chalices, royal jewels, expensive clothes and paedophile scandals...

Prayer:

– Who are you?
– The Messianic dynasty of Christ
The origin of divine humanity
From the holy family
Of Mary Magdalene, Joseph the son of Christ
and Joseph of Arimathea
Our mother conceived in the anguish of mortal yearning
Her Bridegroom came to the fiery Solovki
There the candlelit wedding took place
Of the Brides of Christ and their patriarch, Golden-Mouth.

The tabernacle of Aristotle is a broken trough. Aristotle is the favourite classical scholar of the Roman Inquisition. Using a volume of St. Augustine they prayed before interrogation, and held a copy of the four Gospels in their fat, sweaty hands as they sat perspiring in their privileged seats to watch the hellish spectacle of the burning at the stake of those following in the footsteps of Galileo Galilei, Joan of Arc and so on...

The saints have long since disassociated themselves with them and those who were thrown into the castle moat have risen again. The depraved whore which is the Roman Harlot was replaced by the immaculate army of the incorruptible, pure and eternal Knights of the Grail. All of humanity hurried on behind them.

The Holy Grail, the embodied and sealed multiplication of Christ, preferred to remain in a state of holy passion. This does not mean it is weak (among His descendants were the monarchs of Western Europe). It was just because the time had not yet come. Humanity was not yet ready to receive the news of Christ. Christ is in a state of holy passion. The Eucharist works with the help of the Last Drop of the Grail from the knight's great lance.

However, the time has now come and the conditions have been fulfilled! The Seraphites have come into the world bearing the mark of purity on their foreheads. These are the people of Christ: they are His progeny and His dynasty, and He is their father.

29.06.2005 Deris Island

The Sparkling Grail

My Lord! My Lord! What a pearl I have found through the generosity of the Most High! The sparkling Grail led me to the gates of Orthodoxy. I camped out there somewhere near the monastery rubbish dump, like a homeless person from Smolensk near the Odigitrievsky Cathedral. I was a misfit in a strange land… I had no father or mother: I was an orphan.

The hypnosis of those serpents is still working now – it is as though all you need is to 'have patience'! This is in spite of all the vile informers, paedophiles, scum, vermin, fags, and murderers of Christ who only know one thing: do not love but hate, curse and rebel. Yet they cry, 'There is no other church! Where else can people turn?'

This is the same as, 'How can there be universal virginity? Who will bear children?' Here the enemy has taken the initiative, transmitting the message, 'Make love not children.'

My Lord! My Lord! How glad I was when the True Church came to me in the wilderness of France, near the Côte d'Azur! During an outing in the village of Maramar, near the mountains of the Revelation, where the throne of Founding Virginity is placed, the Grail was revealed and began to speak.

'I am the true Blood of Christ and the Church of the Holy Spirit. I am the Blood which is collected in the Inexhaustible Chalice, whose grace multiplies by the hour. My Blood was not spilled out onto the sand.'

The more I came to understand the divine scrolls, the deeper the bliss in which my soul reposed in the Castles of the Grail.

It turned out that the inflated Byzantine inquisitors and executioners are the stupid thieves who borrowed its dogma from Byzantium and the Roman rational theologians. It has nothing of its own except for the deadlock of the sin-obsessed mind and the Josephite germ which debilitates from within and gradually turns a person into a galvanised corpse (this was what the 'third Rome' was transformed into during the martyrdom at Solovki).

How glad I was to rediscover the church for myself! My Lord, what a Chalice! It has made me fragrant and rapturous with ecstasy! It is the brotherhood which I was striving for. It is the virginity which I yearned for. It is purity, faithfulness, nobility, and aristocracy. Betrayal, lies, and treachery have no place here. It is the true humility of the spirit. It is the true treasure house of mysteries. It is the True Church of Christ, which was created by the Lord.

I was so shocked when I saw the three branches of Christianity through the eyes of the Grail: Orthodox, Catholic and Protestant (which emerged from the Catholic Church). They are three apostates (different manifestations) and three distorting mirrors for those who are equally false and who sleep in concrete tombs in space. It is only a short step from there to believing in flying saucers and the 'spirituality' of UFOs.

The Church which was founded by Christ is such a divine miracle! It is just as inexplicable, paradoxical and *yurodivy* as He. Everything is miraculous, not of this world and completely sacred. The Bride is the reflection of the Bridegroom. They share the same composition and the same blood. She is the perfect image and likeness of Him, her Beloved.

The double mystery of the Grail lies in the fact that, having been enclosed behind the gates of the Holy Being and the catacombs, the Grail is communicated more than anything else in the world. For example, where is the Grail? It is impossible to say. However, Mary Queen of Scots, who was executed, was a virgin of the Grail. The Merovingians and the Swedish kings,

Teutonic and Breton dynasties, duchies and castles belonged to the royal dynasty of the Grail.

The Gospel has been cut short. It is insulting for the Lord to see overlooked so much of the great mystery, such as His miraculous, threefold Immaculate Conception by the harlot which was transformed through the Myrrh power of His powerful holy rod into the second divine child, Joseph the Sweetest. The indescribable, unattainable and perfect Templars, who were slandered in the Middle Ages and are still misunderstood this day, are the knights of the Grail, children of Christ through His Blood, and the royal messianic dynasty. The Sons of the Most High, who have come down from heaven, have been immaculately conceived.

The whole history of the Old World from the 12th to the 20th century is one continuous battle between the true church and the whore, the imposter and the predatory villain. It is all about imitating, adapting, executing saints and putting scribes and Pharisees on thrones. The Lord tolerated this two-thousand-year history of His Church, during which time He gathered together an amazing number of enlightened orators, minnesingers, virgins, glorious knights and invincible warriors.

The Grail fought amazingly. In its hands was the sword of David, the sword of the Grail, the Holy Lance and the Last Drop. It had satin, velvet, brocade and patchwork, and its banners and heraldry were designed in heaven.

This is the other Church of Christ. It cannot be said that the Roman Harlot defeated it and displaced it. No! The Grail with its Chalice has confounded the Roman Harlot whilst remaining in the shadows, in the Holy Being and another time. That same Roman Villain, claiming to be universal and to have conquered the whole world, was eventually disgraced and recognised itself in the vengeful Gorgon – the terrifying old woman with snakes instead of hair, who lives in the caves of dark Hades.

In the legends of the Grail, Joseph the Sweetest is Tristan, the mournful one. At one point the young Tristan fought single-handed against the 'vile monster' which had gone over to Ireland.

The pure knight decided to fight the dragon. Having armed himself with the robes of the Most Pure Virgin and the sword of Christ – the mystery of the Immaculate Conception – he set out to meet the dragon, which is described in the apocalyptic books of the Grail as follows:

'It had the head of a bear (obstinate, aggressive stupidity) and its eyes were red like burning coals (he has drunk the blood of the saints and is still thirsty). It had two horns on its head (Behemoth, aiming its horn at the stomach), its ears were long and hairy (a 'Big Brother'-style device used for eavesdropping; a Dominican torturer from the time of the Inquisition with long and terribly hairy ears), it had the claws of a lion (if you go near it, it will tear you to shreds), its tail was a snake (there is nothing but hypnosis in its rituals, mysteries, ideas, theologies and views) and it had the scaly body of a griffin (this bird of prey feeds on carrion: the accomplice kills the saint and keeps it for itself).' This funereal religion has turned dead saints into idols. The 'scaly griffin' element is also about being remembered posthumously, a decorative Panopticon, supposedly of their saints, with icons depicting their victories and, behind them, endless torture chambers with cries of anguish and the scores to be settled from thousands of years.

The battle was terrifying. The dragon bit through the lance of the Grail. Tristan's armour turned black, like dying embers. His horse (the knight's strength) fell beneath him. The unsheathed sword of Eternal Virginity came into its own – its absolute protection began to work. The monster retreated and surrendered.

Tristan thrust the holy sword into the monster's jaws. The blow fell directly on the jaws – it is forbidden to lie to the face, according to a cunning theology. The sword penetrated the dragon's body and sliced its heart in two – a sign of the reversal of the hypnosis. The dragon let out a plaintive cry and perished. Tristan cut out its tongue – it is forbidden to preach slanderously against the saints or Christ in church (in the Grail it is forbidden for clerkly churchmen to preach at all, and the saints remained silent!). He hid the tongue of the enemy in his pocket.

However, even though it was dead, the dragon's poison was transformed into a fever and the Knight of the Grail was poisoned as he inhaled it. The despicable Roman symphonist, the French king, Philip the Fair, features in this legend as the cowardly knight, Enguerrand the redhead, who coveted the hand of the fair-haired Isolde – the Church of the Grail. When he realised that the dragon was dead he claimed the victory for himself.

In the castles of the Grail there is a healing Myrrh ointment which consists of particles of the Immaculate Conception, particles of proximity to the Most High, particles of Divine Wisdom, and particles of waxen and Myrrh immortal bodies. They work infallibly against the bite of the snake.

Here is another paradox! In the annals of the Grail it seems that the knights always vanquish black dogs, dragons, bloody barons etc. and the Templars almost seized power over the world (the religion of the Grail). However, once again it has ended with the triumph of the Roman harlot and the 'commercial popes' have taken the bit between their teeth.

It is impossible to read history as if from the outside. 'From the outside' ends up being 'another way', or 'through a forbidden door', like robbers and thieves. The history of Christianity and the world can only be read with eyes from heaven. If you look at it from the throne of the Inexhaustible Chalice, it is one great triumph.

The Most High ordered that it should be so. People should bear witness through being *yurodivy.* We should go where He wants. There are no definitive texts. No institutional administration should be set up and one should continually strive towards self-perfection, grow up, and experience rapture on the one hundred and fifty steps leading up to the castles of the Kingdom. The perfect manuscript telling of the glory of the knights and myrrh-bearing women of the Grail is still being revealed. Thus, the Grail, which is forbidden now and cursed secretly by Roman swindlers and Vatican and Byzantine executioners, is being revealed as the true All-Powerful One and the King. The whole world (alas, Christians are last of all) will be shaken by the revelation of the True Church: it is so great and indescribable ; it is so beautiful and perfect – it is a radiant Virgin in white robes. The Grail will eclipse all the fallen ones in this world and the Chalice from the hands of the Lord will feed the many suffering people in the world.

*

The claim that the Templars attended Roman Masses every day is just another in a series of a thousand slanderous claims made against these holy descendants of Christ. In no way could the knights have been attracted to Roman Masses in cathedrals with professional choirs. All they needed was the Chalice of the Grail. This is the original Chalice and all others are copies and imitations. The robes of virginity and faith in the miraculous presence of Christ were their armour. Their temple was the place where Christ had dwelt (Jerusalem).

The liturgy at the knights' round table was filled with ecstasy. The participants were enraptured and filled with holy passion after the first few words and the Grail fed them generously from the Holy Being.

The conscience of the Grail remained clear. They became saints after a very short time and jealously guarded the purity of their faith, not admitting outsiders into their inner sanctuary.

The liturgical rite took no longer than half an hour but its nourishment kept them going until the end of their earthly days and a thousand years more. Being of the same composition and the same blood as Christ, the knights partook of His Flesh and Blood in a special way and considered it a great honour to serve the two-fold responsive Grail, in other words, to give their blood to Christ on the battlefield. The Templars drew their divine spiritual strength from the holy passion of the liturgy which they experienced during battle. In the history of human warfare this was the very rare entry into the Holy Being during earthly combat with swords, bows, chain mail and other weapons.

The Chalice was their heart's desire. There are so many visions of the Chalice! What a profound theology of the Chalice. It is a Chalice of such a profoundly mystical theology! The Chalice is greater than the Cross. The blood crystallises in myrrh and the blood of a martyred knight becomes Myrrh. From his seed the immaculate humanity of Christ is born. There is no other way to continue the work of Christ except through suffering, so that the last drop of blood of a disciple and heir can spread the great miracle-working Grail, which means spreading the new seraphitic (scarlet roses and white lilies) human race. Martyrs joined the ranks of the crowned kings of the messianic dynasty and knew that Christ would rule with them for a thousand years in ineffable bliss.

There was a fundamental difference between the knighthood of the Grail and the monasticism of the Franciscans, Dominicans etc. The monks spent their cloistered lives theologising and praying. The knights, though, were filled with rapturous ecstasy, yearning for the union of love and going into battle as if to a wedding feast.

The Templars believed in a different Christ to that of the Roman Politicians. Rome is the 'bear whose eyes are red with fury like glowing embers', who has come to destroy the saints. It has the tail and the habits of a scaly snake and the sword of the Grail must be thrust into its jaws, penetrating down to the very heart so that it perishes and can no longer lie, slander or bring any new evil or universal catastrophe into the world. This dragon is capable of anything; it is capable of all sorts of dirty tricks to destroy the world.

*

The legend of the evil baron Stolzenberg has a surprising ending. After his castle was cursed by the Knight of the White Lion and vanished without trace, the villain's spirit was left to wander around in the form of a black dog, as if it were guarding some buried treasure. There was no treasure, though.

The Vatican will leave behind non-existent treasure. They boast about the treasure, but there is nothing there, just as Christ, in Whom they 'believe' after their own fashion, is not there. The treasures of Solovki, though, remain intact, and the treasure chambers of the 150 castles of the Grail are bursting at the seams.

Oh, Alleluia!

30.06.2005 Deris Island

❧

The Spirituality of the Grail

The Grail is a radiant, resplendent, spotless virginity which does not compromise. There is a law of virginity: once it is threatened it can no longer be restored. Christ guarded His virginal Church like a caring mother.

Perceval was unable to help the kind and wise Sir Bron, the first keeper of the Grail, and remained indifferent to the Chalice, simply because he could not rid himself of the attraction of beautiful women and tournaments. His human nature gained the upper hand and his spirituality was insufficient. Only after a spiritual crisis and having confessed to a hermit, was he able to go to Monsalvat and see the magnificent Grail.

It is senseless to attempt to enter its white castles and glorious mysteries without first undergoing a spiritual transformation. The ascetic practice of self-mortification is only the first step. It is followed by igniting the flame of the heart, love for the Most High, the grace of the Holy Spirit and the burning of icon lamps.

The lamp of the heart must be lit i.e. the inner Grail must be present. Then the future of the True Church will be revealed.

At the same time the Roman Harlot became increasingly involved in fornication with world powers, making compromises with monarchies in the interests of expanding its own geographical boundaries, the virginal Church remained faithful to its Bridegroom, Christ. It showed itself to be the perfect image of Him and born of Him in the truest sense – from His origin (Abraham's seed), from His breath and from His molten pearl. It is born of his being and his *divine humanity*. It has grasped that which the Roman shadow is unable to even vaguely grasp, in spite of all its cunning, theological efforts to trace its origins 'back to the apostles' and to define itself as the 'only one worthy of the blessing of Christ' and 'ruler of the world'.

The spirituality of the Grail is beyond compare and is superior to all others. Its mark is to be found everywhere. It is important to give oneself fully to the Grail and to love the nature of its structure: strict morals, a life of supreme love, the brotherhood of chivalry, sobriety and the unsheathed sword of David to fight against lust. The constant struggle with snakes, dragons and all kinds of monsters, conjured up by the 'whore of Babylon' is effectively the main occupation of a virginal knight. Of course, what is hidden behind 144 doors and castles is the ecstatic mortal yearning for the heavenly Beloved, the rapturous perception of the Eucharist; seeing Christ through the eyes of Mary Magdalene, the Holy Mother and myrrh-bringer of the Grail, clinging to Him with all one's might, clothed in the robes of virginity, which have been retrieved from the white palaces of the Grail.

The Roman dragon exhales and the whore hurries into the other world. Her infernal shadows, false seduction, and abominations are replaced by the pure, radiant and undefiled religion of the Grail. Thus Christ affirms His Kingdom on Earth.

What should this deadened sacred place be called, filled as it is with confusion like that of the second Temple of Jerusalem at the time of Judas Maccabeus? Confusion can lead to disastrous consequences.

If this liar and hypocrite is not exposed in time, she will bring about such abominations! The Popes gave their blessing to fascism. The Metropolitans collaborated with the communist butchers, on whose conscience lies the swamp filled with the blood of millions, where ghosts shrouded in smoke are ready to condemn the whole world to be executed. Priests bless nuclear warheads, cardinals invoke the blessing of the Holy Trinity on 'healthy sex' ('Catechesis for the Lost' by Ersilio Tonini) and cover paedophiles.

*

An atmosphere of heavenly love reigned in the castle of Monsalvat. In accordance with the Eye of Temperance and the Tower of Happiness, not a single serpent was allowed here. Tournaments and glorious victories in battle were of little significance. It was important to undergo other tests; the spiritual tests of discerning the seals and unlocking inner chambers.

If a knight was accepted into the brotherhood of the Divine loved ones, he would be able to experience the highest raptures of ecstasy. The flame of the beloved's heart burned constantly. The heavenly masters of the Grail came out of the Holy Being and revealed Christ internally (in the causal world). It was impossible to remain indifferent.

The soul remained captive forever and was kept within His disciples. This was the beginning of a life of ecstatic love for a virginal knight who had been initiated into the mysteries of the Grail. Everything else only led back to it. It was necessary to conquer fear, ancestral agendas, thoughts, lust, attachments, pride, rhetoric and so on, simply to prevent the devil from closing the gates of the heart.

According to the mystic teaching of the Grail, the inner castle, with its gates of the heart which bear the seal, had been transformed into a damp crypt. The flame was gradually being extinguished. The Bridegroom no longer came to visit His bride, leaving her alone in the depths of repentance, until something profound happens to her: until a burning crisis frees her from the darkness which has engulfed her.

Obedience comes from the madness resulting from the self-sacrifice of love. A willingness to serve one's brother can only come out of love. The Templars had some sayings which they used as greetings: 'Sir, out of love for you, I am ready to serve you tomorrow and do as you order', 'Out of love for you, my lord', or 'Know that, out of love for you, I am ready to fight this evil villain and risk my life for you'.

The daughter of the master of the White Castle asks Perceval to wear her favour during a tournament with the bravest knights in Brittany, such as Sir Gawain and Sir Lancelot. Perceval responds with the words, 'My beloved sister, out of love for you I am ready to fight anyone who can use a weapon.' They are guided by only one motive – love. There is no higher or nobler motive. When a knight rides out into battle, his strength comes solely from the love he has for his father, his brethren, his homeland, the Divine Mother, Christ, and all those who are hurt or suffering.

The only motive is kindness, empathy or love. It works perfectly, but on one condition – the soul must be cleansed of all sin.

The way to the Grail lies through obligatory chastity, i.e. the complete purification of a person. Virginity, like chastity, reveals the true Divine wisdom, and only through this is it possible to approach the castles of the Grail.

The prophet sang: I will not bow my head until I have found You, Lord. The knights of the Grail, who wandered the earth, vowed to the Most High that they would not spend more than one night in any house (if they had to stay there twice they must use different quarters) until they found the Grail. The Grail ordered that they should have no home on this earth, and no attachments.

The Grail is jealous, like El Kanna, the Most High, who revealed Himself in the laws of Moses: I am He who will reveal Himself to anyone who loves me, as a Father of boundless, rapturous, divinely passionate, exalted, unfailing and ecstatic love.

29.06.2005 Deris Island

The Love Potion

To the priest of the love which is not of this world:
My son, the greatest treasure which I can give you as a father, and which you can inherit as a son, is the love which is not of this world. Search for it! Go out into a field and dig up this priceless pearl. It will grant you the finest companions which cannot be found on earth – a spiritual bliss which is unattainable to mortals, and riches which are not even found in heaven.

TRISTAN and Isolde is the gospel of the Grail. It is not possible to unravel the whole plot without having first been anointed in the white castles and without the mystery of the Sacred Chalice.

It is said that, once, two knights drank from the Grail and immediately fell down dead. It is impossible to go back to one's former life, after having participated in the Grail. At this point there is a penetrating and fiery *metanoia*. One must become a thousand times greater and be capable of victories far beyond one's normal human capacity.

What is this? They are sailing on a ship when Brangäne (Isolde's maid) gives her the love potion which was prepared by Isolde's mother for her daughter and King Mark.

She knows that Isolde will not be able to love the weak-willed, worthless excuse of a king. Her daughter is destined for a different and greater love. She makes the drink from herbs with magical healing properties and says to Brangäne, 'Give this to my daughter! Let her drink it together with King Mark.'

Isolde is the other, non-institutional church. On the outside, she must marry the unfortunate king, the weak-willed symphonist who is in constant conflict with his four barons. These barons continually threaten to renounce their king, return to their castles (dioceses) and wage war against him if, he does not agree to their secret demands. (This is precisely how the hierarchy of the Orthodox Church blackmailed the Russian Tsars. It is as if Tristan and Isolde were taken from the chronicles of Nestor or from Kostomarov's 'History of Russia'...)

However, Divine Wisdom arranges for Tristan to drink the mysterious potion at the table on board the little ship as it sails towards the harbour of the Kingdom, instead of King Mark. What! Like the Knights Templar he will be bound to serve the king. He himself is the prince and heir of the Lap of the Most High – Loonois. However, he has left behind his royal quarters, his trappings and regalia in order to take on the role of a humble knight and servant of King Mark.

Brangäne, what have you done? You, holy virgin of the Grail, have allowed Tristan and Isolde to drink from the chalice containing the love potion!

Tristan drank from the Chalice of the Grail, and became forever an apostle of supreme love. Isolde followed suit. From that time on, whatever happened, be it separation, slander or mysteries, they were miraculously preserved and led by this supreme love of the Last Drop of the Eucharistic Blood of Christ.

I would like to dedicate a sermon entitled 'The Elixir of Love' to all humanity, so that the millions of suffering orphans might drink of the sacred Chalice of the Grail. I would like to use it to feed the children of Singapore, Thailand, Malaysia, India and Sri Lanka, and all those affected by the catastrophe of the Asian tsunami and to those caught up in subsequent world disasters. I would like to bring it to all those suffering orphans of every modern-day nocturnal megalopolis. I would like to give communion to idle tourists and inhabitants of criminal dens.

Anyone who has tasted the Love Potion will live forever. It is impossible to drink twice from the Chalice of the Grail. Having drunk from it for the first time, a single drop generates a vast ocean of divine love within a person. The heart is set on fire forever. The composition of that person's blood begins to change...

What is this? Is this the setting on fire of the Eucharist?

Yes.

*

The Grail, which leads to the White Castle, is so near! A communicant is a junior christ. In becoming like Christ, he sacrifices himself. Particles of restauration are awakened within him, giving rise to one of the immortal bodies.

Restauration (participating in the Atonement) is the greatest mystical term of the revelation of the Divine Virgin of the Grail at Fatima. She asked for restauration, promising Her maternal protection and a place in heaven after death for all who took part in it.

Oh characters of the Grail and people of the Grail! Noble knights. The fire of the Holy Spirit burns in their enlightened gaze. They are so courageous and pure! They are so gentle! They are so fervent!

Perhaps I have not yet mentioned the most important thing about the saints which I have described. Of course, they are unique. They are not to be confused with the parameters of 'Orthodox' sainthood, which depend on how far they are embedded within the false, institutional norms.

The final thing that I can say about my holy mother Eufrosinia is that she is one of the characters of the Grail. Although she went around barefoot and stooped in prayer, she floated along in a golden boat. It was in pure Grail fashion, despising the rules of the Pharisees, to bow in prayer 3000 times during the Pharisees 'endlessly drawn-out vigil! 'I was simply floating in the air after the service!'

All around the flies were sleeping through their hibernation. There was a portly lady in front who resembled a strapping soldier from Suvorov's time... 'Can you not see: those three angels in front of us are standing under the dome of the church and bowing in prayer?'

She had witnessed the sacred springs... By the grace of the Wondrous Vessel, this is the source of all mercy and grace!

Saint Innocent, who gave us the silver chalice from heaven with beautiful inlaid work, is a true saint of the Grail. This knight of the Roaring Lion (his voice could be heard 12km away, when the frail Innocent was preaching to his flock), like Lohengrin, King Solomon of the Grail, the much-insulted Sir Bron, Perceval, Tristan or Owain, he bore the bloody stigma in his heart. Innocent was stabbed in the chest by a Red Army bayonet. His wound was enormous and possibly damaged his lungs. What ordinary mortal could have survived this without the mark of the immortality of the Seraphites (the wondrous anointing with the oils of the Grail)?

And such tears! His eyes were never dry again. He was the great guardian of the Chalice from Balta in Moldavia!

Wherever the Grail goes it leaves behind a burning trail!

Another holy mourner of Russia is the patriarch of the Gulag, Seraphim the Tender, the last Russian emperor *Mikhail Romanov II,* who abdicated from the throne to be given a different crown – the golden crown of eternity.

He is the father of indescribable love and the great mourner of Russia who worked miracles from within the Grail's castles of the Holy Being. He walked barefoot through the White Sea of the air. Then, from their lofty heights, the white castles sent down to him oils for anointing, Gospels, crosses, medical plasters, iodine and antiseptic ointment for treating wounds. The mystical library at Solovki was seen and read by Sir Bron at the beginning of the 20th century, with its countless volumes which have been read in heaven. It is like an inexhaustible Psalter of which 100 000 copies were produced. Each one is unique and multidimensional in its own way.

150×100 000 psalms of heavenly history! Oh...

The sceptre of the Grail is in the hands of our knight of the White (transformed from the black) two-headed eagle and the transformed heathen Egyptian Lion of the state and the monarchy, in the form of a concrete sphinx. Once again, he never ceases to shed tears over those under his protection: the Mishas, the Natashas, the 'eyesores', and the *yurodivy.* What about those whom he has rescued from hell on earth, the dozens of soldiers whom he literally pulled from tanks crushed by an atomic bomb during the 'rehearsal for the apocalypse' – the detonation of an experimental atom bomb in Orenburg in the 1950ies?..

The black cassock remains fragrant to this day. The kamelavkion is scented with myrrh. The skull is waxen. The Gospel, which has lain in the ground for over half a century, bears no trace of corruption.

But what of the mysterious Mikhail? And what about the most blessed Ia? Or mother Mary of Heavenly Kindness? She came to bid me farewell:

'Father, I am going away...'

'Where are you going?'

'To the Mysterious Church.'

*

Is there a more powerful witness to the destruction of the demonic hordes than that of the Grail?

In the legend of Perceval it is said that, having taken the Chalice from the hands of Sir Bron, the most glorious and invincible knight of the White Swan and Eternal Virginity freed Brittany from a magic spell which had been cast upon it by a medieval wizard.

Clattering and grinding their rats' teeth, the demons never tire of repeating, 'Who is this?'

There is nothing like this either in heaven or on earth... and there are no plans for it either.

*

The dome of Istanbul's Hagia Sophia was torn away from the stone walls of the Islamic Mosque and raised heavenward. The white silhouette of the virgin of the Grail stood in a suburb of Cairo for several hours from two o'clock in the morning until five o'clock...

It is impossible to comprehend any of her appearances without the Grail! Prayers without the Grail are nothing but dust in an abandoned tomb.

Centuries have gone by.

People have learned nothing about Christ.

Emptiness reigns...

The Orthodox Christians have been struggling for half a century. They received communion almost every day. On feast days they administered the sacraments. And what came of it? They have disappeared without trace, like a mediocre wine. No grace has been bestowed upon them: not even the slightest token. Not one of their sins has been forgiven. Yet how many bows and confessions have passed under the black vestments of the priest!

They have disappeared without trace. It is impossible to achieve anything without the Grail.

What exactly is the Grail? Oh, my child, the Grail is that LOVE WHICH IS NOT OF THIS WORLD.

Light a candle and become speechless with delight as if time had come to a standstill and the Lady of the Grail of Zeitoun Herself had appeared before you. A white silhouette... If you look through the eyes of the Grail, though, you will see the 30-year-old Jewess, the Holy Virgin of the Grail, transformed with unearthly beauty.

'Who are You?' you, my young friend, will ask the Most Pure One. But She will not reply. A large crystal tear will fall from Her eye and onto the Ground. The person who witnesses this will experience an inexplicable attraction towards the Grail. He will remain forever with this Lady in White who, when She appeared, brought with Her the unearthly and divine fragrances of the castles in the air where She dwells with their countless inhabitants.

Where is She and how can She be reached? It is not possible to reach Her by natural means. It is only possible through grace. The origin is the source of grace for everyone alive. It is the Creator's foundation for the City of God on earth. It is the basis of existence. Remember this and tie it [to your hand] like the mysterious name of God.

'I am the love which is not of this world. It is impossible, unique and real. It is all-embracing, overshadowing, omnipresent and alive. It is both hidden and revealed, the Beginning and the End, Alpha and Omega.

My divine screen is switched on. My child, you must read the mysterious signs of the Book of Life. Read John's Apocalypse and the canonical volumes... My child, see how much there is! Read, read the pearl-like manuscripts. Even the Gospel of St. Eufrosinia is greater than her fruitful life and a drop of its myrrh.'

*

I carry with me the wooden Grail decorated with a white dove in an octagonal bush – the insignia of the Marian priest of Melchizedek.

Is there no bread? It does not matter. We can use French brewer's yeast instead, which was brought by my friend M. Superleveur de Bieore, en paillettes. It is rich in vitamins B1, B2, B3, B5, B6, and B9, proteins, magnesium, phosphorus, zinc, iron... It also contains particles of restauration – the golden pollen of Divine Wisdom.

The wine is magnificent! The *yurodivy* Professor Bukovich has brought it and it is clearly from the Grail! He has been repenting for twenty years for having performed abortions. He is taking on the rest of the world alone: he is standing alone to oppose artificial ovulation, stimulation, artificial fertilization and inhuman practices. He has been nicknamed 'Doctor Bible', or the devil incarnate. The medical mafia have promised three times to kill him for divulging the 'secrets of Hippocrates'. 'Drink, father! Take communion from the Chalice of the Grail!'

My disciples consider it their duty to bring me a bottle of the finest Moldavian, French or some other incredible wine:

'Drink, father! Take communion from the Chalice of the Grail.'

At the bottom of the Chalice, the dazzling formation takes place of unifying particles, like the glittering of the sun on the surface of the sea – the theotic pollen of the twelfth immortal body.

Oh, my Beloved, Oh!
Such rapturous bliss.

It seems that it is possible to get by without the Byzantine Troparion or the Seraphim, 'Do not sing, do not sing, nightingale! Do not disturb my prayer'. The right hand of the Most High is stretched out over my small travelling wooden Grail. We have been wandering for twenty-five years now and have made a vow, like Sir Perceval, or any other saint of the Grail, or even King David, not to sleep in a bed but to wet it with tears until we have found the Holy Grail – this pearl of Divine Wisdom – and until it envelops us, fills us with the Holy Spirit, and transforms us beyond recognition.

Tristan prevails. This handsome, golden-haired man, the most handsome in Brittany and the finest knight of the whole of humanity, smeared himself with disgusting filth in order to appear ugly and thus gain access to the castle of Queen Isolde.

Being a *yurodivy* also means having the right to the truth. No one can object. It doesn't result in a death sentence but with the reaction of the little dog, Petitcreiu, – a ridiculous laugh.

No-one understands anything... And that is exactly what is needed.

The heart is set on fire by the words of the ultimate truth. Tristan, the dazzlingly magnificent and finest knight of all time (the archetypal Keeper of the Chalice of the White Castle), is transformed into an ugly mortal, so that such poor, ugly mortals can become beautiful, like the knights of the Grail.

What is there to offer to young people? What would be best? 'The Bishop of Maitreya'? The pathetic Franciscan brethren? Archbishop Kondrusiewicz?

Offer them the love which is not of this world. Offer them Christ, whom nobody yet knows. Offer them Mary as she was before she appeared to anyone.

The Lord is on fire. The Divine Mother fans the flames. In the castle of the Grail the Most Pure Virgin is worshipped as the one held most dear.

Have you seen Her in any Council? Have you seen how fathers Gleb, Nikolai, Theodosius and Athanasius, noble knights of the Grail, worshipped her with great honour? In their hands they held the invisible swords of the Grail. They nobly clasped their hands to their hearts in a chivalrous sign of honour to the Holy Virgin. They think the world of Her. They want to be like Her. She loves them infinitely. Again and again she gives them a hundred times more than they had dreamed of.

It is only possible to speak of this using 'apophatic' or negative language. It is a covenant with the Most High who is not of this world. The undefiled origin has been overlooked on earth. The grace of the Holy Spirit is not present in people receiving communion in church. And so on, and so on...

Oh! Just one drop of this Myrrh potion is sufficient for the flesh to become steeped in myrrh forever. You cannot receive communion from the Grail twice. The same is true of Blessed John's chalice. I give real communion only once.

'What is this all about?' I hear you ask.

I, who have delivered 150 000 pre- and post-Eucharistic lectures, say to you, 'It is the Sacred Love Potion.'

The maid, Brangäne, prepared it for her mistress, the fair-haired Isolde, and King Mark. Isolde had been promised to him in marriage against her will. 'By accident' the king of the Grail willed that the potion should be drunk by the young and handsome Tristan. (Tristan is the archetypal keeper of the Grail; the heir of the Grail; the son of the Lord by Mary Magdalene and Christ; 'Desposyn' – father of the other church, who sampled a different kind of grace and believed in a different Christ...).

Tristan and Isolde drank the love potion, which was made of 140 different herbs, and were intoxicated forever. They lost their minds in their union and became intertwined in ecstasy. They had to experience such great sorrows and mysticism! The glorious Tristan, the prince and heir of Loonois, who had exchanged his crown for a suit of armour, disguised himself as a repulsive creature. He was deceived and betrayed. He was cursed. He, who was loved by the whole nation after having saved Brittany from the four metre tall Rephaim, Morholt, was sentenced to death for 'breaking the law'. She, the most beautiful queen of all time, and the favourite lady of all Brittany, was sentenced to burning at the stake, like Joan of Arc, because she, who was not subject to any law, 'broke the law'.

Who am I? At first I was a monk (seeker), then a holy vessel (conductor), and then an *anointed* one, of the love which is not of this world.

How can I explain my actions? What is my reasoning? The love which is not of this world. Before its sacred and perfect holiness all laws are rendered numb. The monsters of hell retreat. Hell opens its gates, becoming humble and gentle and avenging the sins of Adam. It is perhaps worth feeling the pain forever.

Are the yurodivy novels of Jonathan Swift, Rabelais and Thomas Moore actually from the sources of the Grail? Troubadours, minnesingers, Orphics, and buskers have captured the hearts of millions with their wonderful songs, which originated from the Grail. When John, the mystic visionary, realised, 'they shall have no more songs or psalms, the sound of the harp or the ten-stringed lyre shall be heard no more, and they shall no longer have any form of art', he was speaking as the first anointed one of the Grail.

*

Oh, He was That Which is not possible on earth. He was unique. Crowds buzzed around Him and His disciples kissed His feet...

I am talking about Christ. He brought about that which no-one else had been able to bring about simply because he possessed the love which is not of this world.

There is no other like Him in the world (with regard to the purity of faith). There is no other in the courts of earth, heaven, mysticism or eternity. Have you clothed yourself in the robes of the love which is not of this world? Has the Most High given you a pearl from heaven which lies molten in your little Solovki and in your permanent holy passion?

If you cannot manage your own small project of realising the *Divine humanity* within yourself and becoming a conduit for the love which is not of this world, then you are worthless and have accomplished nothing. You will not be accepted into the Kingdom and you will not be welcome into the white castles of the Grail.

The legend of Tristan and Isolde (although the Pharisees' censors and, it would seem, Wagner's opera of the same name, are unaware of this) constantly excites the human mind. There is such rapturous love in such appalling circumstances! The potion is intoxicating. You only need to drink it once in order to find yourself in a permanent state of ecstatic holy passion.

Oh, I would like just one thing; for just one drop of the Myrrh love potion to set your heart on fire, my son. Then, from being an orphan, uncertain, not knowing what to do with yourself or where to go, not knowing which church to spend three hours in or which role models to follow, partake of the Last Drop of the Grail and become a conduit for the love which is not of this world.

Is this possible? Yes. First you must undergo 144 000 tests. Show the Most High that you are not from 'down below', that you are not a serpent, who has come to kill and maim innocent knights with its venom. Prove that you will not misuse the wisdom of the Grail for your own evil purposes. Prove that you are selfless, renouncing all earthly things and virginal.

You must have renounced everything for the sake of the quest for the Grail. You must be prepared to sacrifice not one but 10,000 lives just to drink the inexhaustible Love Potion again and again. Prove that, like Beethoven, you are prepared to go against the whole world and that the final movement of his ninth symphony the 'Ode to Joy' is resounding within you: 'Be embraced, ye millions of brothers!'

It stands alone so that you can give up everything else for its sake.

My friend, are you fascinated by Zarathustra? Praise the Lord! Both the ancient Persian version of Zarathustra, or even Nietzsche's version ('Also sprach Zaratustra') are better than Ignatius Bryanchaninov or Joseph Volokolamski, the 'holy fathers' who are the pillars of the ecumenical councils. The Lord be praised if the love which is not of this world is revealed to you through this ancient prophet of the Fervent Power. The prophets Zarathustra, Mohammed or Sun Myung Moon will light the eternal flame within your heart, dispel fears and light a silent icon lamp within you.

The stairs on the way to the Grail require an introduction to the Immaculate Origin through the origins of Christ, which are realized through the Messianic Branch. There is one more condition – a calling from afar, or the sacred calling of the Grail. It is as if one of the maidens was blowing the sacred Horn of Plenty and calling out from the ends of the earth, such as Quito in Ecuador or Havana in Cuba.

Oh my friend, you realised this architectural project when you finished the Academy of Fine Arts and Contemporary Painting. You became a great designer and creator of exhibitions. You understood yourself to be a teacher of the faith and an eternal disciple of the Most High... Did you become an apostle of the love which is not of this world, though? If so, then you belong to the True Church of Mystery. If our Father has prepared many anointing oils containing myrrh for you, then hold them in your hands and wait for the brides of Christ to come to you dressed in white. They will open their bottles and, like the 'other Mary', they will pour myrrh onto your head from an alabaster jar.

My son, the greatest treasure which I can give you as a father, and which you can inherit as a son, is the love which is not of this world. Search for it! Go out into a field and dig up this priceless pearl. It will grant you the finest companions which cannot be found on earth – a spiritual bliss which is unattainable to mortals, and riches which are not even found in heaven.

Homo theoticus. Oh mio Dio, Oh my Lord! The human who is being deified is becoming divine!

Empty your mind of everything else. If this idea hits a nerve, then become a conduit and a vessel, a witness and a confessor of the love which is not of this world. Forget about the protestant celebrities, Billy Graham the American televangelist, Metropolitan Anthony Bloom in his church in central London, and the finest preachers and teachers on earth. Clothe yourself in the garments and the mentality of Christ, the priest of the love which is not of this world.

However, this Kingdom, which is not of this world, is now being established on earth. There is nothing else. There is no other prospect for humanity except to become a sacred vessel of love, which is impossible for the Adamites and those in their care.

How many orphans can you make happy! Your gaze alone leaves its mark on them forever. How many souls can you endow with a trace of goodness to last for a thousand years!

Search and search again for the priceless pearl, harvested in some field, goodness knows where... Perhaps you will find it tomorrow in a cheap souvenir shop among the plaster statues of monkeys and models of medieval castles. Lord knows!

*

The Knights of the Grail and their myrrh-bearing women are sacred virgins of the love which is not of this world.

Through this love they have achieved eternal virginity and worship Christ, their role model for perfect and supreme love, who came down to earth and left the burning trail of blood in the hearts of millions. There is nothing higher than this love. Nothing at all.

It is unthinkable and impossible.

It drives people insane and mad with desire.

If you drink the love potion of Tristan and Isolde just once you will be driven mad with the ecstasy of a love which can overcome all distances, circumstances, separation, enemies, death or hell. The potion renews itself through deep sleep, temptation by the devil, endless deserts, parting and leaving...

Here is a love letter which was left on the table.

> Oh Where are You, my beloved?
> Come to me. I cannot go on any longer.
> May I die in Your embrace.
> Let me kiss Your hands and touch your garments.
> Let me see You, if only for a few moments.
> Let me whisper a few words to you.
> Oh my Beautiful One...

This is the Song of Songs about the Divine Beloved, Who is more beautiful than anyone else on earth, and about the love which is absolutely not of this world...

It is only this love which makes it worthwhile coming into this miserable world where seven billion flies sleep lost in oppressive dreams and caught in the devil's great (spider's) web.

'Father, it seems that I have drunk a waking potion! I have woken up five million sleeping flies.'

'Alleluia! Now take them to the Ark and prepare suitable clothes and a meal for them.'

In the parable of the Prodigal Son our Saviour spoke as a true teacher of the Grail. When his son returned from his wanderings, the happy father killed the best calf and prepared expensive wine for the occasion – the Love Potion from the Chalice of the Grail.

…I once knew a fool who was the Son of a famous Russian theatre director. In Soviet times he would receive communion at 9 o'clock in the Orthodox Church in the suburb of Ilinsk, and at 12 o'clock in the Catholic Church in the Lyubyanka district of Moscow. He later became a Polish priest. He converted his father. He read the preaching of the catacombs and said of himself, 'Every day I die and rise again.' Then he left the priesthood. Did he find the love which is not to be found among mortals?

If so, he will have found peace.

The Holy Spirit, who comes with the sacred Chalice of the Grail in His hands, says, 'This is the sacred drink. Drink it. It will bring you the love which is not of this world. You will become citizens of heaven. Drink it just once and you will live forever.'

Lord, Lord! I have received communion myself so many times! Would partaking of the Last Drop just once have set me on fire? So many people have received communion from my hands several times a year! Has the love which is not of this world been ignited within them?

If there had been a revelation from on high, then it did not last long – just a few moments during the liturgy of the 'Requiem Eternum. Open the doors to the faithful', or after a private concert where my daughter Frances performed a solo. If this is so, then the Lord be praised. I did not risk my life in vain when I came to the Three Fools' Cultural Centre, embraced you, exchanged a holy kiss, tired myself out and preached... I managed to do what I wanted – to give you the holy love, which is not from the world of Adam's descendants.

*

'Seraphites? You have invented them. Priests of Melchizedek? The Grail? Solovki? Nightingale Mountain? Altar of Union? White tents? Wedding chambers? The Most High?'

If this entire list is fictional then there is no reason for anyone to come to this concentration camp for displaced persons.

There is no reason for him to get lost in the loneliness of a night club or to sit with sweaty palms on a chair in the waiting room for the passengers of flight 205.

My soul is hesitating... Should I really be going there? The Mad Dog raves, 'No, not like that! Do not hold the chalice like that! Do not preach about that...' Well you go and serve instead of me. Show me: how is it possible?

'Whatever you do, it will not be quite right...'

In the face of doubt from the oppressive, biting, stinging midges that were my thoughts, I relaxed and felt sufficiently intoxicated. I had attained the love which is not of this world. That is why I have so many followers. More will be added to their number into eternity: from one to a thousand.

Is it not true that it is wonderful to bring into this world the love which is not of this world?

'Have you not read the Revelation of the Divine Mother yet? Have you not been to the church in the House of Culture of the Three Fools? What have you been doing for the last 35 years if you have not known the love which is not of this world?'

Oh my child! If only all those poor visitors who frequent night clubs, bars, casinos and trans-meditation shows, or if all traders, producers, realtors, opera singers and soloists at La Scala in Milan merrily singing Verdi's 'Aida', the principle director of Moscow's Malaya Bronnaya or Tagan theatre, the late Anatoly Efros or Yuri Lyubimov, Marina Tsvetaeva or Albert Einstein, the genius of mystical physics, could see just once the light of the love which is not of this world!.. Then all churches would be closed, and the earth's 'information pool', used by military generals, psychotronics, and those developing space technologies for the 25th century, would evaporate. Then the Kingdom of the Most High will come down to earth.

Nothing else is necessary beyond dying for the one worthy calling. A person is greater than himself just like the Most High who, having sent his only begotten Son into the world as a God-Man, showed that He is greater even than Himself.

I believe in Him Who is greater than Himself and always new. His name is 'Behold I make all things new.' However, if the Creator is greater than Himself, then His creation, made in His image and likeness, which includes you and me, that tiny ball of earth and sand in the great vault of the universe, is greater than itself. Therefore, being called from nothing, born of a sinful mother and a son of man, I boldly dare to profess the love which is not of this world. The Father of this love, Christ of the Burning Eucharist, is the only one worthy of praise and a perfect role model.

They asked Him on whose authority He was acting, healing and bearing witness to Himself as the Messiah. The love which is not of this world. With what power did he raise Lazarus, who had been dead for ten days, back to life, or confound the teachers Gamaliel and Shammai in the Jewish synagogue, when he was a 12-year-old boy? With the power of Him Whose love surpasses all earthly conception.

The Grail teaches, though, that it is unattainable in the present.

With what power did Tristan jump from the chapel before he was due to be executed? With what power did he manage to avoid the thousands of traps which lay on his path? With what power did the beautiful Isolde free herself from the spell of the hundred lepers and from the great dishonour of having to eternally await her death? With what strength did they survive together in the forest (the holy cave) of Moriah, where Adam managed to beg forgiveness for original sin? With what power were the evil and wicked baron Ganelon and the other four villainous black barons scattered in different directions when they saw Tristan transformed with burning power?

'By the power of the love which is not of this world.'

Oh, in what way is it possible to forgive unforgivable sins? It is one more miracle on top of another.

With what power did He multiply the loaves and the fishes so that there was enough to feed the 10 000 who had come to listen to His preaching? With what power did He heal lepers and give strength to the weak? What exactly was He speaking about in the Sermon on the Mount? He was speaking about the love which is not of this world.

He was speaking of this love when He said, 'Happy are those who mourn – with tears full of emotion! – for they shall be comforted. Happy are the peacemakers – for they shall be called true sons of the Most High.'

It is impossible to understand a single word of His teaching without an internal revelation concerning Him and the love which is not of this world! His descendants will praise Him forever and, in the third millennium, He will be proclaimed King of the love which is not of this world.

'My children, what do you wish for from the divine civilization?'

'The love which is not of this world, Father. We have already been through a lot, but have not yet known this love.'

Then my dear mother Eufrosinia began to cry.

'So much evil! They beat me so much! They wanted to cut off my head. I begged so much but they only responded with more cruelty. When I knocked on their door after forty days of fasting, they would not give me as much as a baked potato. Then you tell me about the love which is not of this world. Because of that I became a child again and read the psalms, nodding my head. I fell asleep thinking sweet thoughts about the nature of the love which is not of this world.'

This is the one thing which makes life worth living. It opens all the gates of heaven for anyone who has understood their calling. Having humbly accepted the image of Christ as the King of the love which is not of this world, Lev Tolstoy abandoned 'Anna Karenina', 'War and Peace', 'What I believe', 'What is art?', his collected translations of the four Gospels, and his visit before his death to Ambrose at Optina Pustyn as well as to Shamordino, humbly assuming the image of Christ as the king of love.

No-one can object. The law against it is powerless.

Oh how can I thank Him, Who died instead of me, Who took my affliction upon Himself and shared my cross? He has done a thousand times more for me than I can even imagine. He gave me riches a million times greater than I deserved.

I asked for only small things, such as an orphic egg, a magic wand, a straw cross and two neighbours with whom I could pray...

However, He gave me His Kingdom and Himself, the incorruptible Divinity. He proposed that 'I who am greater than myself', am myself plus Christ whom I have accepted and of whom I have partaken.

You and I are one. Oh!

Oh love which is not of this world! Why was it that I went up Nightingale Mountain and was honoured with a revelation of the Altar of Union and *divine union*? It was so that I can spread throughout the world the teaching and the gospel of the love which is not of this world. It is the Kingdom of the *myrrh-anointed* disciples of the Holy Spirit. When the Paraclete comes, He will renew it on earth and confirm in His disciples.

*

...And so they crossed the Treacherous Ford. According to the 'black barons' (the bishops), Isolde had broken the law.

There, in the presence of King Mark and a hundred knights, she demanded 'Divine Judgement.' She stood there in her innocence, holding the burning hot iron.

'I have committed no sin against love. I have not broken the law of the Most High.'

Tristan proposed a duel to protect Isolde from slander.

'Get out of my land, you traitors! May you never be shown mercy again!'

Oh, would that the eternal court, with its burning hot iron, could have proven her innocence! And so, pale-faced, she approached the fire.

'Not one mortal man has ever embraced me, save Christ.'

Everyone fell silent. The iron was white-hot like the furnace of Nebuchadnezzar from the time of the three youths who confessed their faith.

Isolde removed the jewellery from her wrists and neck and gave it to some beggars. Then she removed her purple mantle and her other clothes. Her beautiful body was covered only with a light, sleeveless tunic. Trembling, she stretched out her arms in front of her and, like Lady Macbeth, her eyes closed and shaking, she walked toward the fire.

Silence reigned all around. Even her enemies and accusers were silent.

The iron was as hot as can be. The executioners were hot and stepped back with their red-hot tongs and feverishly red, predatorial eyes.

What would happen?

Isolde raised her eyes heavenward in ecstasy. At that moment a divine body (one of the twelve) came down to her – the theotic body of the bride at the wedding. Then she called for anointing oils of myrrh and the sword of the ultimate truth. The holy bride of the divinity, the priestess of the Most High and priestess of Melchizedek boldly stepped towards the furnace and placed her snow-white hands into the coals. Then she picked up the red-hot iron. She took ten steps with it as if in a holy trance, still dressed in white. She tossed a piece of the hot iron onto the ground and opened her arms in the form of a cross.

The witnesses saw that her hands had not been harmed.

This is how the Lord protects His immaculate ones and the spotless holy virgins of the Israelites.

Oh, to what end have I been virginal, *a yurodivy, an Elder,* a father, served the Eucharist and preached for the last 25 years? I have done these things so that, one day, I might reach the level of Seraphim the Tender, my father, the last heir of the

Holy Chalice, taking it to the Russian Grail. His is the level of a father of the indescribable love which is not of this world.

I go to visit Buzuluk. There I find one marvellous old woman, and then another... Maria, the 'mother hen' is eagerly trying to say something. Lydia, who was close to him for 20 years (she baked cakes and his favourite cabbage and egg pasties for him), is attempting to say something but she is already half paralysed. Her master gave her an icon. Then another icon. She introduced the *yurodivy* and *starets* himself. She did this without uttering a word. How could it possibly be put into words?

However, if she could have spoken and her half paralysed body had been able to move, she would have said:

'How can it possibly be put into words? He was the father of the love which is not of this world. He is the Christ of the *second Golgotha*.'

100 000 prisoners were his daily audience in the appalling church in the Solovki Archipelago. Among the 100 000 convicts were guards and former priests, who were destined only to lie in frozen piles in the Siberian earth. They had known the love which is not of this world. This is the Gospel of Solovki.

*

'What is this?' they say. 'Is it another miracle? Sorcerers can walk into a fire without being burned, too. Yogis walk across burning coals. Has the legend of Tristan and Isolde really come from Roerich or from Tibet?'

No, this is a divine body and the robes of virginity.

The holy fire, which burns in the heart helped saint Elizabeth (Isolde), or the mother of the Grail, who had borne her heavenly sons and daughters for Christ the First Anointed One, to enter the fire without being burned. It helped her to take hold of the burning hot iron while her beautiful hands remained perfect.

No, no! That holy love kept them both safe on earth.

Tristan died whilst fighting seven opponents single-handed to defend his friend Kahedrin. A black knight wounded him with his lance...

Yet death did not exist. Death had been vanquished long ago. He died in the arms of his beloved. Death was only granted in order to enter an even greater holy love.

Oh, immortal mortal! You dared to break all the laws of the universe in spite of the devil's zodiac programme and the horoscope which was compiled for you: you dared to become acquainted with the love which is not of this world.

Pass through the last gates of mortality in order to know the LOVE WHICH IS NOT EVEN TO BE FOUND IN HEAVEN. It is a love which is greater than itself. Is it not true that this love, which you have professed, has no limits? So, finish your journey worthily.

It is only possible to die out of love. Anything else is unworthy.

Were not Tristan's victories all because of his love for the beautiful Isolde? Was his outstanding courage and strength in the face of thousands of temptations not fed by his love for his virginal bride?

Oh Isolde, where are you? Kahedrin, hurry to Cornwall! Bring her back in 40 days! Disguise yourself as a merchant and, when you are granted an audience with King Mark, go to Queen Isolde. Show her the ring of green jasper (the symbol of the knights of the Holy Grail which represents loyalty to the last drop of the blood). Then say, 'Tristan is dying. Come quickly!'

Love is greater than death. You must die in love and of love.

The other Isolde, the 'weak-willed' (the symphonist church) deceived the dying knight. She accused her husband of being passionately in love with the other Isolde, the wife of King Mark in a far away land. She lied to his face.

'Isolde, Kahedrin's ship is approaching. Tell me, if its sails are black or white?'

'Black' (the colour of mourning).

'Oh, no!'

Isolde was not coming to him... Perhaps it was better that they were apart.

Tristan would die without seeing Isolde. He met her as he was drawing his last breath, as the last drop of myrrh and Eucharistic blood were flowing from his heart. Christ, his Father in the flesh, having given His spiritual family to his mother Mary Magdalene, died in him in holy passion. Tristan died of love in the arms of the Lord.

Isolde, who was driven insane, like Lady Macbeth in Shakespeare's tragedy, arrived on land.

'Where is he? Where is he?!'

Then she saw Tristan already laid to rest. He was so handsome! His deathbed was one of prayer, of passing and of light.

'What have you done with him?! Go away', she said to his wife, pushing her aside. 'I loved him more than you. You are not worthy enough to do what I am going to do.'

Isolde died of love for Tristan. Tristan died of love for Isolde. They conquered death.

Jealous King Mark, who had been deceived by both of them, who loved them both infinitely and who had sentenced them to terrible deaths (handing his wife over to be mocked forever by a hundred lepers), ordered that they should be laid in tombs – chalcedony for Tristan and beryllium for Isolde. He took them on his ship to a white castle and laid them beside each other in the same chapel.

During the night a bush covered in thorns grew over Tristan's tomb. Its branches laden with fragrant flowers grew around the chapel and on Isolde's tomb. The fragrance of the flowers spread all around. A wondrous bed of flowers had blossomed. The people living nearby were mad about them both.

Isolde healed Tristan from the fatal wound he received during the struggle with the Rephaim Morholt. Why was Isolde unable to save Tristan as he was dying? Why, if Tristan knew he was dying, did Isolde rush to him from Cornwall without her healing oils?

That was how it was meant to be. That is how it is today.

He had drunk from the chalice of love and the chalice of death and he had been betrayed by the baron and by an evil dwarf...

Isolde was led to the fire and sentenced to death... However, their holy love was so great that, in the dense forest of Moriah, they slept blissfully on the ground with an unsheathed sword between them – the symbol of eternal virginity!

'Tristan, if you must suffer, then I want to suffer with you. I want to be wherever you are. My body is here, but my heart is in you', was Isolde's reply to Tristan's question, 'How can I live?' The ring of green jasper, which Tristan had given to Isolde, was a symbol of the bonds of holy union between two anointed ones. 'No one, no towers and no strong gates will ever prevent me from carrying out the will of my beloved.'

Where did they come from?

They came either by magic (hypnotic snakes) or out of supreme love.

*

What is this Lamb, which features 14 times in the Revelation of John, as Christ the Lamb or as the Lamb of Sekirnaya mountain, which gives itself as a constant sacrifice?..

The love which is not of this world is all-conquering, crowned and glorious. Its kingdom is coming. It is already gathering more and more supporters and followers. Even if I shut myself away in seclusion and they seal my lips fast, I will constantly proclaim the love which is not of this world. I have known it. I have seen it once. I will never renounce it.

The relics of mother Eufrosinia are beautiful. The miracle-working drops of myrrh on the photo-icon of Mary of Heavenly Kindness are a sign of the genuine nature of our faith.

I will never renounce the fire of repentance, the cross as the key to the door of the Kingdom, or the priesthood of Melchizedek. I will not go back on any of my teachings and I will not renounce the New Holy Rus', the divine potential or the unifying particles. I will not renounce anything, because those whom I have taught and preached to from the beginning, from the first teachings in Barybino and Mishina, have been led to the Kingdom of the love which is not of this world.

You must believe: this is the one thing which humanity is waiting for. This is the one thing which is worth living for. The only way to live like this is to overcome thousands of obstacles and temptations.

*

Today, my son, I have not prepared the liturgy. There is no bread and no wine... This does not matter, though. Let us finish our teaching and partake in communion, just as Seraphim did with a bottle of Cahors in Buzuluk.

While I was dictating this sacred text to you, the Chalice was raised three times to the fiery throne of heaven. It was blessed by the Right Hand of the Most High, Seraphim the elder and mother Eufrosinia. The Most Pure Virgin kissed it Herself and then sipped the heavenly potion. Let us taste it now and there will be peace for all those who belong to Christ. Silent, eternal peace.

Poor old woman and hundred-year-old orphan! Look at yourself running after Father Joseph with your dishevelled grey hair, saying, 'Give me communion!' Is that not why you are here in this wretched hospice lying stiffly on damp, dirty beds with rotten, mattresses – in order to find the love which is not of this world?

You were abandoned and insulted. Your kindness was forgotten and betrayed. The evil cats howled at night...

Time is marching onwards. The hour is close at hand when the Kingdom of Supreme Love will come.

There is a supreme world: it is the world of supreme love.

Its king is our Bridegroom, A Lamb languishing in the wilderness.

The bride yearns to die in the arms of You, her Beloved.

*

I have already forgotten a lot. Prayers and events slip through my fingers like water through a sieve... I remember almost nothing. If only I can stand firm in this expanse with the silent icon lamp burning as the heavenly love, which is not of this world, pours out in the night.

Oh my child, have you managed to get yourself a job as a laboratory assistant in some stupid company for a pittance, while your brother is graduating from a high-class technical institute in Jerusalem and will become a first-rate computer scientist? Well, that is great. I know that he excelled both at chess and in matters of the heart... That is marvellous. There is something better than this, though: one day he will leave all this behind and become a priest of the love which is not of this world.

It is amazingly simple. It is both opaque and transparent, and it is crystal clear. It can be found everywhere as it is the guiding principle behind all things. Take, for example, the genius doctor who earns a pittance operating on incurable cancer patients, or Professor Bukovich...

'I made 50 million Euro for Croatia through my operations, but in return they only cursed me and ranked me among the Satanists.'

'My friend', I tell him, 'I have brought to Russia the royal gift of the New Holy Rus', which is the most wonderful ideal and superior to anything on earth. I have enriched the treasure of Orthodoxy with the *Second Golgotha* of Solovki. I have brought the most precious of all pearls, which was embedded in the crowns of Russian emperors and metropolitans, to the altar of my Fatherland. Russia has rewarded me with a slap in the face and with poison. Then they hastened to thrust a lance with a poisoned tip into the anointed one.'

All that my Queen, the Divine Wisdom of the Divinity of Holy Theogamy, asks is that I enter the mansion of love, having surpassed myself.

*

Father, You have abandoned me... The memory will be erased over time. Their minds have become weak. They are being pressed in a vice. Everywhere around has been deserted.

Two people remained with Christ on Golgotha: Mary and John. There were also three myrrh-bearing women...

Now, though, the impossible is happening.

He tried to express the love which is not of this world through words and healing, but no one paid Him any heed. Now, he is giving them His Blood, the three-hour fiery blood of the Gospel and a letter written with the drops of the fiery Blood.

The sight of Him Crucified reflects this great love which is not of this world! He dies and rises again. He comes to the immortal bodies and transfigures them. He says, 'I died, rose again, and will live forever.'

Such is the love which is not of this world.

The Most Pure One takes Him from the arms of Joseph of Arimathea. She weeps over Him and washes His wounds. She gazes upon His countenance and repeats the same phrase over and over:

'Oh Divine Jesus, You are the Love which is not of this world!'

I have not yet written an *akathist* for the 25th hour of the all-day, 24-hour prayers of Chrysostom. It will be an akathist, an ode, a eulogy, a Magnificat, a royal song of praise to Him, Christ, the love which is not of this world.

All nations of the earth join together singing Schiller's new 'Ode to Joy'! Rise again in Beethoven's new Ninth Symphony! All peoples be embraced! Be united as one! The love which is not of this world has come into our world. Rejoice!

*

...Yes, yes, my brother. Forgive me, forgive me.

My heart has been pierced. Now I understand why I came into this world. I understand why I have suffered and what I have been seeking. I have undergone so many trials! I have passed through pits of snakes. I have been turned away so many times! They told me it was too early! The time had not yet come. I must wait a while. Then I was simply rejected and told I was not worthy. Who are you to profess this superior Supreme Love? You are a pathetic slave to sin.

The Most High handed me over to the devil, who tormented me. He called me with those last words. He indicated the countless covenants I had with him and my endless failings, saying,

'Can you see who you are? You are the most pathetic, vile creature. How can you possibly be the channel of the Most High? You only give out evil, hatred and poison. Take a look at this corrupt world with its miasma of modern cities, you disgusting nonentity and piece of filth! You noxious germ, infected with all the diseases of the world, and bringer of evil: who are you, you proud freak, to claim to be the bringer of Supreme Love?'

This terrible vision then disappeared, and was replaced by my dear Mother Mary. She took me down from my – tiny and entombed in sleep – cross, and comforted me, saying:

'That is how it must be. Do not be afraid. From now on, do not look at your path from the perspective of sin. Do not be ashamed. Do not bear grudges. See how gracious is the Most High. Your eight languages, your different adventures, your travels, your interests, your passions, your tears, your conversion, and your conversion of others, your liturgies, your magnificent gatherings and your vows of chivalry all serve one end, which is to celebrate the love which is not of this world.'

Stretch out your arms, my child, and pray. The hour is at hand when all of humanity will be embraced by the burning bush of the love which is not of this world. Then we will rise again and enter the Ark. Our Divine King will announce the arrival and the beginning of the 85th immortal civilization.

It will only be possible to say one thing about it: that the obstacles in the way of supreme heavenly love have been removed. The devil's intrigues, particles of evil within the blood of Seraphites, forbidden entrances to earth from 'down below', the gates of Lucifer, Ben Elohims (fallen angels set free at the end of time) winning over modern humankind with their in vitro fertilization and grotesque experiments with artificial creation of homo sapiens sapiens (homo cosmicus), will all disappear forever.

The obstacles have been removed. The composition of a human being has been altered. His heart is a waxen relic. Alleluia and Hosanna, My son! The hundred thousand enraptured new martyrs of the *Second Golgotha* did not suffer in vain. It was not in vain that Seraphim the Tender lit five thousand candles as he entered the hearts of the deceased of Solovki in the bottom of pits or frozen into the ice of the White Sea.

The time of the Kingdom of Christ has come! Nothing else will hinder the spreading of the love which is not of this world throughout the earth.

What was being written about? What was Schubert writing about in his sublime sonata or Beethoven in a song from one of his miniatures, which comes chiming out from mobile phones? They were writing about the love which is not of this world. Composers wrote music about it. The Castle of the Grail sought out poets, minstrels, minnesingers, orators and preachers. Fearless soldiers, officers and generals gave their lives for it. Mary Queen of Scots went to the scaffold for it and Nikolai Romanov II was tortured by the Communists for it...

My child, lie down on the Altar of Holy Union, and never worry about anything. However difficult things may be, when God hides His face so that His Grace seems not to touch the soul, whatever abuse or intrigues the devil may come up with (your old followers and friends renounced you with their curses), you are the conduit of the most precious thing on earth: the Gospel of unimaginable love.

There is no need to even think about anything else. It is at the very heart of all things. You do not need to do anything.

You do not need to read sermons or weave baskets like the ancient ascetics. There is no point slaving away at work and earning a living for your family. Do not think about taxes and visas or ecumenical councils and wandering the earth.

You have discovered the love of Tristan and Isolde which is the last thing which could be revealed on earth.

My son, at 3.35 this morning, you drank the Love Potion with me.

*

What links me with Father Paisius? The love which is not of this world. 'Father, I am living in your love.'

'I love you second of all after the Divine Mother', (Eufrosinia said to me). 'I love you, too, mother, second of all after the Divine Mother.'

The sacred bonds of love are the foundations of brotherhoods, sisterhoods, and human communities filled with Grace. That which does not exist on earth is a chaste, eternal and pure love, which surpasses that of Adam's race.

However, within a person, the Lord has hidden a supreme, angelic potential for love. He gives him his cross to bear, his holy passion and his despair to be endured in the desert. He tests both the strong and the weak. Some things He forgives and some things He retains – only so that they might be anointed with the sweetest love which is not even to be found in heaven.

The Saviour considered it an honour to come down to earth and to suffer for Adam's race. He was able to express the love which He could not even reveal in heaven.

*

I would like to begin my endless song. I would like to sing it to all of my dear friends and to you, my dear daughter, and to you my dearest, so that you may be clothed in the garments of supreme love. You will be able to say that there is nothing more beautiful or perfect. One day you will find it and nothing else will concern you. One day you will say:

'Father, it is in your power. Grant me the Love Potion.'

Oh, my children, the Eucharist of Blessed John is somewhat different to the Sofrinsk chalice, which can be found in every Orthodox Church! There are thousands of them and they are worthless. The pearl of John is worth all of these Sofrinsk chalices and the Holy Gifts put together. The love which is not of this world can be tasted from within it.

This chalice is special. For forty years it has lain in the damp earth in a village known as 'Raiski Sad' (lit. 'Garden of Paradise), in honour of St. *Innocent Baltski* who once preached there. Now he preaches in our church.

Have you understood anything in the Bible? Did the Soferim, the Jewish scribes, learn anything from the glorious Torah? Did they ignore the commandment of supreme love: 'LOVE ME WITH ALL YOUR HEART AND WITH ALL YOUR SOUL'?

'Why should I love You so fervently and wholeheartedly?'

'I am a Jealous Divinity and the Father of the love which is not of this world. I am bringing its holy grace to the temple of Jerusalem. Today my blessed hand is here. Tomorrow it will go far away and the angels will close the temple. When this happens, do not enter it.'

*

It is 4:40 in the morning. The bodies of the poor Adamites are wrapped up in white sheets. The others are sleeping peacefully in their bridal beds...

If only they knew how many prayers lit up the Altar of Union of the love which is not of this world, in the still of the night! Then they would enter into their union with Him, who brings supreme ideals, supreme love and supreme bliss.

I am willing to move to a higher plain and to make any sacrifices necessary in order to drink from the spring of unspeakable mysteries! I am only interested in them.

01.07.2005 Deris Island

The Way to the Castle of the Love-which-is-not-of-this-world

Perceval

In that hour of triumph, the lady of the castle entered the room accompanied by ten young virgins and four pages. They hastened to remove the knights' armour and weapons. The young maiden was so beautiful that Perceval fell in love with her at first sight. He began to proclaim his love to her and request her hand in return.

'Oh handsome knight! I have devoted myself to the invincible Chalice and the heavenly treasure', replied the maiden. 'You shall have my love and I shall give you all the riches of the earth if you complete one task for me. A white stag lives in this forest. Kill it with an arrow and bring its head to me. I will lend you my hunting dog. As soon as you let her go she will run after the stag's trail. Then follow behind her as fast as you can ride.'

Perceval took heart when he saw how the dog followed the trail of the stag, eventually hunting it down and killing it. While he was busy, an old woman caught the dog and made off with it into the forest. Realising what had happened, Perceval caught up with her:

'Madam, kindly return the dog to me!'

The treacherous old woman replied:

'You have stopped me in vain, Sir! Is this really your dog anyway? I know more than you think. I will return the dog to its owner as you have no right to it. It is you, not I, who have stolen the dog!'

Perceval was incensed:

'You old witch! Please give it to me! If you do not, I shall have to take it by force!'

'Noble knight', pleaded the witch. 'Your power is bad if you can use it against a defenceless old woman! However, if you do as I ask, I will gladly return the dog.'

A knight in black armour appeared from a grave somewhere. Perceval was not afraid of him and, crossing himself, he prepared to fight. Meanwhile, the another knight seized the stag's head and the dog and galloped off with them into the forest.

Perceval continued to fight the Black Knight. His strength increased. He suddenly attacked his enemy with the strength of the Most High.

*

...What is this? Is it a stupid fairy tale? No! It is an encoded document which shows the way to the Castle of the Love Which is not of this World. It can, of course, be read by a three-year-old child. The key is as follows.

The white stag is the symbol of the Psalms of David, and a keen and passionate yearning for the presence of the Most High. Run like a stag to drink from the heavenly spring!

Once, though, this monk (very active, i.e. having overcome all generic obstacles almost instantaneously and having converted early) fell and, in the blink of an eye, was overtaken by a dog which was full of energy. He must profess his faith like the Domini canus – the dog of the Lord – powerless and surrendering. The greatest faith is that of the Son who did not judge His Father, even when he was dying on the cross, the Last Drops flowing from him as he said, 'Father, it is finished!..'

The stag is sacrificed. However, the dog is followed by the pleading witch who says, 'Does the Grail belong to you? Nothing belongs to you!' She promises to return the knight's faith (the spirited dog, which the lady of the castle gave to him to help him) if he runs to a certain tomb and reads the mysterious incantations there.

The tomb belongs to some corrupt priest... He emerges from the grave as the Black Knight. Perceval begins to fight with him. Meanwhile another evil villain steals the stag's head (the fruits gathered from climbing the 15 steps on the spiritual path) and the dog.

I chose this legend out of a whole host of legends about the divine Perceval, who was more than divine, immortal and crowned three times, along with other knights who had a perfect faith, for one purpose: so that my precious reader can understand where he is going.

He must pass through a dense forest along hidden paths, where it is possible neither to turn back nor to move forward... So, must he lose his way? This cry is the most important of all.

On the path to the Grail there stands a grey-haired, nagging witch – the old church. She is highly unscrupulous and jealous. She is aware that the son of the Kingdom is standing before her. In spite of this, she brazenly holds the dog in her arms and says, 'This does not belong to you. The question is, who is the owner of the dog and which of us is the thief!' Then she lays out the conditions of returning the faith to the Most High – to go to a particular grave and summon the spirit of the deceased person.

The naïve, pure-hearted and noble knight zealously saddles his horse and hurries off to a new adventure. This burial vault seems like a great and holy place to him, rather like the limestone sarcophagus where the remains of St Francis of Assisi have lain for 800 years, along with his follower and spiritual daughter, Clare... It is completely different, though! The faces of saints and silver caskets containing royal relics ought to emerge from such a sacred tomb, but instead, out jumps a black villain and repulsive apparition.

What a terrible thought! What kind of saints lie in these vaults?

The malicious, jealous old woman (the old hag, the superficial church and Rome) will return your faith to the Most High, if you do as she bids – summon the spirit of the unclean deceased person from this grave and tell it to go away.

Just summon the spirit of a dead person and see what happens to you.

Tristan and Isolde

The sacred allegories of the Grail! Having dressed in the clothes of a wanderer – a pilgrim's cloak on his back and a staff in his hand – the mysterious king of Loonois (the heart of the Most High) spends the happiest hours hidden away with his beloved in the dense forest of divine virtues, where nobody could reach them.

There are traitors all around, though. They scour everywhere with their eyes. They are just waiting for the right time to pounce on the two divine lovers.

Tristan stopped near a tall fir tree whose branches hung over a water trough of white marble. His face was reflected in the clear water and a few drops fell from above.

Should Isolde be summoned in the usual way? No! Her beloved will come no more. They must part from each other once more so that their love can burn even more brightly from afar.

Adventure, separation, the deserts of hell, obstacles and injustice... Oh! Anyone who has tasted the love potion knows that the fire burns much hotter in a concrete hell and in a hidden underworld – anywhere but the way it was yesterday when all was as well as can be and when they lay naked and virginal on the ground on the faded grass and dry leaves.

Isolde's careful, light footsteps will tread here no more.

Tristan comes to the castle. Isolde, will you leave your white rooms?

What is this? At the window of her room, she heard the

song of a nightingale... No, it was not a nightingale! The song's inexplicable beauty delighted her all night long. Then she suddenly realised it was Tristan!

Somewhere in the distance was heard the unpleasant, insistent tolling of a bell. It was a call to prayer from some dragon's den. It proclaimed that anyone who did not come will suffer eternal torment. It was the bell of the Inquisition. The lovers, though, were blissfully immune to these temptations. The sound of the mad old woman's bell seemed like black magic to them. It made dogs howl and killed flies. This bell of the Inquisition spread shock and terror in its wake. It liked to sentence people to death, to cook them alive, to impale them, and to simply mock them.

No! It was very different in the castles of the Grail.

Isolde came to her senses and listened to the song of the nightingale. She could understand what it was saying. Her secret lover was singing like a nightingale. Then she understood that this was his 'last farewell'. She was filled with such sorrow! This was their parting. So, at the end of the summer, the nightingale bid farewell to her in the forest of Moriah in the midst of great sorrow.

'My dearest! How long will it be before I hear your voice again! Just call me and I will come.'

They spent that night in the garden in the 'Divine Bower'. They could not stop talking to each other, gazing at each other and kissing each other's hands, their hearts joined together, and holding each other in a heavenly embrace.

Meanwhile, they were being pursued by a pack of hunting dogs. The four black barons, Andreth, Gondolin, Dinalin and a fourth unnamed one, were servants of the red dragon. They seized the servant by the throat and asked, 'Where is he?'

'The beast, whom you thought was mad, has returned to his lair.'

The traitors revealed Tristan's hiding place. His refuge was no longer secure.

'Run away now, my dear. Run from the country which you saved! It has done everything it can to drag you through the dirt and to kill you. Run away for the sake of my love!'

'Oh! How will I live with without you?'

Isolde answers with the creed of the Grail:

'My body is here, but take my heart with you. Our lives are bound together and indivisible. We are inseparable and united as one. Run faster so that we can be nearer. Our love cannot be parted. The Name of Him who gave us the love potion to drink is 'I am, and when I am not there, I am there all the more.'

This is news of a great mystery – He is even more present in His absence!

Without a dungeon or a hermitage, is the Ever-present One, like a Madman filled with passion and following His bride, and Christ of the Parousia, really the invisible presence of Christ? I will give him to a great teacher of the Turkish order so that he may anoint the Sons of the Most High. He has many followers in London, Hawaii, the Hague, Havana, and goodness knows where else. He spreads the wonderful news about the Second Coming of Christ, which has come from the burning hierarchy of Solovki and from *Nightingale Mountain*, throughout the whole world.

What is Tristan's warbling all about? It is the voice of a love which is beyond heavenly and which is responsible for all the good in the world! When a warrior reaches ineffable heights, he is given the gift of singing like a nightingale. His voice rejoices and is glad. It is sad. It foretells parting or more happiness... It is beautiful, though, and you will never tire of listening to its strains.

'Do not sing, nightingale! Do not interrupt my prayer', says Seraphim Romanov, the old man with the heart of gold, the great orator of the New Holy Rus'. He is telling a different nightingale to 'not sing' – the one which bursts into churches with its preaching and sings like a goat.

False nightingale, do not prevent the other nightingale from singing its song of supreme love within me.

*

How lofty are the heights of the Grail! Those who reach them assume the forms of radiant animals – the *yurodivy* dog, Petitcreiu, Gilan's faithful dog which was raised by Tristan himself and given to Isolde, the lady of the castle's dog which fell whilst following the trail of the white stag, and the nightingale which sang the divine Song of Songs in the gardens of the Grail. There are other animals, too: the white eagle and the white lamb, the divine human (inhabitant of the Grail). In opposition to the animals of the Grail is the crimson beast with bloody eyes.

'The beast you are looking for has fled from its lair!'

Sound, sound the bell of the nearest Catholic synagogue. Once again these villains are abusing the poor! They do not want to bring into their churches the message of the kingdom of supreme love or the miracle of Christ which had never before been witnessed on earth, and 'he will come down again after many years of indifferent Christianity. Instead, they want to ring the funeral bell. The villains will bring a whole crowd into their bell-induced coma and into the great pestle of the fat, Catholic matriarch who believes herself to be holy and a direct descendant of the third generation.

The war cry goes like this, 'Apartments!' Neurotic landladies rent out apartments to holidaymakers for the summer. 'Apartments, money, money! Bring your money here!' we chant together with father Paisius when we hear this cursed bell of the official state religion calling people into the ghostly crypt.

Which is better: a closed Orthodox church, permanently boarded up and used as a hideaway by Mafia chiefs, or this ever-open tomb which fills you with terror as you enter it? It makes no difference whether it is a plump businessman wearing only his underwear and stricken with grief, or a sunburnt young boy in T-shirt and shorts who enters. He will scratch his head at the abject prostration and will come out throwing his hands in the air:

'I cannot find anything here. He is not here.'

*

'The lion sat in the castle and listened to the sound of the horn' (this is a reference to the White Lion, which is Tristan's protector).

'Where is my Tristan? What have you done with my Tristan?'

They welcomed the hour of death as if it was Easter. Therefore the resurrection is close at hand. Their love must pass one final test.

A creeping blackthorn spreads from her shrine over his small tomb and is covered with the fragrant blossoms of an unearthly beauty. Even their graves are joined together! They were not put in the same shrine – it is as if they were laid in different parts of the chapel of the world. The Most High of the Grail, El Kanna, made it this way so that a green arch of the branches of the blackthorn could grow between them...

Oh, my daughter! My body is somewhere in Croatia, but my heart is with you. On leaving my home and having taken a vow of homelessness on the relics of saint Eufrosinia ('master of seven castles', as my enemies put it), I say:

'I have no earthly dwelling place. I will remain with you and will never leave. When you dine, leave an empty chair at the table for me.'

01.07.2005 Deris Island

Yurodstvo of the Supreme Love

Oh Tristan! I have not yet fully learned how to sacrifice myself. I am afraid of the cross... This means that my love is still inadequate. I must drink more and more! My dearest, quench my thirst with your gaze, your heart and your chalice. Caress me still more. I have not yet learned enough about supreme love.

*

The indisputable task of supreme love is yurodstvo, or acting like a *yurodivy!* Without it, there is only the hypocrisy which is so hateful to the Most High: the letter of the law, authoritarian rules, and the black shadows of the Inquisition which arise from out of these.

'What has become of Tristan because of his love for me!' exclaims Isolde, the queen of supreme love and the archetypal Virgin of the Grail. 'Tristan should have lived in a palace surrounded by hundreds of bodyguards who were worthy of his nobility and purity of heart. He should have been able to ride from castle to castle in pursuit of glorious victories. He would have administered to the people and been crowned as a great monarch... For my sake he left behind his victories as a knight, was banished from court and hunted. He covered his face with repulsive black filth. He was hunted like a wolf. He was beaten and made to live under the stairs like a dog...'

Supreme Love seemed to pay no heed to this. On the contrary, its yurodstvo engendered a kind of inexplicable inner happiness.

Through this yurodstvo, it can speak about the final truth. Yurodstvo is the only way for a prophet to fulfil his mission.

*

'See how he has taken leave of his senses!' They threw stones at him and beat him on the back with clubs. Tristan bore all this blissfully, without feeling any pain. What an answer he gave to King Mark, though!

'Why have you come here?'

'For Isolde, whom I love more than you!' replied the great king and heir of Loonois, the second Christ, disguised as a black African.

'Nothing less than the Queen! Would you not be satisfied with anyone else?' raged the king, who somehow did not understand and could do nothing. 'But if I give you the Queen, whom you 'love more than I', what will you do with her, you filthy swine?'

'I will take her away', the filth-covered Tristan gazed upwards. 'I will take her to the place between the sky and the clouds where our beautiful crystal refuge, known as the Grail, lies hidden. The sun rises and penetrates it with its rays, giving it a heavenly warmth, and the winds cannot shake off its other-worldly peace. I will take the Queen to this heavenly peace and to gardens full of roses which bloom from the moment the sun comes up in the morning!'

The barons covered their ears:

'Ridiculous fool! He is a master of telling tales.'

Tristan (who did not care about them) sat near Isolde and gazed into her eyes.

'My friend!' Mark said to him. 'Tell me how the thought entered your wretched head that the Queen might be attracted to something as ugly as you?'

'I have earned the right, my lord. I have endured far more for her sake than you have. I have been driven insane out of love for her.'

Who could possibly speak like that? Anyone attempting to do as Tristan did would be instantly beheaded.

'So who are you?' asked King Mark, perplexed.

'I am Tristan! I am the one who loves this maiden and will love her until I die and beyond!'

Isolde, who had once drunk from the Chalice of the Grail, did not recognise him. This was double yurodstvo and a double wound! This was the eternal stigma in Tristan's heart! However, thanks to his mysticism this simple-hearted knight managed to reach Isolde, who recognised him through the ring of green jasper – the sign of the eternal bonds of union.

*

This is another legend of the Grail which highlights the *yurodivy* nature of supreme love in this world. Its yurodstvo has two sides. The Grail rejects the unworthy – the 'righteous' (the serpents who imitate conventional morals, writing and rituals).

The Grail can also see inside a person. Only *yurodivy* enter the Grail – those from another world, who are not satisfied by earthly love.

01.07.2005 Deris Island

Mortal Grief as the Climax of the Gospel

Mortal grief... Humans grieve inconsolably.

The French modernists coined the term 'existential pain'. Sartre's novel, 'La Nausée' is about a profound grief which sucks out life.

Grief is clearly an experience which comes from the devil and, within the Orthodox spiritual tradition of the *starets,* it is defined as depression. Meanwhile, mortal grief is the highest state of two virginal lovers. It is a guarantee of victory over death.

It is impossible to comprehend it when not in a transfigured state.

Isolde says to Tristan:

'Our lives are joined and interwoven with one another. How can I live without you? My body is here, but my heart is joined with yours.'

Mortal grief is the consequence of the bonds of union. They cannot be undone by distance, loss or death. Mortal grief is like the saying that 'death has been trodden on by death'. It conquers death and separation, uniting forever. It is the bonds of death which are the bonds of union.

Mary Magdalene conceived Joseph out of mortal grief, through the bonds of *Divine Union* and supernatural love.

Tristan and Isolde, the two anointed ones of the Grail (the Grail and its Church), literally languished in love for each other. They were bound together with golden threads and would not be separated in this age or in the next.

This is the mysterious bond, and the fathoming of the Grail. It is the strength which helps to conquer the majority of earthly temptations or injustices which may befall two divine lovers.

Yet this mortal grief is inconsolable! It brings such divine consolation to another, heavenly dimension.

*

Tristan and Isolde part again and again... The Duke of Gilan shows his benevolence towards his noble guest. He tries his best to entertain him with parties, tournaments, meals and socialising with his friends. Tristan is inconsolable, though. His mortal grief for Isolde is weighing him down. His heart is aching. Lost for words, he begins to sigh as if during the deposition from the cross.

The Grail is grieving for its bride. Mortal grief is one of the most exulted Myrrh states of His knights.

Further along in the story a mysterious character is woven into the narrative – a little dog named Petitcreiu ('miniature creation of the Most High'). Petitcreiu is ingeniousness itself. Its soft fur shimmers with a range of colours. Its neck is snow white. One side is a purplish red and the other is a saffron-yellow. Its belly is azure blue and its back is pink. It wears a gold collar with a bell which makes such a pleasant, clear and pure sound that it comforts and calms Tristan's heart and consoles his grief.

This is where the little bell ringer of the Grail first appears in the story. It provides amusement, entertainment and *yurodivy* comfort to neighbours and to the world. Each of the divine lovers has a little dog named Petitcreiu. Nothing and no one in the world could comfort them more than this comical creature, whose bell rang every time it moved, as if they were communicating their thoughts and ideas through the dog's movements.

This legend of Petitcreiu, the multicoloured dog with its strikingly perceptive and friendly gaze, tells of the mystic comfort which the knight of the Grail found for his mortal grief over his Divine Beloved.

Mortal grief is like a 'concrete tomb': it is as dark as night, abandoned, deserted and oppressive. However, the Most High sent a source of comfort to the knight of the Chalice. This was something unexpected and wonderfully spontaneous. In this case, it was in the form of the little dog, Petitcreiu.

'Do not despair, do not despair, My child! Life goes on. Look how spontaneous this world is!

Do not give way to your grief. Take heart, My Son!'

Only a lonely knight of the Grail can find a little dog like Petitcreiu. This is because he has no beautiful maiden. He is not of this world. He is often tormented by depression, grief and disquiet. The Most High has gone away. His friends have betrayed him...

Then a priceless treasure comes to his aid: a comical African parrot which can only say one phrase, 'Lord, have mercy', like a stupid priest, or a dog such as Petitcreiu, or perhaps a canary in a cage.

Such a mysterious creature is hard to find!

The Duke of Gilan loves his pet dearly and would not part with it for all the money in the world. So Tristan turns to cunning methods.

'My lord! I know that your country is suffering at the hands of Urgan the giant. This monster is demanding a heavy tribute from you and your people. Sometimes you are forced to sacrifice the finest sons and daughters of your land to him.'

'My dear knight, I would gladly give anything, even half of my kingdom, to the one who could defeat this monster. But who would dare attack this giant? With one look he can burn you to cinders or grind you to a pulp with his teeth.'

The hairy giant Urgan is a symbol of the generic programme which must be conquered in order to purify mortal grief, so that they may enter the divine, virginal ecstasy of holy passion. Without this mortal grief there is no meaning to Sartre's 'La Nausée', existential grief, or the 'existential condition' of the

European intellectual, Karl Jaspers. The hairy Urgan is the destiny as prescribed by Tibetan horoscopes. It is impossible to reach the Grail and to achieve true holiness without first defeating this.

Such sorrow! Rome did not defeat the hairy Urgan, and so he is now demanding large sums of money from them. Generic Christianity, with the blessing of the world order, has turned into the exact opposite of itself.

Tristan defeats the hairy, aggressive order. The monster gives way to him. The sword of the Grail triumphs over the hefty club. Slicing off the giant's right hand (cutting off the right hand symbolises the monster's loss of control over his soul), Tristan takes it to the duke as proof of his victory.

'My lord! I beg of You to give me just one thing as a reward. Give me Petitcreiu, Your miraculous dog with the bell!'

The duke kept his word. However, in spite of being granted Petitcreiu, Tristan was not satisfied for long.

No, mortal grief is inconsolable! It will eventually reignite like a magic candle and will lead to a holy madness, a state which is unattainable to the human psyche, but which can be understood by those who give their lives to the theology of love and unfalteringly follow the way of Divine Love or the covenant of the Holy Spirit. Thus, when the Heavenly Father gave the command to 'love with all your heart', he was talking about the burning and jealous love for the Most High.

Tristan is pleased with the dog and is comforted by it for a while. But can he really survive without his beloved?

'No! Let the dog comfort Isolde! Is it right that I alone should find comfort?'

Tristan asked a travelling juggler to take Petitcrieu to Cornwall. However, Isolde found herself in a similar predicament. At first, the little bell and the dog's penetrating gaze are a source of comfort to Isolde but then she began to reflect:

'How can I be comforted when Tristan is unhappy? He is

so chivalrous, sending me Petitcrieu, his pride and joy, to make my own grief more bearable. No! It must not be. Tristan, I want to suffer as you suffer!'

Isolde untied the bell from around Petitcrieu's neck, rang it one last time, and then threw it out of the window into to the sea below.

This great sentiment, 'I want to suffer as you suffer', is reflected in the creed of the Grail: 'I came into this world to enter a union with the Most High through suffering humanity.'

This union is possible here and now.

Isolde untied the bell from around Petitcrieu's neck, rang it one last time, and then thrust it out of the window and into the sea. A virgin must be as brave as possible, setting free one of the mysteries of the theogamite calling – to be joined by the bonds of divine love, to become one with the Most High and to become divine.

At this point another law comes into force. There is no place for egotism. Union with the Most High is a union with the whole of creation all at the same time, demanding unlimited compassion and inclusivity.

The promised threads of the Eternal Covenant join a person to his Divine, Beloved Christ. These gold and silver threads multiply and spread to those close to him, eventually joining together the whole of suffering humanity with threads of light.

In the castles of the Grail, a knight cannot rest, even on the Sabbath, as long as there is suffering in the world. Such is the capacity of the hearts of the noble knights and maidens of the Grail to love and to be loved.

*

Petitcrieu, with his bell, is a knight of the Grail...

What a marvellous way to be comforted and unwind! To hear a street musician, see a ridiculous advert or admire some village show, is to see this same directness in all of creation which it never loses, no matter how hard it has fallen. Such directness leads to innocence and virginity.

This dog, Petitcrieu, is very hard to catch! It can only be done by someone with a pure heart. There is no way for anyone else to catch it and so their existential grief, or nausée, is inconsolable.

01.07.2005 Deris Island

❧

The Attraction of the Grail

According to legend, Sir Perceval, in his quest for the Grail, came to the White Castle with the chambers of the Holy Being which belonged to his uncle, Sir Bron, the keeper of the Grail. Seemingly by chance, a wondrous procession passed by Perceval as he was speaking with the Fisher King (who catches the church of the *anointed* ones in the net of the Most High). Maidens carried white stoles and behind them followed caskets decorated with precious stones, a wooden vessel, a lance, a sword, vestments and other items. Sir Bron was suffering with an incurable illness. The wise old man could only be cured by the question, 'What is this?' (Just as Mary asked, 'But how shall this be?' at the Annunciation)...

After much time spent wandering, the Prodigal Son (the parable of the Prodigal Son is about the Grail) confessed to his hermit mentor (the superficial church's obsession with repentance is only a step towards the great mystery of Christ and the true church) and returned home. Once again, the Chalice of the Grail and some other items were brought out from another room. 'The Chalice of the Grail is a miracle-working vessel; it is the holy of holies, it excludes all sin and it is the Chalice of all blessings and grace. Only a pure knight who has taken a vow of eternal virginity can be its keeper.'

'What purpose does this vessel serve?' Having experienced the attraction of the Grail, Perceval wanted to explore its mysteries. At that moment, the great and wise man was cured of his illness.

Just like Perceval with the Chalice which was carried past him, so, too, does the world remain indifferent to the great chalice in the hands of the priest of Melchizedek. The mystery of the Chalice is not understood and the Grail, which is wounded together with Its keeper, suffers terribly, as this miracle-working vessel has been turned into a cursed chalice filled with filth and impurity.

'Oh, that miracle-working vessel! It contains the Blood of Christ and, within that Blood, lies the myrrh of His divine love. This Blood is the origin of our dynasty. In it are all the mysteries of the Most High and the divinisation of humanity. All of His love, the Saviour's wisdom and the three hours of His sacred passion are stored within it. Through it, the perpetual mysteries are realised.'

'My son', continued Sir Bron. 'The Blood is never the same. The Saviour gives us more and more. When the vessel is empty, it is replenished. The composition of the newly replenished blood is altered. The last drop of the true disciples, who have been brought into the holy passion of the cross, has been added to it.'

Anointing in the Grail shows that it is possible to be a priest for 50 years, taking the chalice into church every day, carrying out the great rite 'neither judging nor condemning', making the sign of the cross, and yet still fail to understand the mystery of the Chalice and the Gospel of supreme love, which is filled with holy passion. It is also possible not to understand about the Myrrh scrolls contained within the Blood which deifies and alters the internal composition of the bride, or about the miracle-working potion of eternal life and the immaculate origin.

'In the true Church, he who approaches the Grail must live in purity', explains the King. 'Remember: supreme holiness is not possible with even the slightest stain of sin, not to mention fighting, victories and maidens.'

Perceval was so attracted by the wisdom of the Grail that he literally froze, kneeling on one knee. The whole of his life thus far flashed before him and Perceval understood how worthless and pathetic it was in the face of the victory of Christ, the great Bridegroom of Glory, and his own relative from the line of the Fisher King – the old Sir Bron.

As soon as the enlightenment of the Grail dawned in Perceval's mind, Bron was cured of his illness.

The Grail is sick! The Chalice has been consigned to oblivion. There is no Christianity: it is dying. The Grail is in a constant state of holy passion. It can only be cured through insight into the greatest mystery of the Chalice. In order to achieve this, one must reject the institutional prejudices of the old faith, with its pre-liturgical examination of conscience, its 'Drink of it, all of you! This is the cup of Christ', or 'We have seen the true Light! We have received the heavenly Spirit!' rather like the early Christian agapes. However, the life-giving mysteries of the Chalice are not revealed and the Miracle-working Vessel is redundant. 'There are only poor copies and cheap craftsmanship in place of the unattainable original', is how these services, which follow the letter of the law, are described in the Grail.

Oh, those who dwell in the white castles know how to weep. There are so many mourners there. Thus the Kingdom of the eternal Grail miraculously spread to Solovki. The Grail fed so many! Was it not the Grail which sent Seraphim myrrh from heaven in three vessels which were hidden in the hollow of an old oak tree? Was it not the Grail which gave them the gospels on faded paper, plasters, iodine, ammonia and other medicines? There was also some miraculous ointment – you only needed to apply it to the plaster over a wound which would not heal, and it would be healed.

So many were healed by Seraphim's miracle-working Vessel! As soon as Seraphim held the Chalice of the Grail in his hands, at -20 degrees centigrade he was swept away to the bottom of the sea, whence he gathered up all those who had been drowned, lit an eternal flame within their hearts and raised them up (often a rainbow appears as a heavenly bridge) to heaven or handed them over to be buried. Often a rainbow would appear to them as a bridge to heaven.

Oh how the Grail reigned in Solovki! How it was decorated with the victories and crowns of the new martyrs of the True Church! So many priests were enlightened by the mystery of the Chalice and, like children, asked questions such as 'what is it?' , as if they had never studied the catechism or any other simplistic theological textbook for schoolchildren. They were distracted by the cold, lifeless rituals, instead of reaching out for the true mysteries and the holiest of holies. They are called to a life of purity and to be completely faithful witnesses to the glory of the Most High.

The troubadours and trouvères of Brittany told of the Grail as a source of all good; in other words, a source of gifts, mercy, ideas, icons, revelations, and clothing. All grace comes from this Chalice. The Saviour put more into this than into His preaching. His blood is priceless. It has a Myrrh composition for the purpose of transforming the whole of a human being.

Perceval was so fascinated by the teaching of his kind uncle, Sir Bron, who had been healed by his nephew, that the young man turned at once and promised his uncle he would leave his old life behind. 'Victories are meaningless in the face of the great mysteries which are revealed to you! I am your servant', said Perceval, kissing the hand of his recovered uncle. Tender tears flowed from the old king's eyes. This time, though, they were not tears of pain from a wound which would not heal, but tears of inexpressible joy.

Sir Bron was transfigured and from his heart there came a white cloud of wisdom. Sir Bron understood that the sacred net had caught a priceless fish. A new keeper had been bestowed on the Holy Grail. Perceval was the true heir and a true son. By means of the cloud which moves from one heart to the other, from father to son and from healed to healer, the wisdom of the chalice was passed on to Perceval. Thus Brittany would be disenchanted.

Is the Grail redundant? It is taught in the White Castles of the miracle-working chalice that the world is bewitched by magic spells. When the Grail is revealed, all evil and black magic is powerless. Spells are broken. The land awakens from its dream.

Holy Rus' needs the Grail of Solovki now more than ever, in order to free it from its age-old, death-like sleep.

Holy Grail and altar of Christ, You will be revealed to those who come to You, trembling on their knees, and who naively ask You the child-like question, 'What is this?' , which the young Perceval himself asked. Then, a message will appear on the screen of the Grail:

True Blood of Christ,
Church of the Holy Spirit.
Holy of holies.
More holy and passionate than holy passion.
Inexhaustible Chalice.
Grace which increases hour by hour.
Amazing mystery
Of the Gospel of the Saviour's Blood.
Holy Grail feed us!

The Grail shields itself from prying eyes and from the devil's meddling ways. It does not permit any impurity to come near It. However, anyone who does reach the miracle-working Chalice is thrice blessed. Oh! The Beloved will feed him forever. It is safe to say that this person would have already become part of the divine civilization on the Altar of Union, and the Son of the Most High would have bound him in the covenant of holy union for all eternity. His heart is filled with a wondrous joy.

However painful the retreat into holy passion may be, there is such joy which increases from day to day, and hour by hour, as a result of the grace and mercy which flow from the living tabernacle – the place where the living Christ, the Grail, is present. Where is the Grail? It is here in this wooden chalice, in the great heart of this servant, in this young girl filled with holy passion and weeping bitter tears, and in this sorrow and weeping. This is the inner Grail.

Honour each one in the same way as the miracle-working vessel, 'filled with every blessing and grace' and hidden within each one of the sons of Christ.

You must find it within yourself by passing through the 144 gates of introspection. You can find it in your neighbour if you look with your spiritual eyes. Rest in the arms of the Pieta. The Divine Mother will take you down from the cross and will give you the same comfort as that which was experienced by the knights and the myrrh-bearing women of the Grail as they drank from the Chalice.

*

'Be filled with the seven great mysteries and they will reveal to you the perfect Christ', said Sir Bron to his successor, Perceval ('partzuf', meaning 'face' and 'El' meaning 'the Most High', i.e. contemplating the face of the Most High). 'The highest form of holiness', continued Sir Bron, pointing to the Grail, 'makes its companions equal to the companions of Christ, and more besides, my child.'

The Saviour does not come, even though He could, simply because He has already done much more. Just imagine how it would be if He had guided you, converted you and healed you. The chalice of His Blood, though, is greater. Through it, He enters into you and transforms you. Through it, He becomes one with you, nourishes your inner self, gives you that which cannot be expressed in words and divinises your humanity. He enters the mystery of mysteries where you could not go yourself, let alone others.

After receiving communion from the Chalice just once, the communicant is greater than an apostle and finds himself dumbstruck and entranced. My child, never be tired of repeating, 'What is this?' if you want the Grail to be constantly renewed and to reveal itself to you in different forms. Do not expect the stereotypical image of the Chalice which you will always have in mind. As soon as you find the Miracle-working Vessel tiresome, boring or 'too commonplace', the Chalice will go away for a long time. It will be replaced by a lengthy, passionate quest and a period of absence. After this, the Grail will reveal itself unexpectedly, no one knows where: through a thistle at the side of the road, through Balaam's donkey, through a senile old woman, or through a *yurodivy.*

My child, the highest level of anointing promotes the vision of the Chalice of fire within the sons of Adam, whose spiritual hearts are lavishly anointed by the Grail with oils, which are understood to be the penetration of Myrrh sticking particles with the Most High.

The messenger of the Grail leaves the White Castle with its most precious relic, and establishes the inner Kingdom of Christ. Never setting down the Chalice of Melchizedek containing the bread and wine of the Eucharist, he feeds all those who are suffering, before clothing them in the robes of virginity, lighting a flame within them and melting the inner chalice.

'What is this?' they will say. 'How can the Grail, *Nightingale Mountain*, the Holy Spirit working through Seraphim Sarovsky, Eufrosinia of Pochaev, Seraphim Solovetski and Monsalvat, the medieval castle of the Knights Templar, all coexist?'

The Divine Wisdom of the Most High is unique: the Chalice is at the centre of all human striving, as the place of the Holy Being, the Second Coming of Christ. 'Where is it?' I hear you ask. It is spread throughout the whole of the earth. It is in the hands of the priests of the new church, the Melchizedek priests of Solovki, the new martyrs who were our crowned fathers, the keepers of the Grail of Solovki and the myrrh of Seraphim. It is also with those masters of ceremonies at the bridal chamber of some inmate of a Saratov TB-clinic, unloved old women in a hospice near Kostroma, or those dying with AIDS.

One drop from the generous Chalice is enough to fill the soul with bliss. It sets it on fire. The underworld is extinguished within it, the black flame is put out and the black sun dies. The singing of angels can be heard: 'Be still, be still.'

Drink from the Inexhaustible Chalice! Drink and then drink again.

The Chalice is misunderstood. The Chalice is replenished. The Chalice shields itself and relies on that which is perfect and familiar. The facets of the transfigured Grail are countless – there are over a thousand colours, each one reflecting the Divine Wisdom and the inner state of the perfect mystery of mysteries.

Taste, My child. Taste Christ. Taste your Beloved. There is no other Wedding Feast apart from the Eucharist. Find the greatest mysteries and do not abandon the Holy Gifts of the Flesh and the Blood, but see them in a different light to that of the lost sons of earthly lust, the institutional priests. It is not obvious, My child: it is always for the first time, always a revelation and always from on high. There is always the ever-changing blood, the wine enriched with oils, the 'Ever more', and 'Oh, my Beloved!'

Drink from this Chalice of Divine Wisdom, the chalice of the highest bliss. In order to drink the last drop just once, you endured your concrete tomb, iron vices, mercury in the blood, and so on. The devil is constantly attacking those who love the Chalice. On the way to the Grail there are many trials and monsters, each one more cunning and treacherous than the last. My Child, this abuse will not lessen – on the contrary, it will increase. Do not wait for it to weaken.

But my child, how wonderful it will be when the angel of the Chalice comes and the triumphant procession begins with wise maidens in white stoles, bearing mysterious caskets, anointed with oils and carrying horns of plenty made of silver and ivory. Then the hot wine of Christ will enter your being. Oh! Oh! Oh!

This mystery of the future requires a permanent state of ecstasy and rapture, giving way to the withdrawal into holy passion and the peace found when taken down from the cross.

The saints never cease to be surprised when receiving communion from the Chalice. Not one of them has ever experienced anything like it. My child, even after two thousand years of receiving communion, it is always as if they are doing so for the first time. They tirelessly search for the Grail as its mystery is inexhaustible in the present as well as in the future.

Therefore one must seek the Grail with a virginal and pure heart and mind. One holds the chalice with such trepidation even though it will not burst into flames or incite the wrath of its guardian angel. One must partake of it with such love and thirst with holy passion to drink from it again and again, begging for a greater understanding of this miracle-working vessel.

26.06.2005 Deris Island

The Perilous Stream

Saint Perceval, a knight, finds the Grail in his quest to seethe face of the Most High

The caves of Tibet, where sages of the 25th (Lemuria), 40th (Creon) and 16th (Atlantis) civilization have been resting for millions of years in a state of *samadhi*, are no longer a secret. Some 'black horseman', an upstart sorcerer, travelled to Tibet and, sticking out his belly, which was scrawny from hunger and fasting, happened upon the trail of Elena Roerich.

Was it not in this monastery that Elena Roerich first heard of Mahatma Moria? Didn't Madame Blavatsky walk through this desert? He, who came after them, is the one who revealed the 'Yoga of Fire' and the 'Inner Transfiguration' in Russia. A whole stand was devoted to him in a bookshop on Arbat Street in Moscow.

Though, the Church of Mystery was not mentioned.

On the other hand, there is more than plenty being said about the masonic cult (beautiful maidens, knights and armour). But, who knows of the Grail as the True Church?

Where is it? It is impossible to answer this question. However, it also is impossible not to answer, just like with the question, 'Where are You, Lord?' Wherever He is, there also is the Grail.

*

The legend of Perceval is a Grail legend about one of the greatest Keepers of the Chalice, the perfect Elder of the True Church known as, the Divine Visionary of the Beautiful Eyes (Partzuf El – 'the one who contemplates the Face of the Lord').

On the way to the White Castle (where he would eventually remain forever as a Keeper of the Chalice, his life stretching out over centuries like that of his forefather, Joseph of Arimathea, who was tormented by Pharisees), Perceval reflected on the mystery behind names. 'Loonois' is the crystal land where the inhabitants of the Kingdom dwell on earth. What does the 'Lo' signify? Lohengrin, Lancelot, Alain (his father)... Amazing! 'L' is the letter of the Grail. It is in the vibration of the white castle, the bliss of silent prayer and the transformation into bliss, which comes through ineffable peace in a state of ecstatic holy passion.

'Lono' is a Russian word meaning 'bosom', 'lap' or 'heart'. L and N are the two mysterious letters of the Mother of the Grail. From the bosom of the Divine Virgin Mother, comes 'Loonois'. It is the 'Lono', infused with 'nous' (Greek, meaning 'mind')... And so it went on, as he explored the many aspects of language, as in the games he had been taught as a child.

His father was Alain (L-N) – the Most High (El) in the Church of the Kingdom, who is known to be the most perfect of all the saints.

His grandfather was Bron (B-R is Bereshit – the first book of the Torah, which is also the beginning of the Bible, and tells of the creation of the world. BR is also the 'Bria' sphere of Jewish mystics. 'On' is the sound of a taught string, like the cosmists' 'aum'.

Sir Bron (an alias of Joseph of Arimathea) was a kind, wise man and the father of the True Church. Perceval thinks about him on his way to the Grail. His grandfather suffered immensely. Thousands of ointments were unable to soothe this wise man and miracle-worker. His wounds were incurable. The worst wound of all was the lack of a successor and the absence of interest in the Grail. Perceval must ask 'What is this?'

Joseph of Arimathea did not have a worthy successor. His son was called Lohen-grin, meaning green fields filled with the blissful sheep of Christ, or a wonderful meadow with fresh grass and wild flowers in the kingdom of Loonois.

These names are so wondrous! Oh, El, there is such rapture and bliss on finding the Most High in the True Church. Mother Eufrosinia can hear its vibrations even now. Lyres of ivory, onyx, emerald, gold and silver ring out from twenty turreted castles.

The sound of the Grail is in the resounding 'Ou-e.' If it is played on David's new lyre, you will find eternal peace. No-one on earth knows this prayer yet. However, if you seek the love which is not of this world, you must be prepared for an unprecedented range of prayers, dense forests where no-one has gone before, curses, lances and arrows which have never been seen before, and deadly poisons from which no-one has ever recovered.

Perceval recalled the trials which he had endured. There were a thousand of them in one day. In his thirty or so years he had lived several lifetimes. He would record his memoirs for posterity later, when he became a very old man and, like the father in Christ's parable of the Prodigal Son, he would wait for his beloved son who had set out on a quest to find the truth (the Grail). Then he would have time. For a long time, between tearful prayers and fervent entreaties to the Most High to bring his son back home, he would lose himself in fond reminiscing.

The scorching sun shone mercilessly. Then the sweat-drenched knight (the prophet armed with spiritual knowledge) noticed a large, bright stream. He could not take his eyes from it. The sun shone on it like a blinding disk, making its surface glisten.

'Such heavenly light!' thought Perceval. 'This is the vision of the Church of Light and the knowledge of the final mystery which I have been seeking!'

Near the stream was a green meadow and, near it, stood an ornate tent, like a cloud of fire enveloping the tabernacle of the Jews of the Old Testament. It was the tent of the Most High and the tent of the Commander in Chief. Perceval made for the tent (there was no way he could have passed by), when suddenly the ground shook under his feet. Was there anybody there? For whom had the Most High built such a beautiful dwelling place?

'This tent is bewitched', thought Perceval. 'Perhaps it will transform into unearthly spectra and de-materialise. Maybe it is a vision. Could it be a dream? Where am I?'

The young Perceval, son of Sir Alain, rode his tired horse towards the stream. They both were in need of a drink... At that very moment a handsome, armed knight leapt from out of the tent and shouted to him:

'I swear by our Heavenly Father, knight that you were not simply planning to water your horse in my stream! You must join with me in mortal combat and earn your place among the 150 other knights lying here before you.'

With a sinking heart, Perceval looked at a nearby tree and saw 150 shields hanging on it.

'Ha, ha, ha!' laughed the guardian of the tent. The bright Stream faded and everywhere around grew dark. The Black Knight of the Bright Stream raised his weapon. Their lances dealt heavy blows but their armour was stronger and the lances broke. The Bright Stream turned out to be the Perilous Stream – the most perilous adventure in all 30 years of this monk of the Grail's *yurodivy,* spiritual, truth-seeking life.

As soon as the battle with the Black Knight drew to a close, the earth began to tremble. Perceval heard a woman's voice shouting out a curse like those found in Greek myths:

'Curse you, curse you, curse you, Perceval, cause of so much evil!' cried that woeful voice, like rolling thunder. 'May you be cursed for having brought so much evil to the church of our fathers. You have broken the tradition and deprived the priests of their daily bread. You have brought irrevocable grief. You have caused thousands of righteous people to mourn their fate. Why have you come down to earth? Have you come to deprive us of the light?'

Only the Pharisees in the Sanhedrin or the Grand Inquisitor (from Dostoevsky's legend of the same name in the 'Brothers Karamazov') could speak about Christ in such a way!

Perceval was showered with curses, one after another, until he could bear it no longer. It was all the more difficult for his having just engaged in battle with the Black Knight.

'Bron, my grandfather, Alain, my father, and Evra, my sacred mother, come to my aid!'

Almost immediately the wise Sir Bron (Joseph of Arimathea) appeared before him. In his hands he held the Chalice.

Perceval fell and prostrated on the ground. His body was pierced with thousands of tiny needles. It seemed as though his blood was poisoned, and yet the curses continued to rain down on him, one after another.

'You are cursed! Anyone who comes to drink from this stream will be cursed! You wanted to find complete holiness, but you will find only the mysteries of Satan, which no-one has found before, and you will be content with them. You wanted to enter the heavenly light. Are you not satisfied with that which your fathers revealed to you? You are a rebel! You wanted to erase the Law of Moses and the religion of the wise men of Jehovah with just one word. Of course you are cleverer than Rabbi Akiva and Rabbi Gamaliel! You are cleverer than all the wise men in the world whom you have taught for the last 12 years, showing them your unrivalled superiority over their theological wisdom, which is considered perfect in Israel! See how worthy you are!'

Perceval was half paralysed and literally bleeding.

'Father! Grandfather, Mother, come to my aid!..'

*

Let us now refrain from exploring further the subject of medieval legends. They clearly reflect the Universal Divine Wisdom, of which Perceval was a follower.

The Stream which was once Bright is the babbling holy water of the old church. It is the babbling stream of the Orthodox liturgy and the Roman Mass. It is the life-giving spring in which to wash and be cleansed of the sins of the past. So much holy water has flowed since washing its mortal wounds dozens of times! So this is the ultimate and most perilous test: the Bright Stream has been turned into a cursed place.

In order to understand this great mystery of the metanoia in which the church, as mother and the only saviour, turns into the place of curse, you must be the philosopher Baruch Spinoza, the Jewish reformer Uriel da Costa, Samuel Frank, Israel Bescht, John Chrysostum, Seraphim Sarovsky, St. Eufrosinia, one of the pillars of the Church of the Divine Mother of the Transfiguration, or one of the hundred thousand rapturous Solovki angels with wings of fire, who were taken to heaven whilst still alive and formed the unimaginable, indescribable Council of Solovki, the *Second Golgotha*. The angels around that bright stream were transformed into fearsome vultures with savage beaks which aim for the eyes and try to peck through the helmet to reach the most precious possession of a faithful follower – his spiritual vision and his yearning to see the unfading light of the Kingdom.

In Grail terms, this level is known as the metanoia of the church. Only select ones can pass through it.

For the majority, it is unattainable. We know how difficult it is to turn one's back on the world, on ourselves and on our inherent programming. It is a cross and a double-edged sword which we must seize in order to cut off bravely that which nourished us, gave us life and is dearest to us. We are talking about something different. The prophet Moses had to renounce the religion of Abraham, which had been such a source of pride for his forefathers. That was why his enemies Dathan and Abiram defied him, 'Is Abraham as nothing to you? What is the purpose of this guiding cloud? Every one of us is a prophet! We are all prophets – not only you!'

He waited at the Bright Stream for a blessing from the angels of the Life-giving Font and the angels of the Most Pure

Virgin. Yet the mother-church (holy Orthodoxy) showered him with curses. Then a voice like rolling thunder sounded from somewhere in the abyss, ringing out like the Synod or a Patriarch sentencing some holy dissident such as Father Gleb Yakunin who had dared to violate their sacrosanct canons.

Any of the saints who have not endured the Perilous Stream (the *metanoia* of the church) during their days on earth have done so in heaven.

It is a terrible truth that the saints are cursed by the institutions to which they once belonged. The Most High allows this to happen so that they can shake off the dust of religious prejudice and enter the purest light.

'Yes, I have already been cleansed in thousands of springs, through repentance and with fire. Now, though, I must pass through the final spring with the cursed water', thought Perceval.

In his days on earth a saint must endure the most difficult level of damnation, which is in essence the death sentence, pronounced by the holy Inquisition, from the superficial church. 'Do these half-wits and wretches (by this he meant those who love burning anathemas, those scorching blows which leave a permanent mark on a person's heart) not realise that, in heaven, they will be cursed by those whom they cursed on earth? All those, like me, who enter the black ark of a religious institution in search of the blessed throng, are subjected to a shower of curses.'

The way to the Kingdom is so complex! It is easy to step over the threshold of an ever-open Catholic chapel. However, one day you will have to jump with Lohengrin from the chapel on the cold rock into the river Elbe, where a green boat with a white swan awaits the glorious knight.

Perceval endured a 40-day hermitage, where he was visited by dancing skeletons with phosphorescent green eyes like cats, demons with scythes and swords, planes, hammers and nails... He had never seen the likes of this before.

The cursing voice, which belonged to some entranced maiden living in an impassable forest swamp, fell silent. What is this? There was a sudden sound of wings. A huge flock of birds attacked Perceval. These vicious creatures surrounded him and obscured the sky. They were cunning and malicious with terrifying beaks. They were black with fearsome plumage on their breasts and they threatened to peck out Perceval's eyes through the opening in his helmet. It seemed as though his visor would fall off with the unbearable electric charge, and then the birds would be able to peck at his face.

At the same time Urban, the black guardian of the stream, sprang into action.

It turned out that a Black Knight dwelt in the great tent of the invincible Most High! What was once a glorious synagogue for Jehovah, giving us the great prophets, Isaiah, Elijah, Ezekiel and Malachi and the great kings, David and Solomon, was now guarded by a ghost known as Urban, the Black Knight. This once invincible warrior was bewitched by the same spirit of the forest and the swamp, who's cursing voice Perceval had heard.

Glorious Israel had been turned into a kingdom of mud, a dense forest and an impassable swamp. Were these black birds really fallen angels and the saints of the Old Testament? Indeed, so it is!

The black birds were nothing other than the shadows of the beautiful maidens of the radiant castle. They were so aggressive, though, these saints whom he had honoured whilst confessing the faith of his fathers! They were sent by that same cursing beggar woman who had accused him of abandoning tradition and the traditional church.

'You accursed werewolves, vampires and ghosts!' Perceval raged, gnashing his teeth. Suddenly he noticed one of those brazen birds was about to peck out his eye through the opening in his helmet. He struck it with his sword and a maiden fell to the ground, dead. The rest of the birds let out a loud cry, seized him and carried him away.

That aggressive bird, which had hovered over his helmet ready to peck out his eye, killed by Perceval, had once been close to him and had now become his number one enemy. They were his Dathan and Abiram, waiting for the prophet on his way to the Grail. So, Perceval was destined to die as Moses did, from the fervent kiss of Jehovah on his forehead which was glazed with perspiration... Then the Most High took him into His embrace after his long adventure on the road to the Heavenly Kingdom.

The black birds of infernal damnation were once the radiant angels of the church which is dear to your heart. However, it is necessary to pass through this stage on the road to the kingdom of Perpetual Light – the Holy Grail. It is so difficult! Only someone who has endured the unbearable curse of the Black Stream knows this. Perceval knew.

The cloud, which suddenly hung over the Stream of Light, and the black birds swarming around him, are the cursed prayer which is uttered by thousands of priests, monks and other sorcerers of the church which they have left behind.

This is perhaps the most dreadful temptation for a faithful person! It is easier to win thousands of battles with strangers. Here, though, one must exceed oneself and let go of that which you once held dear. Only someone who is truly courageous and who is able to renounce the ideals which once sustained him, throwing them off like superfluous clothes, may win this final apocalyptic, cataclysmic battle. This person holds the sword of the Grail in his hands.

*

Just like with the prophet Isaiah, after seeing the angel of the Lord, a burning coal of the heart of the Grail was laid into Perceval's breast with burning hot tongs, and he lay motionless in his hermitage. Suddenly he heard repulsive laughter. Following that first battle, an even more perilous temptation began at the Perilous Stream. The devil himself came.

'Do you want to drink from the Chalice of eternal life? Wretched creature! The Keeper of the Chalice of Christ is condemned by people to eternal damnation. You are a wanderer incognito and an anonymous wise man. No-one recognises you. The names of a thousand saints who are as nothing compared to you will be recorded in the church's calendar and will be remembered in the liturgy by the priests of the church. People will read about their lives, invoke their names in prayer, celebrate their victories and follow their signs. And you? Do you know that, if you drink from the Chalice of the Grail just once, you will die an ignominious death?'

You are seeking eternal life from the miracle-working Vessel. Christ said that whoever drank from this Chalice would live forever, and if he died he would rise again. Are you are seeking to partake of the real, burning, fervent, transforming Eucharist from this Chalice? Wretched creature! There is no-one who has ever drunk from this Chalice and not died an ignominious death. This is the fate which awaits you, too, as a disciple of the thrice ignominious Christ. He is ignominious in the eyes of His Jewish teachers. He is ignominious in the eyes of His teachers who witnessed His shame and His crucifixion. He is ignominious in the eyes of His most distant followers whose thoughtless pursuit of His faith has resulted in delusion and a gulf.

'Cunning enemy!' said Perceval, barely moving his lips. 'Death does not exist! Why are you frightening me? I am not afraid of anything. In my concrete gloom and hellish isolation, with my deranged mind and congealed blood, I am dying out of love for my Divine Beloved. I am no longer that same Perceval, the knight with sword and visor, who was once victorious in tournaments and who was proclaimed by beautiful ladies to be the bravest and most gallant knight in the world. No, I have left all of this behind in order to engage in a spiritual fight. Therefore you will not be able to lessen my yearning to drink from the Cup of the Grail, even if it ultimately ends in death... out of love. Nothing is more beautiful than this.'

I made a vow to climb the stairway of temptation – the stairway with 150 steps on the path to the Grail. One of the last steps is the gates of death. I must pass through them without fear. I am not afraid of death because I know that, beyond it lies the path to the kingdom of a much greater, infinite love. The Grail is the divine potion of burning love. It cannot be found on earth. Anyone who comes to know it and tries it just once, brings it into this world at the cost of his life. However, when he passes over into eternity, he enters his Father's embrace.

You were lying, you worthless cheat! You were lying from beginning to end, pointing me towards the image of the Bright Stream (which was then cursed and made dark), the magnificent tent (the former tabernacle of the Jews and the Law of Moses, and which became the tomb of the Black Knight). The former sanctuary became a home to malicious, demonic birds. Instead of revealing the Kingdom of Heaven to me as angels, they looked for little holes in my helmet, so that they could peck out my eyes. You were a liar from the beginning and wanted to lead me away from the True Church! However, with your words you increased my desire to live in Tintagel – the white castle of my father, Alain, and my grandfather, Sir Bron!'

*

Perceval worked many other miracles and saw even more. There were so many miracles; they were impossible to count. The Lord saved his life countless times. The black birds could not reach him and the hostile knights with their cursed hordes had been defeated...

The temptation was over. But what was this? There stood the most beautiful of trees. Perceval shut his eyes and breathed in the fragrance of its branches. It permeated his whole being, like the natural scent of pine, and like the resin, which Seraphim extracted from the frozen blocks of ice on the Archipelago, for anointing wounds.

Was this not the Tree of Life, as it stands at a crossroads leading four different ways?

Perceval hurried along, then stopped his horse and stood admiring the tree. Above it stood a Virgin in white. 'What is this wondrous miracle?' thought Perceval. Then he saw all the apparitions of the Divine Mother: Cova da Iria (the bushes, where the Divine Mother appeared to three shepherd girls in Fatima), the three oaks (the site of the apparition in Garabandal) and a somewhat old and ominous tree at Montichiari with the Rosa Mystica... Orthodox Christians cite a young boy's vision of a miraculous icon, which was revealed in a blinding light, somewhere near three fir trees in the midst of a dense, overgrown forest.

Perceval glanced heavenward: there was another tree standing above him. This was the same one, which had ascended into heaven. Again the vision included a tree, children and a cross. It was like Fatima, Garabandal, Holy Rus', the Grail, Solovki, or the prisoner-saints.

Suddenly he saw two seven-year-old boys with unearthly white bodies. Their faces were wonderfully radiant. These angelic children sprang lightly from branch to branch, casting rays of light with their gentle gaze.

'Who are you?' Perceval asked them. 'If you are the creation of the Most High, then nod. If you are demons then leave at once'.

'Sir Perceval, we live on earth at the will of the Most High. We have been sent by Him and we came here with one aim – to meet with you. You seek the miracle-working vessel of the Grail. We know that you will find it. Your grandfather, Sir Bron, Joseph of Arimathea and the Fisher King, will be overjoyed to see you again in his castle. He will consecrate you with the greatest mysteries. You will see and hear that which will transform your path on earth, if it is determined that you will eventually reach the end of it (the path continues on into eternity. The Grail is a source of delight in heaven and then it returns to earth). Happy is the priest, who is not separated from the Holy Grail! He is truly a servant of the priests of Melchizedek. He will live for over a thousand years. He is fed from the Chalice and with special bread – manna from heaven. After your trials you will be worthy of a higher destiny than any mortal, who has ever lived on earth'.

'It will become your great desire to leave behind a memory of yourself in the tender tears of repentance. Not for the generations to come, though. They will each have to make their way along their own little path to the Grail with their own temptations. Hardly anyone manages to reach the coveted goal. Do you want to reveal this mystery to your beloved children? The Most High will give way to you and some of them will inherit the mysteries of the Sanctuary and the Treasures of the Lord. You will pull out a string of pearls and give it to your children. 'Father, we cannot accept so much!' 'My son, this is nothing compared with all my other possessions! Take it for your loyalty and your love for your father. This treasure belongs to you. I have lived for you and everything I have done was for you''.

'Why are you running from branch to branch in this beautiful and fragrant Tree of Life?'

'Oh, we never tire of wandering among the fragrant, Myrrh scrolls and smelling the perfumes in the wonderful imaginary gardens of the Grail. Every saint, who has come to this tree, has left his impression there and we are happy to share in their lives and the flowers of their heavenly virtues.'

'Keep to the right', said the angels before disappearing from Perceval's sight. 'Soon, faster than you imagine, you will see what you desired.'

*

Thus, his trials having ended, he found himself in the embrace of his dear grandfather, the holy and blessed Keeper of the Grail, Sir Bron.

Perceval kissed his grandfather's scarred, wrinkled and waxen hands. He saw him as if for the first time. 'My goodness, such sorrow! There is so much of the world's sorrow in the face of this wise man!' he thought.

'Grandfather, what was the significance of the beautiful water mill, three miles from your castle?'

(Near it there was a boat with three fishermen. When he had moored his boat, the oldest of them stopped and invited Perceval into his home).

'And what of the towers of the Happy Watchmen and Morgan le Fay? Or the lowered drawbridge and the open gates?.. It looks so easy to pass through them, yet it is impossible to enter without permission from on high.'

'The beautiful mill, which you saw, my son', replied Sir Bron, 'is the mystery of the radiant souls, the grain, which has been ground into the flour of Christ, Solovki the Second Golgotha, and the martyrs of supreme love. This final vision on the path to the Grail is Solovki. The fisherman, whom you met and who invited you into his home, is Saint Seraphim the Tender, the father and patriarch of our Church. The grey-haired old man is the fragrant dwelling place of the Grail, and he invited you into his hut to introduce you to the twelve brethren, the burning hierarchy of the Church of the Holy Spirit, the Paraclete. The lowered drawbridge is a sign of being chosen. The bridge is normally raised so that no-one can enter without the blessing of the Most High. The many towers represent the watchfulness of the spheres, whose chambers you must pass on the way to the Grail.'

'Now I understand. My dear grandfather, I have been searching for you for so many years!' Perceval sobbed tenderly on the shoulder of the Fisher-King.

'My weakness tied me to my chair and I ate nothing in the final few days. But I was with you. My gaze was fixed on the blank screen. Look!'

In the corner of the dark room, where the old man welcomed his heir, shone the transforming Chalice. On its surface glowed a screen. Onto this screen flowed an endless stream of letters, and then some images appeared and dates and faces flashed by...

'On this screen of thoughts I saw everything, which has come to pass. The gift of insight does not preclude the gift of miracle-working. But your trials are over, my child', Sir Bron smiled sorrowfully. 'If only I had had enough time! I would have been able to tell you of my experiences: the questioning in the Sanhedrin, the victory over the demon of the Pharisees and my love for the Lord. I would tell you how I travelled to Brittany with the young Jesus and the Virgin Mary. I would tell you of how I took your father, Alain, Joseph the Younger, from the arms of the dying Mary Magdalene. I would tell of how I found a wife for him, who could not even compare with Sarah, Rachel and Rebecca, the wives of Abraham, Isaac and Jacob, and who would give birth without stain of sin... Time is short, though, and I must hurry. Let us go. I will show you my royal treasure and you will be rewarded for your trials and sorrows. Forget your wounds now. Cleanse them. Servants will bring you precious oils and within half an hour you will be completely healed as you enter the rooms of my castle. Know, too, that I have been cured of my illness.'

The Vessel was tilted. Drops of blood fell onto the old man's hand. This was the Last Drop of the Blood of the Lamb. Bron and Perceval gazed heavenward: above them stood the heavenly Crucified One, the Lamb, crowned with seven crowns. It was the Suffering Christ and Supreme Love. Oh!

The Guardian of the Chalice and his heir approached the throne of the Lamb in indescribable holy passion and admiration. Their hearts were on fire.

The miracle-working vessel tilted and they drank the Myrrh wine – the drink which is sweeter than anything on earth...

02.07.2005 Deris Island

The Hermit's Cell

The ascetic church... This is nothing new to the Grail. Tiring of his quest for the Grail, following seven years of victories, Perceval visits a hermit's cell. This gentle ascetic is Perceval's uncle, the brother of his father, Alain, and the nephew of his grandfather, Sir Bron.

The task of this holy father is to come to the aid of the one seeking forgiveness for his sins. Perceval confesses to his hermit-uncle for two days and two nights and is granted full absolution from his sins. The hermit gives Perceval a penance. He wants to visit his sister (the image of the old church again).

'She is no longer living. She has disappeared and you will never see her again.'

Perceval was overcome with grief and began to weep...

Purification is not the ultimate goal. The hermit understood perfectly, who the true keeper of the mystery was: Sir Bron, Joseph of Arimathea.

'The True Church is there! Hurry, my son, and you will find only triumph. May the Most High grant you the crown for all your trials. You have been cleansed of your sin. Evil no longer has any power over you. As an anointed one of the Most High, I welcome you to the branch of original immaculacy. The path to the Grail is laid open to you. Sir Bron, my uncle and your grandfather, is looking forward to meeting you. Go, my child!' repeated the wise old man, who was not of this world, patting Perceval on the cheek. He held him, his heart and kissed him on the forehead, at which they both began to weep.

The hermit gave Perceval the vessel containing the potion for healing all diseases, and blessed him as he went on his way.

*

Asceticism is not the highest level of spirituality (as is believed in the camps of the 'black crows' or the 'night patrols' – the cunning church of the Inquisition). The hermit spoke of his uncle, Sir Bron (Joseph of Arimathea) with awe and told Perceval:

'The True Church is there. Hurry! Absolution from sin and total forgiveness are only a step on the way to understanding the highest mysteries of the Divinity. The highest of all these mysteries is the love, which is not of this world. It is because of this love that your sins have been forgiven. It is because of this love that you were cleansed in the holy waters of the Immaculate Spring. It is because of this love that you have endured so much sorrow. It is because of this love that you came down to earth. Now you will find it in its entirety.'

Rejoice, my child, great chosen one of the Most High! On the way to the Grail, you promised the Most High that you would kill no-one else, until you found the Divine mysteries (the miracle-working Grail and its 150 white castles around the world, in both visible and invisible spheres), and that you would not sleep for more than one night in any single house. Now you must make a third promise: the Guardian of the Chalice will become the Guardian of the mysteries.

'Mine is not the highest level', the gentle hermit told his dear nephew. 'Although I am hidden from the world, you can find me in a hut in the forest, you can talk with me, and I can absolve you from your sins... The Guardian of the Chalice will become the guardian of the highest mysteries. He will be easier to find than me (*yurodstvo* in the world) and also impossible to find. My son, guard with your life the precious mysteries, which have been given to you! Do not let any of them fall into the hands of our enemy and the serpent. This promise is very complex. It presupposes dozens of other gifts of Divine Wisdom, such as sobriety, vigilance or discernment of spirits. It requires the strength to defeat the devil, at the same time as the gift of insight, the gift of the sober judgement of the Most High, Eufrosinia's shield of courage and the sword of the Grail.

Hurry, then, my child, to the castle of your grandfather Bron. Amidst the many treasures kept there you will also find those counted out by me!'

In the old man's cell, an icon was emitting a beautiful fragrance and the old man began to pray.

'Father, I love you!' wept Perceval. He threw himself at the feet of the hermit and began to kiss his hands. 'What would I have done without you? I feel so free after two days of confessing! Your kindness knows no bounds, just as the Lord is infinitely kind. How tenderly you entered the inner sanctum of my divine soul and how compassionately you heard my confession!'

'Well', said the old man, pushing his nephew away and unable to restrain the tears, which were welling up in his eyes. 'Take care of yourself. I am nothing. When you see your grandfather, Sir Bron, you will not recognise him. He is greater than I. You will see things, which cannot be seen on earth.'

'Yes, uncle. Yes, I know', said Perceval.

Getting up from his knees, he embraced the old man and kissed his hands. After receiving his blessing he set off once more.

02.07.2005 Deris Island

The Only One
Who Lingers before my Gaze

He is the only one, who lingers before my gaze. He can only be comprehended as a knight of the Grail. Perhaps a priest of Melchizedek? Or an ascetic? Or a disciple of Christ? No. In the crystal castles of the Grail, our souls dwell in the Holy Being. His name within the Grail is like that of Tristan's friend – Kaerdin, or something similar. In the Grail, a soul is given a name from the white castles...

The divine civilization. The Most Pure One revealed a celestial, triumphal arc, when she last opened her heavenly gates. It was indescribable! Something as wonderful as this can only exist in heaven.

The divine civilization already exists! The quest for the Grail leads to its triumphant heavenly gates.

The divine civilization is being constantly nourished by the Grail. Nothing else is necessary. Why, then, does the ascetic practice of our Church require a person to leave the world behind, to become part of a different world, to be locked away and to ask for forgiveness from their sins? In order to be nourished by the Grail!

Without it, to live an ascetic life is pointless, as shown by the story of Perceval's hermit uncle. The chosen keeper of the Grail was not this hundred-year-old wise man, with his wonderful crown of virtue, the universal mourner, the great confessor, the wise mentor, and the gentle father, entirely holy with his radiant face. No; instead it was the 30-year-old Perceval, once dissolute and frivolous, who was chosen.

Why is this so? Can something like this be explained? I cannot explain it. The mysterious reasons are known only to the Divine Wisdom of the great castle.

The wisdom of the Miraculous Vessel comes from the vision of the divine potential, and from the insight into the particles of sticking. The Eye of Sophia penetrates the innermost sanctum. It seems to weigh on apothecaries' scales the golden pollen of the Bridal Chamber, and the drops of the anointing oil of myrrh, which poured down from Aaron's beard. It is as if they are collected in a cup and placed on the sensitive scales.

Perceval seemed to have much more of these drops. For this reason, the mark of the chosen one shone on his forehead. Nothing could be done to alter this.

His path is a complex one, including beautiful ladies, knights' tournaments, nocturnal iniquity and drinking with friends... However, forty-eight hours of confession with the gentle old man and one liturgy in his chapel with the burning Last Drop were sufficient to purify him completely and for him to glow with the mark of the Grail.

03.07.2005 Deris Island

LOHENGRIN, OR THE KNIGHT OF THE SWAN

Oh Lohengrin, the divine Lo!
His name alone is enough to make him shine.
Alone against the alien and captain of the UFO.

The true sons of the Most High against the Ben-Elohims,
Born from on high, more honourable than the Cherubim,
And more glorious beyond compare than the Seraphim.

IT was he, who defended me during my last 'fateful' conference in the hotel Astoria, when I delivered the latest gloomy prophecy about 2045 and the planned sacramental and cosmic birth of the cosmic monster from the captain of the UFO and the whore, who was designated for that purpose!

The Grail will remove the spells from the suffering earth. The Grail will prevent a war between Russia and China, thereby preventing the third world war. The Grail will proclaim and build the Divine Civilization.

At Solovki in Russia, the Radiant Grail of the Second Golgotha has begun to shine. This is also true of the Divine Mother's Nightingale Mountain. In response, the hundred thousand Last Drops of the lambs sacrificed at Solovki have been collected in the sacred Vessel.

Oh, sacred object which has no equal in heaven or on earth! Riches more precious than any of the wealth found on earth! The Miraculous Holy Grail is the source of all good and all grace. The flames are fanned by an incense burner of Sofrino, like the jaws of the huffing and puffing wolf, which was borrowed from the Holy Grail (just like the liturgy as a whole, which was ascribed to them by St John Crysostum, and their hypocritical ritualistic rites).

Another great son of the Most High from the Messianic dynasty was Lancelot (from Loonois). In the divine scrolls of the sons of humanity he describes the appearance of the Most Holy of Holies in the form of the Ark of the Heavenly Church: 'A white dove with fluttering wings flew in through the window, holding a golden incense burner in its beak. All around there was a heavenly fragrance as if all the perfumes and aromas of the world had been gathered together'.

If the most precious treasure, which a mortal could ever possess disappeared, or if it was thrown away, the Round Table would collapse. The Church would perish, the world would disappear and the universe would be torn apart. Queen Elaine, mother of Sir Galahad and a close relation of Joseph of Arimathea, was aware of this.

This is where the myrrh in our chalices comes from! There was myrrh in the silver Grail of Innocent Baltski. Myrrh also flowed from the small, sacred vessel of the Second Golgotha of Solovki, made by the hand of the Most High, and which was the Grail in the Hands of Seraphim the Most Tender.

*

...Let us simply call him Lo: the Divine Lo and the finest knight of all time.

Using the metaphors of the Grail, the immortal Lo is a combination of all the prophets, patriarchs, heresiarchs, Abrahams, Noahs, Moses, Johns of Damascus, Origens and other religious luminaries, as well as human minds such as the Lomonosovs, Suvorovs, and Kutuzovs. 'Lo En' is a divine person from the 'Lono' [lap, bosom] of the Most High. 'Grin' is the shining radiance of the Grail.

Is Richard Wagner, who wrote the opera of the same name, really the only one, who can fill the vacuum, boycotting the name of the Holy Grail and its divine knights? Let us praise the true descendants of Christ rather than their enemies, the ben-elohims and the would-be sons.

In the Gospel of the Grail, this is one of the most well-loved legends. As the Sun of Suns rises in the east and as the Bridegroom emerges from the bridal chamber, so, too, appears the divine Lo – Lohengrin. He is the finest and the most glorious, invincible, humble and *yurodivy* knight of all time. Like Melchizedek, he is a priest from heaven.

First, sensing trouble in the subtle vibrations of the spheres of the Kingdom, the bell of the Grail sent a falcon with a bell around its neck ringing gently to calm those suffering in the earthly night.

When no one on earth can help any longer and a host of demons swarm down, the soul remains alone in a concrete underground bunker, tearing out its hair and crying out like a prisoner in an underground cell, 'Help! Let me out!' When no one on earth in this deserted, never-ending, hopeless loneliness can help any longer, the Grail hears these mortal cries filled with holy passion and the falcon flies to their aid. Or perhaps the white swan on the silvery surface of the Volga or the Rhine. Or even the firebird or any other bird of the air. It is followed by Enoch and Elijah and then the soul feels completely safe.

Saint Lo! You have sailed to the many prisoners of the Second Solovki in your golden boat, drawn across the waters of the sea by a white swan – the symbol of eternal virginity within the Grail!

Oh, how his father grieved that his son had to leave his father's home and embark on worldly adventures. However... he must save the duchess Elsa in Brabant, who has been wrongfully accused of murder!

*

None of the medieval legends can be deciphered without a simple code. The Templars, knights of the Grail and true disciples of Christ, fought against only one enemy – the Roman Inquisition and its 'crusaders': the hard-core antichrist faction. The Grail on earth had no press, no armies of millions, no state executions or any other means of suppressing non-conformists. Also, the Grail went away into the blessed catacombs, believing the world to be unworthy of the radiance of its divine and glorious light.

From time to time the miracles of the Grail (miracle-working icons, apparitions of angels, the aid of the archangel Michael and Eucharistic communion) caused human minds to worry and so were forgotten. Generally speaking, Adam's race is not yet ready to enter a dialogue with the Most High. The corrupting origin (original sin) harms them from within, destroying the creation of the Most High and leading them towards a fatal ending.

*

...On his deathbed, gentle Gottwald, Duke of Brabant, called for his beloved daughter – the beautiful, innocent, pure-hearted, radiant and golden-haired Elsa.

'My precious one!' wept the Duke. 'How will you manage without me? Who will look after you?'

'Do not leave me, father!' said Elsa, kissing the hand of her dying father. 'I cannot live without you. Without you my life will be at an end.'

The Grail describes her as the true daughter of a true father! Gottwald's fading mind feverishly sorted through the vassals of Brabant, eventually settling for some reason on the violent, savage and disobedient, yet loyal, count of Brabant, Friedrich Telramund. Telramund was an experienced knight who had defeated over 150 opponents. He was compelled to call upon Telramund!

'Count Friedrich', said Duke Gottwald to the loyal vassal when he arrived in his chambers. 'I am dying. Please protect my beautiful daughter. Elsa is defenceless. You have done much for our fatherland. I believe that your loyalty will serve me at this time.'

Gottwald became unconscious. The next day, the church bells rang to announce that the Duke had passed away.

Here, though, is where the next Shakespearian-style, half-detective, half-mystical-allegorical story of the Grail begins, known as 'The Knight of the Swan, or Lohengrin'.

The count turned out to be an ambitious, evil villain. He publicly announced that the Duke entrusted his daughter, Elsa, into his care, and that Telramund should marry his daughter, thus becoming ruler of the land.

Elsa was horrified by this thought. She hated the cold, calculating, corpse-like count. She was repulsed by his bluish lips and his eyes like black coals. The evil look on his cunning face disgusted her. 'Count Telramund is a lecherous villain!' thought the innocent, beautiful Elsa. 'He is a cold-hearted murderer who flattered my father. My dear father will go to heaven, but the devil himself came to him on his deathbed – Telramund the Roman vassal'.

The villain's magic was such that he managed to persuade King Henry the Fowler (catcher of the souls of birds: his loyalists), who believed his every word. If this was so, then he had no opposition to the marriage. He just wanted to listen to the other side of the story, though.

In her audience with King Henry, Elsa angrily denounced Telramund as an upstart and a villain.

'Whilst appearing to serve my father, your highness', she said, looking the King in the eyes, 'he has undermined our state! He hated my father and wished him dead. I will bear witness to this before the Lord. Telramund is lying! There is no place for this ambitious villain in Brabant. He will destroy the duchy, destroy me and destroy the people. Think about it, your highness! Do not make a grave mistake. Do not allow this villain to take charge of me and of our dearly beloved duchy'.

King Henry was in a quandary. He was prepared to believe his loyal vassal, Telramund, but he was convinced by the beautiful Elsa.

Under the circumstances, they would seek the 'Judgement of the Most High'. Would Telramund agree to this?

'Yes', answered the rogue with a sinister smile, knowing that there was not one noble soul – not a soldier, a baron, an officer of the king's guard, or a simple shepherd – who would defend the honour of the innocent and pure Elsa. Everyone was afraid of Telramund (the Roman Inquisition). As is written in the chronicles of the black knights, his name instilled fear in everyone around. This villain's sword had never been defeated and its spell could not be broken. Who wanted to end up with their head cut off by challenging this deathly-pale 'black prophet'?

'My Lord, my Lord! Eternal and true Divinity!' wept Elsa, wringing her hands, like a myrrh-bearing woman seeing Christ led out to His crucifixion. 'Listen to me! Lord, is there really not one noble soul on earth, who can defend the truth in the face of lies and virginity in the face of debauchery. Is the world really as tainted by depravity and corruption like it was in the days of our ancestor Noah?'

The legends do not mention the Roman church. Who else, though, if not the Holy See, this 'representative of Christ' on earth, can help the downtrodden, the poor, the accused and the insulted? The 'Holy See' presents the opposite image here – the Roman Inquisition in the face of the 'black bridegroom', Telramund.

Elsa sighed. Duchess Elsa of Brabant was in a perpetual state of holy passion. What could be done? The date for the tournament (the Divine judgement) had already been set and Count Telramund rode triumphantly around on his horse, confident of victory. Who could possibly stand against him? The heralds blew their trumpets to summon anyone brave enough to make a stand. It was in vain!

A huge mass of people gathered in the square. The crowd was buzzing. A platform was erected for King Henry the Fowler and his retinue. Who, apart from idle onlookers and curious children would dare to set foot in the town square!

Suddenly, Elsa saw a falcon with a fascinating little bell tied around its neck. It sounded so sweet! It was irresistible.

This bell of the Grail thwarts all the devil's schemes. Elsa's grief-stricken face instantly lit up: help was at hand. On seeing the falcon she exclaimed, 'My prayers have been answered! It is the throne of the Most High!' Whether it was in a dream or in reality, she had seen the saviour for whom she had been waiting and for whose coming her pure heart had been hoping.

The gentle falcon flew around the square, looked at her trustingly and came to land on her shoulder, as if it was her only protector. 'Do not grieve, Elsa', it seemed to say in its voice of ineffable quality. 'The Lord has heard your prayers. The Grail will come to your aid. The bell of the Grail is already summoning the knights and they are ready to fight for your honour'.

'Oh, you have come to me from the Kingdom!' exclaimed the innocent maiden, her mind transported far away beyond heaven.

Opening her eyes, she saw before her the grand judge of the duel, the king, and next to him, the menacing Telramund. The king invoked Divine judgement and ordered the heralds to sound the fanfare. If, after one minute, no-one had stepped forward from the crowd, then Telramund would be declared the winner and Elsa would be forced to submit.

In the emptiness of holy passion, when no one and nothing was able to help, the Grail came to her aid. The crowd buzzed, ready to praise Telramund as the winner, when suddenly the sky was flooded with an unspeakably beautiful, ineffable light. A triumphant arch of azure blue was revealed. From out of its glorious light, in a golden boat, sailed a fine knight with a sword. His small boat was pulled by a white swan, swimming rhythmically across the surface of the ocean of the air.

Oh, it was indescribably wondrous! The crowd was enthralled. Who was this? Had the Most High himself come to the aid of poor, lonely Elsa, who was filled with holy passion; the innocent soul, who sought a union with the Most High and a union within the Grail?

The boat sailed up to the place, where King Henry sat with his retinue, and came to a halt. The noble knight introduced himself:

'I am Lohengrin. Duchess, I have come to fight your enemies and defend the honour of an innocent maiden.'

'O my fine knight, my betrothed, and my one and only on earth and in heaven! My fate is forever in your hands!'

Elsa leapt from her seat in excitement.

'What is this? Is this not a wonderful dream?'

That night, she had seen a wondrous knight in a white boat – her saviour. Then the dream had come true.

The duel was held at the place where the mighty Rhine flows into the endless sea, and a luxurious royal tent was erected on the banks of the Scheldt. The hermit monks of the Grail dwell in the Holy Being. They come into the world (they are called to be yurodivy: this is the perfect Grail!) from goodness knows where, just at the right time.

Just as Melchizedek, king of Salem, with the chalice and the sacred gifts in his hands, meets Abraham, and is revered by him, so too does the whole of Brabant revere Lohengrin, the priest of Melchizedek from the Church of the Holy crystal Grail.

According to Roman chronicles, the Pope defeated Jacques de Molay, the Grand Master of the Order of the Knights Templar. The order was dissolved and their property confiscated. The majority of the immortal knights were forced to give false evidence under torture, which they later retracted... This was not really what happened. The Grail is invincible. Whether the Chalice of the Grail is in Camelot or Monsalvat, in Corbenic or Glastonbury, no enemy can breach the strong castle walls of the great fortress.

Lohengrin defeated Telramund! The brutal villain begged for forgiveness like a pathetic dog with its tail between its legs. Magnanimous Lohengrin was ready to cut off the brute's head. His gaze penetrated the frigid coals of Telramund's eyes.

'Foul vermin! Be gone forever from the face of the earth, you Roman villain!' hissed Lohengrin, seething with righteous anger. Then Telramund's strength was all gone. His evil black blood had been neutralised. The strength, which he had borrowed from those, whom he had killed and tortured, no longer worked.

*

Elsa fell in love with Lohengrin and soon they were married.

Thus began the messianic age. New towns were built. There were no more robbers by the wayside. It was as though the land was in a heavenly state of intoxication. The country was ruled by a knight of the Grail – a divine monarch, who had come down from heaven. (The general notion of monarchy comes from the Grail. An anointed one leads his loving people. Where, though, does this anointing take place, if not in the Grail at the hands of the keeper of the Chalice, or in the messianic dynasty of Christ Himself? Without the Grail a monarchy is empty and false, just like a church without the Grail. These two blind caricatures of a church and a state bereft of the Grail have tormented the world with their attempts to establish a perfect social system like the one found in heaven).

In the Grail the peaceful 'combined soul' of humanity is pure and innocent. It is assailed by slanderers and ambitious people, evil-doers and caricatures of Adam's race, like Count Friedrich Telramund. However, these seemingly invincible people, these Rephaim flexing their muscles, and these evil-doers, will be defeated. David will always overthrow the great warrior Goliath with a stone thrown to the head. The saints of Israel (a Grail term – 'Led, saw, invincible') will be triumphant.

The world will rejoice, when the sacred chalice of the Grail shines over them. Everything will succeed. The first psalm speaks of the Grail, when it says: 'they succeed in everything they do and the leaves will never fall from the tree'.

There is such a difference between the mystical anthropologies of the Grail and of Rome. 'A worldly soul' (Elsa, Isolde, Elizabeth) seeks to enter into a union with the Most High). From the Roman Curia's point of view, she is a cursed whore, who needs the 'firm hand' of the Lord.

Telramund's lie about his 'right of inheritance' with regard to the Duke's daughter (as he had been given the blessing of Duke Gottwald on his death bed to defend the innocent and defenceless Elsa) is Rome's lie about the 'inheritance of the apostles' and that of the bishops (as if the Saviour had bequeathed His work and His Church to them.

Lohengrin was a virgin. Two radiant angels were born out of his marriage to Elsa. These unblemished children were born of the messianic dynasty. If the Grail releases a knight, it is for the sole purpose of continuing the race of Christ and is a special cross to be borne.

Lohengrin does not win with his strong 'iron' muscles, his superhuman strength, a blow from his sword or physical endurance (as told by shrewd medieval chronicles, mostly written by followers of the Roman Whore). Lohengrin stood against Telramund just as David stood against Goliath – on the side of the divine truth. Lohengrin is called to defend the ultimate truth. Like a priest of Melchizedek, his righteous wrath leads him to victory. The force, which summoned the evil villain into battle, and which spread terror throughout the land, had already been defeated before the fighting began... Lohengrin was scented with the fragrance of eternal virginity and the people admired their new Duke. He is indeed immortal.

*

Several years passed by. Brabant shone under its new leader. Its enemies had somehow been swept away. Robbers were afraid to attack people on the highways. Barons did not exploit their servants. Truth and justice reigned in the land and all around there was contentment and prosperity. But would it last?

Here it is: humanity's yearning for a perfect social order has been satisfied! Lohengrin, knight of the Grail, is king, prophet and priest in one person. He is perfect theocracy, hagiocracy, the Triumphant Lamb amongst 144 thousand virgins... How long would it last?

The Grail is prepared to defend every soul, who has been wrongfully accused. Lucifer's poison, poured out three times, would have taken its toll long ago. However, just as Lohengrin saved Elsa of Brabant, the Grail has saved me from the serpent's venomous bite.

Every morning a falcon came to me, its little bell ringing, perched on my shoulder and calmed me saying, 'Do not grieve, blessed John! The victory is for the Most High. Be patient'. 'I waited patiently for the Lord', I replied to the falcon, stroking it and gently holding it next to my head. I felt the warmth of its body and it comforted me. The heavenly sound of its bell caressed my ears and my enemies were powerless.

I was declared insane three times under the Soviet regime for being a follower of Orthodoxy. They called me a 'parasite', a 'trickster' and goodness knows what else. In their wickedness my enemies were ready to use me as a scapegoat for their own vices. The Holy Grail has defended its anointed one.

Not one of the symbols of the Grail is accepted in the Roman church, such as the white swan, or eternal virginity... If only the monasteries of the Roman Harlot were decorated with them, then monasticism and celibacy would flourish all over the face of the earth. Now, though, they are full of paedophiles and artists of dubious orientation. If the church had sailed in a sacred, golden boat along the glistening surface of the Rhine, and come down from the Kingdom, just as Lohengrin's boat came down from the Holy Being, the messianic era would have dawned long ago. If the world had followed the example of the True Church and accepted the messianic dynasty of Christ, then the Grail would not have had to remain concealed and what happened in Brabant under the reign of Lohengrin would have happened throughout the whole world.

The world is not ready to accept the knighthood of the Grail. Adam's race is not ready to espouse Christ. It is not ready for the bridal chamber. The Gospel has come into the world in advance and is addressed to a different race – the Seraphite race III.

Brabant bears witness to that same unfortunate spirit. Less than three years had gone by when the inhabitants of Brabant forgot, what could have happened if the evil, malicious Telramund had taken Elsa as his bride and, together with her, he would have seized his other bride – the Duchy of Brabant – in his scrawny hand. He would have imposed taxes, duties, compulsory conscription to the army, poverty, hunger, strict regimes, injustice and a tyrannical system of government.

Religious fundamentalism only fits in when the social system is based on authoritarian despotism. It is more closely related to Pol Pot, Pinochet, Stalin and Mao. It finds the Grail as hateful as the Grail finds the Roman Harlot.

The world still does not know that the greatest confrontation in its history is that of the True church against the false church, or the 'hypocrites' as they are referred to in the Book of Psalms.

The rejoicing over Lohengrin's victory had subsided and the people wanted to know, WHO this knight was and how he had managed to win. Telramund, in his exile, did not waste any time. He sought revenge. This hideous beast rolled up his sleeves and hungered for power. All was not yet lost! Who would dare stand against him, this invincible black Roman knight?

This Lohengrin was the devil himself. He was the son of a whore! It would not be difficult to prove – all he needed was the help of the Roman Inquisition.

So, rumours began to spread. Let Lohengrin reveal his true origins! Was he not the son of the devil? Did he not come from hell to turn up here out of the blue? Did he not bewitch our dear Duchess Elsa with his magical charms? And were his sons not conceived by the devil?

'What is going to happen, my dear gentlemen? Will our Duchy fall into ruin! We invoked the judgement of the Most High but have received that of the devil instead!'

'Do not forget!' said others. 'Count Telramund is a malicious rogue! Our dear Duchess called upon the Most High as there was no-one on earth who could help her. The Lord can, though! The Most High sent His angel from Heaven. The Lord Himself is ruling over our land! Can we appreciate the countless mercies with which the Lord has showered us for no apparent reason? Brothers, let us give thanks to the Most High!'

They rang the magic bell again and again, but they were on their own and no-one listened.

*

Once again, Elsa was in a state of holy passion. She called Lohengrin only one name, 'My beloved!'. She was head over heels in love with him. She was the happiest ruler of all time and she had a wonderful family. The people, too, were in love with their divine leader, Lohengrin. The black barons, though, constantly nagged Elsa:

'Let him show, who he really is! Is he not of the devil? Count Telramund proved his true loyalty in the way he served our country. He won so many battles for his country! But who is this Lohengrin? Who is this sorcerer who stands before us? Is he of noble birth? Has he not violated the immutable law of Brabant, which was passed by our fathers?'

Elsa recalled the terms of her marriage. She alone could question Lohengrin about his origins. The Grail remained in the catacombs, in the Holy Being. Her nerves were torn to pieces and Elsa could not cope any longer. She essentially lost control. One day, the fatal confession took place in the marriage bed.

'Tell me, my dear, who is your father?'

'I am a knight, who came into the world without being born. I am a priest of the order of Melchizedek, and the whole world belongs to my Father.'

'Answer me seriously, my love!' Elsa gently insisted. 'Can a loving husband not trust his beloved wife? Would I betray you?'

'Elsa', pleaded Lohengrin, 'Do not torment me! Elsa, you must not betray the Grail!'

Elsa could not contain herself.

'Tell me, where you came from, and about your family background! Who are your parents? Who are your father and your mother?'

Lohengrin turned pale and his face bore an expression of deep sorrow.

'You have uttered the fateful word! You have asked the dreaded question and broken your vow. Elsa, your doubts have destroyed our happiness.'

Elsa was bewildered. Her heart was wounded. She gazed through her pain into the distance. What did she see? A white swan was swimming across the waves, pulling an empty boat.

'The swan! The swan! What a dreadful sign. The white swan has come once more', she trembled and fell unconscious at the feet of her husband.

'Yes, yes, my dear. The time has come for me to leave.'

*

Poor Elsa! She could not stand against the world. Her nerves, which were already in pieces after the attack from the Throne of Rome in the guise of the evil villain Telaramund, simply gave way. The spirit of the world had its own way. Was it really so important to know about her husband's unearthly origin? Was it not clear that heaven had come to her rescue? Now it was as if there was no Divinity and no help from heaven. Earthly doubts and arguments had prevailed.

Brabant was not ready to become a 'heavenly state', to be ruled from on high and to be born from on high, as stated in the Gospel of the true followers of Christ. Thus Lohengrin left Brabant.

A huge crowd gathered on the banks of the Rhine to watch the boat. The people bade farewell to their great leader. Many of them wept and pleaded:

'Forgive us, Lohengrin! Forgive us!'

King Henry the Fowler was there, too. He was deeply upset. The heavenly bird had been caught in a snare this time. It could not be kept in Brabant's cage any longer.

Lohengrin blessed Elsa and their children. He left them under the protection of the Most High. The messianic dynasty must be continued.

Lohengrin returned to the Grail.

That was the end of the story.

04.07.2005 Deris Island

The Power of the Scepter of the Gradulation in the Hands of the Priest of Melchizedek

Within the legend of the Grail there is another scroll called, 'The Power of the Scepter of Gradulation in the Hands of the Priest of Melchizedek'.

...In the Middle Ages, there was once an impregnable castle which belonged to the evil Baron Stolzenberg (as an impartial reader might have observed, this is another image of the Roman Inquisition). The castle stood in a dense forest and was feared for miles around. The Baron's name alone was enough to strike fear in throughout the whole of Germany. His soldiers destroyed fields, trampled people to death with their horses, and set fire to peasants' huts. The Baron himself loved to hunt people down like animals; such was his attitude towards mortals. He used them as a target for his sharp arrows!

Rome wanted to conquer the whole world and create a worldwide Catholic empire. They believed that the Kingdom of the Most High would come down to earth when the Roman emperor became the universal ruler and all the monarchs of the world bowed down before him. However, the ugly kingdom of the devil, or the distorting mirror, came instead.

The villain's power grew day by day and his success spurred him on. However, all his deeds had an element of evil in them, as if the devil himself were standing behind him, hiding under the name of the Most High...

'O, those servants of the Most High! They sold their souls to the devil long ago', people in the crowd said of the Roman villains. One by one they walked towards the noble knights of the Grail (the knights Templar, keepers of the Chalice, and guardians of the true Church of Christ).

To the greedy, stout Baron, this seemed very little. In spite of his vast amount of land, possessions, and barns full of riches, he was constantly waging war on his neighbours, bringing the spoils back to his castle.

His cellars were packed full and there was no room left in the stores. There was nowhere to put anything yet Rome continued to steal and take other people's lands until the universe was spiritually bereft and morally void. The Roman rulers rubbed their hands as they walked around like women draped in gold and pearls. Few people realised that, during their night-time prayers and long Masses, these Roman criminals opened the gates of hell, and that they did not walk with the Lord, but with the devil. They had consigned the glorious Gospel to oblivion long ago, exchanging it for the holy Roman Inquisition, with its treatises such as 'Malleus Maleficarum' (Hammer of the Witches) and 'The teachings of our holy father Aristotle on rational logic and theological dogma'.

*

One evening, Stolzenberg was sitting in front of the fire with his repressed young wife. The fire was blazing away when the arrival of two minnesingers was announced. The Baron was annoyed at the disturbance but he dare not send them away: it was customary at that time to welcome singers into one's home and show them hospitality. The neighbours were called and many came to listen to these lovers of the truth and wanderers from heaven.

The older of the two minnesingers held a wonderful harp in his hands and the old man sang a tale of ancient battles, campaigns and victories, and of the saints of the Church. He sang of many ancestors and owners of the castle. The stern inquisitor listened to him with pleasure and expected that the minnesinger would eventually sing his praises (the Roman Inquisition). However, he nobly fell silent, bowed to the audience and walked over to the wall of the great hall.

Stolzenberg bit his lip and contained his anger.

The old singer was followed by a youth wearing a sword in a damask sheath, with handsome legs. He was still young with clear, bright eyes. He sang of heavenly love and of the first love which has been abandoned by humanity. He sang of the eternal Virgin and of true virginity. He sang of the chivalrous glory of the true saints, their endless courage and their purity of heart in the face of evil and malicious villains. He sang of the suffering of Christians tormented by their greedy pastors, these bald sorcerers and black magicians of some wedding rite which is open only to them and is performed hourly by them. It contains much hypnosis but is fruitless.

(The people were confused about faith in the Most High, as professed by Rome. In the castles of the Grail it was said that 'they invented their own Christ. No such Lord exists on earth or in heaven, or indeed anywhere else, be it in the dungeons of another world or in vacuums'.)

Ah! The young minstrel sang with such inspiration! He gave such a sermon at the altar of the royal gates of the cathedral! It seemed as if the Holy Spirit Himself was speaking from his mouth. Then his wrathful gaze turned to the baron, and their eyes met. Filled with righteous anger and the fire of the Holy Spirit, the young minnesinger began to tell of the divine retribution which awaited those priests who did not follow their calling and instead became saviours of those who destroy the world; the priests of Satan.

The baron was incensed with rage. How dare this holy preacher, who had come down from heaven, say such blasphemous things in the Roman church? Go and preach elsewhere! This anger was then mixed with jealousy as Stolzenberg's young wife threw the singer a rose (the sacred prayer of the rosary).

The powerful tones of his voice rang out like the strains of a church organ. His voice became ever stronger and his teaching was carried to the heavens, proclaiming to visible and invisible worlds alike...

The Baron grew weaker by the hour as fear gripped those loyal to him. It would only take another half an hour of this preaching and they would turn against him, his charms reduced to nothing! No, no, no!

Clenching his teeth, the Baron seized the spear he had been playing with during the sermon from the singer of Supreme Love, and thrust it straight into the heart of the golden-haired youth.

The young singer fell, drenched in blood. The crowd were struck dumb. Who now would teach about the Christ of Supreme Love, the Kingdom of Heaven, virginal love, the Immaculate Conception, Original Purity, the beauty of a person who has conquered sin, the kingdom of the Seraphites, and the fragrant, scarlet, white and orange roses?

The Roman villain got his way. The hunchbacked Stolzenberg smiled and strode out of the hall alone.

Dazed, everyone waited to see what would happen next.

The old minnesinger (the Heavenly Church) approached the body of his young friend, wrapped him in a cloak (a distinguishing feature of the Templars), lifted him onto his shoulders and left in silence. As he was leaving the room, though, he turned round and, in despair, he smashed the young singer's harp. Then he faced the castle and uttered a terrible prophecy.

*

Let us stop here. Whose scepter was the most effective: the church anathema or the knight's sceptre of gradulation?

This is the essential question! There was one thing the Roman villains did not consider: Jacques de Molay before the martyr's death at the stake called on the Heavenly Court of Philip the Fair and the Pope – two symphonist villains who condemned the keepers of the Grail to death, thus crucifying Christ in him.

Philip died during a hunt on the very day and at the very time predicted by the Holy Knight. Soon after, the Pope passed away in his malice and all trace of him disappeared, as if he had never existed.

The Roman sorceress and master of anathemas on holy people underestimated the strength of the sceptre of gradulation which was directed against the evil spirit behind Roman Inquisitors! The Most High, though, revealed and exposed this evil spirit, who in his wrath destroyed the castle and evil black baron.

Now and forever this proud castle was destroyed! His song, accompanied on the organ or the harp, would no longer sound within its walls! Henceforth only wails and moans would be heard here! (At the Second Golgotha the wails and moans of millions of tortured victims, who now wait for their scores to be settled, could be heard beneath the sweet strains of the liturgical organ). Not one tree would grow in the gardens of Rome! Not one flower would bloom on its hillsides! This blossoming church would be transformed into a grey, deserted slope, from which all living things would flee!

Jacques de Molay pronounced a similar prophecy over the Pope and the French King for they had decided to defile and slandere the greatest and most noble knights of all humanity, confiscating their property and erasing their names from history.

*

Stolzenberg was unmoved by matters of conscience.

'Will there be no more singing? Praise the Lord! Things can be kept under control with the sword and dagger.'

'Missionaries and crusaders with armed conquerors can be sent to natives to swell the ranks of the Catholics...'

Gentlemen, are you afraid that the death of the Roman Whore will mean the death of the Church of Christ? Don't you see! That is not the case! On the contrary, it will be reborn. The Holy Grail and its 150 castles of white ivory will come down to earth. The warriors of Elijah and Enoch are the greatest of all humanity. They will seal the gates of Lucifer and those of Beelzebub, Behemoth and Tibet, and they will open up the indescribably beautiful gates of union with the Most High. Then humanity will enter the ark of salvation and will remain there 'until the end of time and beyond'.

*

While the people mourned for the minnesinger, Stolzenberg was feasting in his castle with his 'diabolical company' (as his associates were called).

The Baron held the great feast to celebrate the sorry demise of the Church of the saints, which he hated! How could he have such little respect? How could he thrust his lance straight into the heart of the singer of ineffable love (the anathema of Rome)?

Oh, Church of eternal youth! Where are you?

This is how the legend of the Grail describes the 'three days of darkness' and the killing of the Roman Whore.

'...Suddenly a flock of black crows launched themselves at the windows of the castle and began to hammer at them with their beaks. As the glass shattered, the crows swooped into the hall and swarmed round the baron who was feasting with his guests. The candles, in valuable candlesticks on the table, were blown out. A shroud of darkness fell all around.'

The 'three days of darkness', cataclysm and universal misery began when the evil villain murdered the old church. The Pope is aware of this and thus guard the Third Secret of Fatima: the Antichrist will sit on the throne in Rome and, at the same time, the judgment of the Most High will begin...with the trial of the church, not of sinners. It will begin with testimonies showing how it has brought corruption and ruin to the world, how it has failed in its mission, and how it has brought about universal darkness by crucifying Christ and His messengers.

'What will the host do with the bad grapes when he returns? They will be subjected to a terrible death.'

This 'terrible death' – suddenly disappearing from the face of the earth, like a leaf in a hurricane – is described in the legend of the Grail which tells of the evil Baron Stolzenberg, his 'diabolical company' and two wandering minstrels from the sacred Grail (noble Templars).

...Stolzenberg went pale with terror. He opened his mouth and tried to whisper the 'Pater noster' in his traditional and hypocritical way, but he was paralysed. As soon as the Baron moved his lips silently to call his brethren to join him in the prayer of salvation, the 'Kyrie Eleison', a terrible banging could be heard from under the ground. The rock, on which the castle stood, opened up and the throne of Rome, in the form of the castle of Stolzenberg, disappeared without trace into the abyss, as if it had never existed.

The next day, the inhabitants of the surrounding villages, recovering from the dreadful commotion, went to the place where the black Baron's castle had been and saw a gaping abyss filled with foul-smelling smoke.

Thus, according to the legend of the Holy Grail, the Most High dealt with the Roman Inquisition.

There was only one way it could repent... Repentance does not end with a few tears and promises 'never to do it again'. Rather, repentance requires a metanoic conversion. There is only one way in which the Roman Whore can repent: the cardinals and bishops must vow to the Most High that they will never again torment, persecute or crucify saints, bear false witness against them, or operate the machine of state repression. On the contrary, they will become the church of the saints and will finally pay heed to the sweet voices of their blessed singers and to their first love (which they had forgotten in the same way as the community at Ephesus in the time of John of the Apocalypse).

There is not much point in waiting for this to happen. The administration is crumbling.

The sceptre of gradulation of the priests of Melchizedek turned out to be stronger than the Roman anathema (the blow from the Eucharistic lance). The True Church has come down from heaven and the sword of the priests of Melchizedek has sliced the dragon in two.

*

No trace remained of the castle at all, and all that was left of Stolzenberg was darkness and shadow. Afterwards, the people in the surrounding villages (Christians) often saw a black dog which seemed to be guarding the treasure buried in the castle. No-one was ever able to find it, as if it was in the world of the Holy Being.

In fact, the treasure had never existed. The treasure trove of the Roman Thief and its accomplices, which was full of stolen property, had long since been dismantled by the noble knights of the Chalice and everything returned to its rightful owners.

As the great legend says, the prophecy of the Church of the saints was fulfilled. The bare rock face towers ominously over a moat. There is nowhere for any living thing on this cliff, which was once covered with a dense forest and meadows filled with flowers.

In the place where the castle of Stolzenberg once stood, there is now only emptiness...

29.06.2005 Deris Island

The Sword of Eternal Virginity

Oh, black louse on the body of Christ! May the Most High expel you from His wondrous heart.

'The disastrous place'...

The Divine Wisdom of the Holy Grail is a constant source of rapture. The knights sat at the Round Table. Further back, to the right of the Grand Master, was the 'disastrous place'. Seeing that this chair was empty, one of the knights asked Arthur, why nobody was sitting there. It was explained to him that no knight has yet been born into this world who would be able to sit in it.

This is the philosophy of the 'siege perilous': it is both sacred and doomed. The 'siege perilous' is the lot of a leader. He will always be envied. People will try to subvert and overthrow him. The 'siege perilous' has nothing in common with witches' spells and curses, although it does have connections with the complex contortions of black magic.

The 'siege perilous' must be won in order to prevent a scribe or a Pharisee from sitting on your throne.

*

Once, Lancelot was compelled to fight in the Chapel Perilous. The magnificent image of the castle of Korbenic is the Chapel Perilous!

'No traveller has yet been born who would give his life to hear the secrets of the Grail', whispered the Maiden of the Divine Castle whilst in a wonderful dream. Thus, the history of the Seraphites (Desposins) against the Adamites is the revelation of those secrets through yurodstvo. The heralds of the Grail ride out, blowing their apocalyptic horns to warn of disaster and appeal to the conscience. The Grail stands against the huge beast that is the corrupt mafia system of modern humanity. It stands against the European Parliament, and medical, automotive, computer and food conglomerates, amongst others.

The time had come for the philosophy of the 'siege perilous' or the 'chapel perilous' to be sentenced to death. That was where holy warriors of the truth stopped, until Galahad came along and, one by one, cut off the twelve heads of the fiery serpent, the guardian of the secret of the Roman Thief (the 'Chapel Perilous'). Then, there were no more parasites on the body of Christ, proclaiming the great mysteries in the guise of 'catechesis', 'new evangelisation' etc. It disappeared from the face of the earth, when the most noble of knights, Sir Galahad (a direct descendant of Christ through Mary Magdalene and Joseph of Arimathea), killed the dragon and threw its twelve, bloody heads into a ravine.

My dear lady, I would not dare to reveal the secret mysteries to those who are unworthy. However, the world is dying because of an abhorrent, overweight curate. Like a real thief, the higher echelons of the Roman clergy go around with twenty-five suspicious keys hanging from their belts. They use these to open the forbidden gates of hell.

How could I not show someone the Cross as the key to the Kingdom? How could I not teach him the attraction of the Cross which came into this world to be shared with all of humanity – the cross of Christ? How can I remain silent as a fervent admirer of the holy Templars, Owain and Lohengrin, and the Second Solovki (this is the worst crime of all humanity, a bloody swamp, where a hundred million innocent victims are buried)? How did they pass by it, as if it was not there? There they are again, those black crows with their Masses made to order and their indulgences for murderers.

May you be cursed forever, with your churches built with blood money taken from innocent victims!

*

A whole divine sonata could be composed out of just a few names such as Elaine (meaning the inaccessible heights of the Most High), the mother of Lancelot (lan – long, length – prolongation of the Most High, celot – settlement; overall meaning – settlement, dwelling place of the Most High), King Ban (the sound of the bell of the Kingdom), and Queen Guinevere (Divine Wisdom).

Lancelot fell in love with Guinevere. Her wisdom was the object of his worship. However, an evil twist of fate led him to find himself in bed with Elaine, whom he thought was Guinevere, and the miraculous and immortal Galahad was born out of their union...

When did they live? Time has been compressed. Its continuum with its predictable, worn-out measurements and its tedious timetable is restricted by the Adamites' routine: being born into the world from a sinful mother, following a mortal programme of events, and becoming involved with some visiting hypnotist or astrologer...

To be mad about Queen Guinevere, like Sir Lancelot, is the cherished dream of a knight of the Grail. Fate leads you to share a bed with someone and then the most pure maiden El-Aine (daughter of the Most High) gives birth to a radiant, divine child, Galahad. 'Gala' means eternal rejoicing and the island of happiness. Alleluia! Sin is defeated! 'Ahad' is the final word of the mysterious commandment, the Shema: 'Hear, oh people of God, the Lord is our God, the Lord is one' (ahad).

Divine joy is being joined with the Most High and dwelling in his palace of divine peace!

Galahad... Ahad... I will say no more. I will not utter another word. Apart from this, I have already revealed many of the mysteries of the Grail. However, the generous castle of the Most High would like to share its treasure with the world.

In the final days, as the Most Pure Virgin foretold in Her revelations, there will be a new 'beginning of time'. The Most High will be with those who are 'last': those who supported Telramund and listened to the jealous villain's slander about Lohengrin's dubious origins will be bumped off from the face of the earth. In this new age of the Seraphites, like the first scarlet roses of civilization, the Grail Chalice will hasten to reveal itself and let people drink its heavenly wine.

First of all, though, it is important to be familiar with the wisdom of the Grail with Queen Guinevere and those who loved her, worshipped her, like Sir Lancelot, the knight who she loves forever. Where is the Chapel Perilous with its shadows? It no longer exists. A *yurodivy* shrine to the Second Solovki has now been erected in its place. There is no Orthodox priest there with all his paraphernalia, nor is there a fat-faced representative from Rome. Not one serpent slithers into this sacred shrine to the knights of the Grail.

So, in the castle of Korbenic and in the holy dwelling place of Camelot, it is customary to contemplate the mysteries of the Most High. The Grail is the Church of the Kingdom which has come down to earth. Thus the Knights of the Holy Union are obliged to share the wisdom of Christ, meaning that they must reject human speculation and adopt the theology of heaven.

I will not look away from the silver altar with its four candlesticks and four candles which never go out. Four pages brought incense burners from Atlantis to here, each one more beautifully decorated than the last with images of a woman clothed in the sun, the 'New Holy Rus'', the 'Throne of Hiroshima' and the 'New Holy America'. It is here that the key to the defeat of China (this infestation of the 21st century) appeared – the sword of Eternal Virginity which cut off all twelve heads of the venomous, lustful dragon at once. However, I will hasten to reveal the wisdom of the Grail to the Knights of the Inner Castle, without risk of being punished by the Lady of the Kingdom – the Most Pure Divine Mother.

I would close these 'dead' and 'perilous' chapels of the underworld which stand on every corner of Altufevskoe Boulevard and indeed of every other street in the asphalt jungle of deranged and misled Moscow. Oh, how could I arm myself with Lancelelot's sword of the Grail which he used in his endless battles with large and small dragons – with green lizards and tiny crocodiles which are still hunted in our sorry kingdom of Brabant?

*

Lancelot was not afraid to enter the Chapel Perilous together with his sister, Sarah (the mentality of the Word). Lancelot's secret was that he was descended from sea-faring stock. His sailor's body and the wisdom of the sea surpassed all human understanding. In the chronicles, he is known as Sir Lancelot of the Lake.

On arriving at the Chapel Perilous, he reined in his horse by the fence. There, he noticed 150 shields on the wall, each of which had once belonged to a glorious knight whom he knew by name. 'What a terrible scene!' thought the noble Lancelot. 'A hundred and fifty saints have laid their heads down in this Roman field of death. What kind of a chapel of Christ is this if holy Knights of the Lord's truth do not come out of it alive?' Lancelot made the sign of the cross and invoked the aid of the Most Pure Virgin Mother, the unwavering Patroness, and his Protector in his earthly wanderings.

It was a terrible scene: 150 shields spattered with blood! Perhaps his shield would join these 150!

Only with the drawn sword of Eternal Virginity is it possible to enter the Chapel Perilous and this engulfing swamp of worldly lust. Blessed Lancelot was not afraid and so, with sword in hand, he bravely entered the confines of the Chapel Perilous. It was quite small inside: a single icon lamp was burning and there were two indeterminate icons (neither Christ Pantocrator nor the Virgin Mother), which were faded with age and which were copies of a long-lost original. Of course, the original of the Virgin Mother is kept within the Grail, as is the original of Christ. It is only possible to see the face of the Divine Mother from way up in the Heavenly Kingdom.

However, as he squinted in the dim light of the icon lamp, Lancelot noticed the body of the last saint to be tortured here by the Roman Inquisition. It was wrapped in a silk cloth and a pleasant fragrance emanated from it. Lancelot could make out spots of the martyr's blood, just like those on the shields.

What is this? Thirty shadows of black inquisitors loomed up on the walls. The evil villains processed with candles and, in their left hands, they held scrolls containing the death sentences.

'You are doomed, knight! You will not leave here alive.'

The black knights ordered Lancelot to lay down his sword, otherwise he would die a terrible death you would never would ever hear of it or find his body.

Shall I lay down the sword of Eternal Virginity and the sword of Christ? To exchange it for something, such as the glaive of Caesar! Oh no! These black monks and hermits, who have come from the underworld to roam the world, did not slaughter his 150 predecessors with that threat, did they?!

'Virginity is barren and brings death!..'

No! The 'Barren One' gives birth! The sword of Eternal Virginity was in the hands of Lancelot. With it, he would defeat the thirty black inquisitors.

'I come to you, lustful villains, sadists, vampires and murderers of the saints of old, with the sword of Eternal Virginity!' said Lancelot, as he bravely walked straight towards them. The inquisitors parted and scattered, letting him pass through.

Panic reigned in the kingdom of Peril. Something heavenly entered the chapel and vanquished the thirty Catholic monk-inquisitors with the drawn sword of Eternal Virginity! They offered him other swords, such as the sword of careers, the sword of earthly truth, the sword of Caesar, the sword for cutting off the enemy, etc. However, the knight of the Grail remained loyal to the sword of Eternal Virginity. He unsheathed it and attacked the thirty villains.

Eternal virginity is invincible. 'Blessed is the guided, invincible, untouchable son of the Most Pure Virgin!' exclaimed the true sons of the Most High.

Another test awaited Lancelot by the chapel fence.

'Come to me', said a beautiful maiden, 'but first put down your sword. I am a woman. Would you raise your sword against womankind? That would be unwise!'

'You whore! May the sword of the truth of Christ strike you down! I am from the Kingdom of Eternal Virginity. To lay down my sword would be fatal. Is your chapel not called Perilous because it is here that virginity is stripped of its power, the law of lust takes precedence and the place is filled with death? Never! It would be better for you, artful beauty and miserable hypocrite, to take off your make-up and become a pure virgin. Arm yourself with a sword like mine, the sword of Eternal Virginity.'

'You are wise. I bow to your wisdom', replied the girl. 'If you had done as I asked, you would never have set eyes on Queen Guinevere again and you would not have left here alive. Oh, woe is me!.. Let me confess to you. I am so sorry!'

Then that serpent in human clothing, the foolish virgin, the papist, priest-following, Roman nun fell on her knees and begged 'Father Lancelot' to let her confess.

'Stand up! Be gone! I will never give you the kiss of a traitor and be unfaithful to my eternally pure Lady.'

'You have done the right thing, knight of the Grail... If you had heard my confession, you would have been burdened with my sins. Our spawn of serpents imitate beautiful maidens and are extremely adept at impersonation and at making a mockery of naïve fools. You should know, Knight of the Grail, that, if you had heard my confession and kissed me out of compassion, you would have perished straight away. I built this Chapel Perilous', said the female werewolf, 'so that I could keep and kiss your dead body'.

Such indescribable horror! Let us stop here. Let us raise our spirits.

From the point of view of the Grail, the endless cathedrals full of relics are 'Chapels Perilous', where the Roman Harlot displays the dead remains of the saints whom she has killed. She is ready to embrace them and kiss them, leaving the imprint of her burning lips on glass caskets decorated with silver inlay. This is not necrophilia or a fantasy about dead bodies. This is the law of the kingdom of 'Chapels Perilous'. If anyone enters and is persuaded to hear the confession of a serpent or to kiss it out of compassion (to enter a dialogue with the Roman Harlot), he will die. Then his corpse will be venerated by thousands of admirers, in spite of the Divine Wisdom of Queen Guinevere who wanted saints to remain alive. There are glass boxes for snakes, and museums containing relics of the saints should use these glass terraria for the dried remains of dangerous African reptiles instead.

'Divine Wisdom has saved you!' said the maiden, throwing off her disguise. 'Do you see Gilbert the Bastard? This knight could not help feeling sorry for me. He resisted the thirty monks of the Inquisition who ordered him on pain of death to lay down the sword of Eternal Virginity. He was not able to resist me, though.'

'May the Lord and the Holy Grail save me from your charms, you cursed witch! May your Chapel Perilous and all who dwell in it be cursed! And may the saints whom you murdered (the 150 bloody shields and the spots of blood on the Grail) rise again and occupy their rightful place.'

'The cunning maiden Hellawes (this was the name of the werewolf of the Chapel Perilous) grew weaker by the hour and withered away out of love for Lancelot, until she eventually perished'. This vampiric witch's pathological love for the saint has been known to the Grail for a long time. However, in the castles of the Most High, the 'Chapels Perilous' were to be exchanged for marriage chapels. When will there be as many of these as there are the 'perilous' types – those ubiquitous white concrete chapels with wooden images of the crucified Christ? They are surrounded only by guards, vergers, exhibitors and tour guides. There is not a word of truth spoken there, and the air is stale.

'An end to the chapels perilous!' said the angel of Portugal. 'Let us build small temples to Holy Theogamy in their place, and then the saints of the Holy Union with the Divinity will come into the world.'

*

That is the story of the great Lancelot's victory over the knights of the Roman dragon. When the monks, after having terrified the knight, ordered him to give up the sword of Eternal Virginity, they were not intending to initiate their lustful programmes. The sword of Eternal Virginity was growing dim because the knight who wielded it was ceasing to appreciate the value of virginity.

It is only possible to emerge as a victor against these Chapels Perilous, which are spread out all over the world, by not letting go of the sword of Eternal Virginity. You will be showered with thousands of curses. Every advertisement in the town will show fornication and say:

'Take our sword! Try the thrill and pleasure of another sword. Cut off the head of your adversary! Use the sword of peace and the glaive of Caesar, and you will achieve everything you ever wanted. Hold our magic sword in your hands!'

'No!' said the knight of the Grail. 'I would sooner die than let go of the Sword of Virginity.'

'Pathetic good-for-nothing! You do not know about the hundred thousand advantages of the sword of peace! A woman gives a man strength. Lust feeds the brain. Libido is spread by astral-mental bodies and grants a person infinite power over the whole of creation. The sword of peace can make a person into a god!'

'Away, you abominable shadows and tempters! The Sword of Virginity returns a person's divinity to him and makes him all-powerful. All I need is the Sword of Virginity, which was given to me by Queen Guinevere, in order to defeat my enemies. With it in my hand I can sit on the Siege Perilous for a thousand years, and no evil power will take hold of me. Armed with the Sword of Virginity, I can win a thousand battles. I can take on thousands of black knights single-handed and they will not be able to lay a finger on me. They will let me pass by undisturbed, just as the thirty monks in the Chapel Perilous allowed the great Lancelot to pass by.'

*

I am bringing these little scraps from the table of the mystical meal to you in order to ignite your love for the Holy Grail, and so that you might set off in search of it like the knights and the myrrh-bearing women from Arthurian times. Saddle the white horse of Christ's truth (a symbol of the messianic dynasty) and arm yourself with the Sword of Eternal Virginity. Bow to Divine Wisdom, just as Sir Lancelot bowed to Queen Guinevere, and the Siege Perilous will gladly pass you by.

*

The castle of Korbenic presented one of the trials on the way to the Grail. Lancelot hurried there to rescue an innocent girl who had been captured and savagely tortured. The cosmic witch, Morgan le Fay, cast a spell on her to make her boil in a pot. This beautiful girl could only be saved by the best knight in the world.

Lancelot was led into a room in the tower, which was as hot as an oven. It was like the fires of hell! What could this be, if not the heat of human lust and the underworld come to life? Inside, Lancelot saw the most beautiful maiden. She lay there, naked and groaning. Her body was in the languor of death. Lancelot was protected by his vow of eternal virginity – neither the evil spirits nor the nakedness of the martyr affected him. Courageously, Lancelot approached the naked girl, took her by the hand, and saved her from her terrible suffering.

After having struck down the thirty inquisitors and defeated the lying whore in the Chapel Perilous, Lancelot went on to vanquish the terrible serpent which dwelled in one of the chapel's dungeons.

The serpent was terrible indeed. This was not so much because of its enormous size, its threatening appearance, its fiery jaws and so on. It is frightening to think that serpents dwell amongst Roman tombs, full of vampires from Catholic churches. On one of the tombstones, Lancelot read an inscription in gold letters, 'A leopard of royal blood will appear in this place. It will vanquish our serpent and then give birth to a lion whose purity and strength are without equal on this earth.' Lancelot is known as the 'Leopard of royal blood', and the 'white lion of perfect purity and supreme strength' is his son, Sir Galahad.

Lancelot lifted up the tombstone, under which lay the relics of the saints before him. Flames of fire flared up from the underworld and a terrible serpent appeared and it set upon him at once:

'How dare you lift off this stone? This is a sacred place!'

'A 'sacred place'?' said Lancelot. 'What are these relics worth if they are guarded by an evil snake and the fires of hell?!'

With these words, Lancelot stabbed the monster in the heart. At that moment, King Pelles entered the chapel, which had now become the chapel of the Grail. Pelles was the father of the beautiful Elaine, lady of the White Castle, and a close relation of Joseph of Arimathea, the secret disciple of Christ. Then Lancelot's heart stopped! Into this chapel, once known as Perilous, which he had won over, the Knight of the White Castle brought the Most Sacred Holy Grail.

The king, the knights and maidens, knelt before it and began to pray fervently. A dove flew in through the window, carrying a golden incense burner in its beak and spreading its fragrance all around, as if all the graces of the world were united as one in it.

A beautiful maiden brought in the Grail – apparently the Most Pure Virgin Mother. In her white hands she bore a vessel of pure gold. King Pelles and his knights entered the Holy Being and their hunger was sated by the Grail.

We may stop at this victory of the Grail over the cursed shadows of the old civilization. The Chapel Perilous had ceased to exist. The serpent had been defeated. Saints now dwelt in the church. Legions of those who were now devoted followers of the Most Pure Virgin of the Grail, carried in the miracle-working Vessel, and a never-ending trail of pilgrims made its way there.

Anyone who drinks from this Chalice just once will know a life of love and will die in love. Then he will live forever in the blessed kingdom of the saints.

04.07.2005 Deris Island

Postscript

There Is No Other Way to Be in Love Except Being in Virginal Love

Virginal love. It can be described as being sent down from heaven and reflected in the mirrors of the Kingdom.

Virginal love reigns in heaven. The commandment from the Torah 'Thou shalt love the Lord thy God with thy whole being' and 'I will show steadfast love to a thousand generations of those who love me', is not really a faithful or adequate translation of the love of those who are in love with the Most High. The word love, as so often used, is trite and worn out.

The Saviour loved his Father so much that, when He was dying on the cross, He did not ask to be freed from His suffering. Instead, consumed by the greatest holy passion, He exclaimed, 'It is consummated!' and 'Father, at last I will rest in Your arms forever'.

He was in indescribable, divine and supremely blessed love with the Father. The flame of this love was kept burning constantly. It could not be extinguished by torment on the cross, crowns of thorns, humiliation, isolation, never-ending holy passion, terror, fear or anything else.

When Christ professes that He is in love with human souls, this innermost profession reveals Him to those whom He loves. From among His followers, He did not seek out those who revered Him, or who recognised Him as a Messiah, a Divinity or a Teacher, as has been written in frigid books which have lain for a thousand years in the tombs of Pharisees, including the four books of the synodical Gospels. Instead, He looked for those who were deeply in love with Him. John described himself in his Gospel as the 'beloved disciple'. He was the only one who was in love and he inherited the blood line of Christ – a race of immaculate ones and the messianic dynasty together with Joseph of Arimathea. Of the twelve apostles, only one loved Him with a profound love, although they were all prepared to die a martyr's death for him.

*

The Inquisition forbade being in love, as if it were a sin, just like fervent love. They wanted to extinguish the flame of love inside the heart and to kill from within.

The censorship of the Inquisition, which for thousands of years has dictated what Christians should read and what they ought not to know has ruthlessly destroyed all trace of being in fervent, profound love with Christ. It was this romantic and fanatical love for Christ, which gave life to the myrrh-streaming relics of Catherine of Siena, Teresa of Avila, Bridget of Sweden, Luisa Piccareta, Blessed Eufrosinia, our own mysterious Mikhail and Ia the Sweetest.

This is a passionate, profound love and a fervent spirituality. Without it, it is impossible to become close to the Holy Being. To be in such profound love is a kind of obsession or insanity. It is not to be found in a passionate, fallen and demonic order, or in idol-worship or fetishes, but rather it is to be found in the highest and most divine ideal.

The religion of the Seraphites is precisely this. The Father is in love with Son, and the Holy Spirit is in love with the Son and with the Father. The three Persons of the Trinity are in love with the Most Pure Virgin, and the Most Pure Virgin is in love with the three Persons of the Trinity. She who is beloved is called the Daughter of the Father, the Sweetest Mother of the Son, the Divinely Immaculate Bride of the Holy Spirit and the Spouse of the Most High in His mysterious Divine Wisdom.

*

The church dismissed being profoundly in love as a charm. It was forbidden to love. Alas, the Greek acclamation 'Axios! Axios!' ('worthy') is only chanted at the ordination of bishops. Christ is 'axios', though, as He gives his followers the last drop, which is heated up to a temperature of five million degrees, during the Eucharist! Axios! He is the only one who is worthy enough for anyone to live for his sake.

You must be profoundly in love in order to take up your cross. You must be profoundly in love in order to desire Him more and more. You must be profoundly in love in order to thirst for Him in the desert even though He sent you to some GULAG for thirty years, exiled in the depths of Siberia with Decembrists, convicts, exiles and criminals, and even though you were locked up with prostitutes and AIDS sufferers.

To be profoundly in love with the Most High is the only thing which befits a person. To be profoundly in love with life and with one's neighbour. To be profoundly in love with our Mother who gave us life. A profound love for a newborn child. A profound love for an earthly and upright father who has given life to his children. A profound love for a blessed mother. A profound love for a friend, a brother or a sister. A profound love for one's beautiful wife and children. A profound love for all those who are suffering, searching and persecuted.

*

Sealing the burning hot divine potential of being in spiritually virginal, profound love, the church of the evil ones welcomed the secretive love. The divine potential had found its sublime outlet into the underworld.

They were so in love with Mammon! They loved their fine pews and their regalia so much and they enjoyed their bureaucracy and lording over the people. They loved their five hour-long services, their hypnotic effects, their singing like birds, their Hail Marys full of grace, their magic and their mysteries. They loved their churches and their institution.

Christ did not manage to spread Himself amongst His disciples, by means of this profound love – instead the devil spread himself among them. The devil secretly spread himself around through paedophilia, homosexuality, alcoholism, sadism, masochism and the Inquisition. Like Gogol's Akaky Akakievich, they liked to record the letter of the law in neat handwriting. They loved to follow it literally. They were in love with their righteous dogma, their order, and adherence to the law.

A hundred volumes would not be enough to show the ugly, inhuman nature of this superficial love and the sowing of the devil's seed amongst those who reject being in passionate, spiritual, profound love. But for the Seraphites, other kinds of love are out of the question. The cold-hearted reject them outright like a cold-blooded serpent, or a tortoise hiding under its shell.

*

To the world, virginity is 'sanctimonious', stupid, nun-like, eccentric, cold-blooded and frigid. Passionate love is about having affairs, or one-night stands, and is associated with sin.

So how is it possible to reconcile heavenly virginity and earthly human passion?

Does humanity know that the holy pollen, the holy of holies, and the most priceless of all treasures (the Lord would speak about this today at his Second or 2002nd Coming) does not sleep, but spreads its radiance around the world like hidden relics? However deeply the holy pollen of the Most High has been buried by modern humanity, who follow each other like sheep, it will make itself known. It will somehow be brought into the open. It will be apparent in peoples' faces. It will even permeate perverted passion or drunkenness. It will even be apparent in the clumsy person who cut his hand on a tin can, or in a sadist, a drug addict, or a teenager blowing his brains out with heavy metal rock.

Oh! There is nothing else but profound love. This person is ready to be driven insane, to leave the normal world behind, to go out in search of victory, and to be tortured for the sake of the Most High, for his faith, for his king and country, for his family and loved ones, or for anyone in need. He is prepared to forgo justice and to give his life for those who are hurt. He will do anything except remain in this religio-psychiatric rut and this frenzied, eternal and deathly dream.

I can see the phenomenal potential of virginal, profound love! I predict that, at first, it will seem unattainable. Thousands of doubts will begin to appear, such as: whom do I love profoundly? Is it the invisible Divinity, a telegraph pole, a theological ideal, a photograph, the deceased blessed Mary of Heavenly Kindness, or the blessed Ia?

Stop. Is it only possible to fall in love with those who are dead?

Stop, I say, my Seraphite children. Fall in love purely and virginally. Preserve your virginity, and only then can you light the eternal flame of profound love. Do not seek profound love first and then virginity.

We are in the Kingdom. No-one takes husbands or wives in heaven. There is no other love except virginal love. If heaven was ruled by those who are coldly calculating and bookish, rational vampires and inquisitors, not one lamp would be lit in the lamp-lit procession. Not one of the wise virgins would have oil in her lamp. In the parable about the virgins filled with Divine Wisdom, our Saviour reminded His disciples to look after their lamps and ensure they have enough oil, meaning that the Kingdom requires lamps to be lit all the time.

There is nothing along the lines of silent prayer or the 'Phos Hilaron'. The Kingdom is filled with the tender, divinely passionate state of eternal profound love. You must believe in its power to work miracles. Through it comes a love for the cross. Through it come the fearlessness of a knight and the readiness to leave this world.

Being in love supersedes fears and norms. Being in love

conquers inherent programming and curses. Profound love rises above the world order and towards heaven. The gates of heaven are opened to those who love and they 'do not notice the passing of time'.

First of all let us recollect that holy Wisdom is divinely and profoundly in love: this is Her nature. It is the Queen Mother who is filled with holy passion. The supreme and insane love in Her soul causes Her to constantly conceive without sin. The 12th chapter of the Revelation of John says of Her that 'and being with child, she cried travailing in birth: and was in pain to be delivered'.

Being divinely and passionately in love comes before the divine letter, which is the sacred scriptures in tongues of fire, the Gospel of the Saviour-on-the-Blood, a letter written in blood rather than ink, the *akathists* of Saint Maximus the Greek who was hidden away in a Josephite monastery for 20 years and who wrote not in ink or even in coal on a wall, but with his own blood.

A person who is in love will become greater than himself. He will forget himself. His gaze will be focused on a point somewhere between divinity and humanity. A Seraphite loves the Most High and, through Him, the whole of creation. God and man are like one to him. He has been joined and mingled with his Divine Beloved. Now, he is joined in union with the whole of creation, by means of integrated and transparent bodies, and his spiritual robes are decorated with thousands of small crosses on behalf of this union with creation. What is this? He is not afraid of suffering. To be in love means to conquer pain.

*

There is not one saint among the Pharisees. The 500-year history of the Josephites has not produced a single true emissary from heaven for one reason: the flame of the heart has been extinguished and profound love has been outlawed. However, monks were forbidden to bathe together with young novices. The sharp eye of the Inquisition was on the watch to make sure that there was no possibility for profound love to appear.

Then, like Dostoevksy's character of Smerdyakov, they gently, tenderly and sentimentally began to fall in love with the Vespers, the Troparion or some saint or other. Or they listened attentively to some priest's sermon, reminiscing about some mythical time. Or they tenderly kissed the fat hand of some archbishop. Or they tenderly watched some fat villain who was short of breath. Or they fell madly in love with some dead saint so much that they travelled from somewhere in Alaska to the provincial town of Assisi in Italy just because that is where the sarcophagus containing the relics of St Francis is kept.

A person will go mad in his own way if he does not know that certain gates are sealed shut to him. These are the gates of divine and virginal, profound love. Without them, though, there can be no faith, no Christ and no Torah. Nor can there be any Gospel, any road to the Kingdom, any life with the Most High or any spiritual happiness. There is nothing.

Love Christ, Mary, our fathers and the church with a virginal love. Then, from the bounteous treasury, you will be given a love which is not damaged or worn out. A love for Christ will make you love all of Christ's creation. I only ask one thing of you: when you are in love, do not let your love fade.

Pentecost, with its tongues of fire, can be seen as the eternal grace of profound love, which was sent to the apostles to help them preach the Gospel of the Kingdom in the third millennium.

Without profound love there is no Holy Spirit, because, according to the Gospel, the Holy Spirit is the Bridegroom. This brushes aside any doubts as to whether one who falls in virginal love can fall for charms.

We must begin with the fact that the Divinity, in whom we believe, is profoundly in love. This is not a fabrication and it is not taken from any dubious sources. It is taken from a trustworthy source thousands of years old – the Torah. It is taken from its central covenant, and from the name of names of the Most High: I am El Kanna, or a Jealous God. I am in love to the point of madness. It will take all of eternity to reveal the full extent of my love over thousands of generations.

May this eternally regenerating covenant be sealed in your hearts. May it be inscribed in you and in the whole of creation.

18.06.2005 Deris Island

***

How can it be possible to be united with Him without being in love? How is it possible to overcome countless obstacles without the sacred advantage of being in divine love?

This is the first commandment in the Kingdom of the third Person of the Holy Trinity (the Holy Spirit). It appears in the Old Testament as 'love with all your heart' and in the New Testament as 'I give you a new commandment: love one another as I have loved you' – madly, piously and eternally.

Satan pressurises the feeling of being in love, be it in a gay club, a disco or a casino, or indulging in acts of abomination, with passions running high and to the extreme. You must love the Most High in secret so that hatred is exposed. That is why He spoke about those who love and those who hate. He did not mention a third group.

*

Because to be in love means to know no bounds, this profound love leads to eternity. To be in love means to get the key to eternal life.

*

Not one of us could make a single sacrifice if we were not in love with the Most Pure Virgin and if we were not still burning with this profound love to this day.

The Queen of Heaven is grateful and rewards those who have a burning love for Her. Her loved ones are so grateful. She protects those who are in love with Her!

18.06.2005 Deris Island

The clock of the Grail showed the time remaining until the coming of Christ. The brides in the lamp-lit procession checked their lamps for Him, to make sure they had enough oil.

*

Now we come to one of the stunning revelations of this journey.

A person changes so much when you look at him through the enlightened eyes of the Grail! He is adored, deified, divine and beyond angelic.

How wonderful it is to find enlightenment through love! Insanity, connected with lust and madness and disguised as love, is the fetish of generic obsession. Enlightenment, on the other hand, is connected with pure, virginal love.

In general, it is only possible to speak of love after becoming a virgin, progressing to the level of warrior-knight or bride. This is preceded by constant temptation. In the world it is believed that love comes together with libido and lust, and that therefore it is aroused by eroticism. This is not the case at all! Beyond this slavish, torturous love, there is a different kind – virginal love, in which the *dabak particles* are inflamed and the flame of eternal virginity is lit.

How humanity yearns to achieve supreme love! They seek it in eroticism, virtual reality, adventures and so on.

A person reveals himself before the Most High when the siren of love begins to blossom within him. Then he will be imbued with the sweet fragrances of the kingdom, he will be at peace, and he will be made beautiful. First, though, all his sins must be purged, his inherent programming must be removed, he must find inner peace, he must make the necessary sacrifices and he must be completely consecrated and anointed. His soul is set on the path towards serving his neighbours and is freed from the drugs of egotism and narcissism.

These are the steps in preparation for divine, profound love. Only then will the true Christ be revealed – not a dark authority obsessed with sin, but the Christ of enlightened confessors, brides and martyrs of the supreme love (virgins).

***

The whole universe is full of divine, profound love. The expectation of the creature waits for the revelation of the sons of God. Only Our Lady of Divine Wisdom is able to proclaim it, though, as She knows the rules for victory over the original curse and over temptation, how to overcome the evil one and how, by undergoing many trials, a person can be crowned victorious.

Without Her it is futile to dare to aim high. She is Divine Wisdom! Day and night, Her praises are sung. She is Shir ha-Shirim, the Song of Songs and the Queen of Supreme Love.

18.06.2005 Deris Island

How the Soul Blossoms in the Grail!

Lord, how the soul blossoms in the Grail! How it is nourished by the kaleidoscope of the Grail, with its rays of sunlight playing on the surface of the Adriatic!

Orthodox Christians go through their own GULAG. They repent, then sin, and then repent again. It is never-ending. It is interminable. It is contempt, loathing, disgust and hatred of oneself. This is the full range of the emotions they experience. This is the best case. The worst case involves malice, treachery, barbarianism, sadism, persecution and murder. Orthodox Institution uses the same Inquisition methods with their innocent flock as those which were used with the saints. They want to open them up to reveal the inside, just like opening a tin with a knife. They want to find something forbidden. Perhaps the person did something, or did not do something. They eternally dig around amongst sins, plunging into inner darkness, and delving into underground stores where it is forbidden to look. The Most High is ready to give them the seal as soon as possible, if only a candle could be lit or a lamp could shine in the underground gloom.

Hail, Queen! Hail, Queen, who rescued us from the righteous hell of the underworld, and from the law-driven Christianity which is worse than Nietzsche's Antichrist.

They invented their law for the sole purpose of killing love within oneself, within one's neighbour, and within the Most High. There was a need for a new law and a new Typikon. The law is the *Second Golgotha* where they nailed Christ to the cross after the Jews. They wanted to make the disciples of the *Anointed* One of them, but only new Jews emerged.

19.06.2005 Deris Island

***

The Roman Pharisees found love to be a stumbling block. They used gentle Christ for profit and they could not fathom the mysteries of the saints. True love is transformed into a deep, burning, profound love and takes on the appearance of jealousy. However, they were jealous Pharisees and they zealously followed the letter of the law. Their Lord told Moses, 'I am a zealous follower of the law'.

Love which is not transformed into eternal and youthful profound love degenerates and becomes nothing more than a cheap thrill.

The Inquisitors are unable to accept the love of the saints they repressed. They cannot. Their cold-blooded hearts of a serpent do not permit these apologists for rational to do such a thing.

The Most Pure Virgin spoke of *Nightingale Mountain*, saying that She met the Lord as if for the first time when He appeared at Ephesus. His love was like never before. After His suffering on the cross in Jerusalem, the Saviour ascended even higher to the throne of supreme love.

Their relationship was that of two divine lovers. Their language was unfathomable. What did they talk about?! What happened between them?! It is unfathomable! Only the Holy Spirit and the Bridal Chamber can help here.

The Gospel of the bridal chamber is not captured in words. It flows 'between the lines' somewhere in the divine worlds. It goes beyond Homo sapiens with his idée fixe concerning original sin.

My Lord! My Lord! I am convinced for a second time, after the mortal passion of the Moscow underworld that bliss is multiplying. It will never exceed itself. You will see. 'Most blessed and blessed of blessed', until the cross is multiplied along with despair, hopelessness and emptiness.

Oh! Divine Wisdom! You reward the *anointed* ones so generously for having successfully passed through their initiation.

19.06.2005 Deris Island

❧

Miracles Come out of Union with the Most High

How can we understand what it is to receive the Holy Spirit ('My mouth is the mouth of the Lord' or as the Most High said to Moses: 'you are My mouthpiece')?

Receiving the Holy Spirit is a sign of the miraculous and incredible entry into union with the Most High and being joined as one with Him. The Eucharist is not yet recognised as a miraculous, glorious union.

El Elyon is infinitely trusting. My goodness, how He gives Himself even to those who are seemingly insignificant! He gives Himself to the dirtiest beggars in a station as well as to sorcerers. He ignores no-one.

A powerful angel stands beside the Grail Chalice in the hands of a priest of Melchizedek. He is capable of throwing an unworthy person a dozen metres with his bare hands, but he never does anything of the sort.

The Eucharist is more than trust, humility, self-effacement, or even love of the Most High. This is His ability, which is blessed by His Divine Wisdom, to be more closely and intimately united than any 'havaim' (a young man in love or a young woman consumed with yearning) could imagine. Seraphites are generally in a state of enlightenment (the opposite of the insanity of constant illumination of the mind through mystical 'bridges'). They continually marvel at the mystery of the coming of the Divinity in man and man into Divinity.

Is the Most High offended as He manifests in creation and is joined with it, forming a unit like in the double hypostatic union of the Son of the Most High? The logic of Aristotelian or Thomist theology does not have an answer to this question.

By penetrating the deepest of human mysteries, and into its Holy of Holies (His ancient dwelling place from time immemorial), the Most High becomes greater even than Himself. He has appeared in a unique and special way through a person. The one who divinises (the Bridegroom) and the one who is divinised (the bride) are completely unique and unprecedented. He carries out something which is not to be found in heaven, on earth or in any other world. It is something which is only conceivable in remote huts or in the Solovki barracks – the unique prospect of *divine union* and the mysterious, yurodivy covenant.

While the priests of the 'church of the former revelation' and of degenerate religions from earlier times discuss the issues of the 'old' and the 'new' testament, the 'first' and the 'second' coming, 'salvation' or the 'judgement over the whole world', cluttering up peoples' minds with distorted views, the Most High is establishing the constant Covenant of Divine Union. He seeks to enter as deeply as possible into the soul of a chosen one in order to become greater even than Himself and to make that person greater than himself.

This amazing transcendence is wondrously blessed and revealed by the Most Pure Virgin. She is the One who unites the Divinity with man, man with the Divinity, the Most High with divinities, and man with man.

Do you want to enter a union, seal the covenant of eternal faithfulness, and enter into a brotherhood or a fraternity? No righteous priest with even the most perfect of rituals can ever replace what Divine Wisdom can do for you, as She is the Mother who can realise the impossible.

What is this holy union? I can tell you that it is greater than simply being joined as one. It is a mutual penetration worthy of the Divinity.

Every being which is joined in union with another being becomes greater than it was on its own. 'We' means much more than just 'I' and 'you' (terms used by the philosopher Martin Buber in his work 'Ich und Du' [I and Thou]).

Why did John of Kronstadt perform endless miracles? He carried them out remotely just by sending telegrams. Thousands of people confessed at the same time and repented, as if they were confessing on their own and in private with a priest wearing a stole. And why did Sergius Stragorodsky or Joseph Volokolamsky never perform any miracles (was it perhaps the miracle of inhuman malice)? Why was Nicholas of Myra called the miracle-worker?

The almost 'charismatic' gift of miracle-working is brought about by the indescribable, impossible, and boundless merging into one, in the covenant of the Most High with John of Kronstadt or Seraphim of Sarov.

It was then that the third Divine Civilization would have come. Three million eternal flames will be lit and will burn constantly for a thousand years...

In the world around us there are more witnesses to the merging of the Divinity with man than it would seem. Is not Mary's Immaculate Conception by the Holy Spirit, which is glorified to this day by the Christian Churches, and which is the First mystery of the classic rosary, just a wondrous sign of the unprecedented, supreme capabilities of humanity? It surpasses itself through Her union with the Most High, which is so profound that the fruit which it bears is the Divine Human Christ, the Son of the Most High, and the King of Israel.

Is the phenomenon of the Divine Human just an ineffable sign of the highest level of fidelity? In what way does the Most High become human and take on the form of an indescribable synthesis in the person of Christ, the Divine human, whilst preserving the two natures which are both 'inseparable' and 'unmergeable'. This represents traditional Christian theology, which is in need of rethinking with regard to the deepest mysteries and reasons).

The Virgin would appear to be an ordinary mortal, born of aged parents Joachim and Anna but in fact Anna gave birth to Her miraculously and immaculately. The Virgin's life is a constant stream of miracles, as recounted in song by medieval goliards, troubadours, minnesingers, wandering minstrels and mystic singers. What kind of indescribable, impossible mystery does the Most High incorporate within a person if the womb of the Virgin can carry His Divine Son! How closely He is united as one!

The Myrrh relics of the blessed Eufrosinia are a living ark. Lord, what else is there? Is this not the ark of the Most High, which was carried into the temple at Jerusalem? Are not the relics of Eufrosinia the Altar of Union? Is this not a sign that the immortal Most High has entered the body of a mortal woman, transformed her and filled her with the joyous oil of the bridal chamber? It is indeed a sign that the saint is now in the spheres of the glorious joy of those who are blessed and have experienced infinite rapture.

Eufrosinia attracted me in her days on earth through the mystery of walking with the Divinity. No, it was more than just walking at his side; it was a mysterious adherence to Him. There is no covenant beyond the ties of the Kingdom of Heaven, the ties of radiance and union with the Most High.

These ties are filled with holy passion which is like chains and weights on their legs. However, there is nothing more blessed than them. The Most High is searching for a bride for Himself in order to perform another miracle with this soul and so be glorified.

Why is it so difficult to grasp the concept of the close, seraphitic adherence of God to man and man to God, which is intended for the new generation?

The curtain is concealing. I would prefer to call it a

smokescreen, a dramatic stunt, or a cheap hallucination designed for the sentimental philistine and vulgar appetites. The concealing curtain (union) was removed long ago! When He rose from the dead, the Son of the Most High tore the curtain between the Sacred and the Holy of Holies. The entrance to the Kingdom was opened up. The distance between the priesthood, which had opened the curtain, and their flock ceased to exist.

The gap has been reopened.

There is the altar, soleas, antimins, panagia, and other sacred objects... Once again, people pray with their eyes blindfolded, as they did in Moses' time. Once again, Paul bemoans the fall of the church... The curtain has fallen with the Second Solovki, though. There, at Solovki, something has been revealed which was not there before. Myrrh and anointing oil have permeated it and all those who suffer torments worse than anything found in the depths of hell, have been infused with a joy even greater than that of heaven. Such is the Heavenly Father's unique plan for *Divine Humanity*. They gratefully united to the Father Himself like brides to the Divine Bridegroom.

19.06.2005 Deris Island

***

I hereby profess the religion of the Grail:

This is the True Blood of Christ, gathered in the chalice by Joseph of Arimathea, multiplied in the chosen vessels at the Eucharist as Myrrh drops of molten pearls, and the ivory of the Grail in the castles of the Most High, at the feast of the priest of Melchizedek.

This is the Second Solovki, where the Lamb was multiplied in the hundred thousand enraptured, glorified, exalted, incorruptible and myrrh-streaming relics, crowned with great and small wreaths, which lay in the earth.

This is Christ of the Second glorious coming and the Divine Civilization which is His universal creation.

I honour my Queen, Holy Theogamy. I find repose in the

fragrance of the Myrrh scrolls of *Nightingale Mountain* and hope to enter the Ark of the last days and the Bosom of Holy Repose.

I profess the cross by the sword of David and the cross of holy passion by the sword of the Grail.

It is the blood of the martyrs, crucified by the Roman Villain and the Monster of Byzantium, which appears like reviving myrrh inside me. In it, there are 12 immortal bodies and, amongst the compositions transfigured by the Immaculate Conception, is the holy pollen of the Most High, which has been released through the power of the Holy Spirit of the supreme love of the Lamb and of union on the Bridal Bed to Your anointed ones, oh Father of Divine Love!

20.06.2005 Deris Island

***

Christianity preaches the unfortunate idea of the Kingdom 'which is not of this world'. Christ said, 'The Kingdom of the Most High is within you'. The fact that it is not of this world is because it is within us, rather than 'in heaven'. Therefore, traditional Christianity is removed from humanity and has falsely created a distance or a Pharisee's soleas. The New religion of the transfigured Christ speaks of Christ who has entered the inner sanctum of a person and revealed his divine potential.

The apostles of Theogamy have something to say to humanity. Humanity yearns to uncover the divine potential within itself, which has now been revealed by the Queen of Heaven on *Nightingale Mountain*. At that time, She proclaimed: 'Just as I invited the apostles here at the time of the Assumption in order to proclaim the mystery of the Resurrection to them, so too, 2000 years later, have I invited you in order to anoint you in the mystery of the Brida Bed of the Assumption and to see you from now on as apostles of the new faith – Theogamy'.

This faith lies in entering the inner sanctum, releasing the stores of heaven, melting the inner pearl, drinking from the Chalice of the Grail, and union and synthesis with the Most High. The mysterious Bridal Bed is at the centre of this religion of the future.

Then we will have something to tell people! A person's soul is focused when there is a Revelation. Something new is being revealed: the adherence of man to the Most High and the releasing of the divine potential within him. Then the apostle seeks the man and the man thanks the apostle.

Christianity bases its religion on a love for cults, catechesis and candles. On Nightingale Mountain the Queen of Heaven established a new Christianity. But within contemporary Christianity, it is impossible to love the Most High, one's neighbours, or oneself in the Lord. 'Thou shalt not love'[11] would seem to be its fundamental commandment.

Is it possible to love whilst serving Mammon? Long ago, institutionalised Christianity made a clear distinction between 'us' (institutionalised faiths, Catholics and Orthodox Christians) and 'them' – the others which were heathen. You only need to be a Christian to immediately feel the distance between yourself and the world. You belong to a particular caste of the Catholic or Orthodox institution. The rest of the world is full of 'devils', 'heathen', etc. You immediately become a bearded Pharisee or a sickly sweet person with a fat face.

*

The following is the fragrance of the good news of the divine potential...

The Most High has abandoned the old church. Do not have any concern about it! The priests of Melchizedek has gone out into the world. Theirs was the light of heaven and the staff of miracles. Their faces were radiant. Their gospel is that of the inner temple. Christ and the Divine Mother are of the Parousia (they are ever-present). They bring the fragrance of the spheres

[11] Do not love the world or anything in the world (1 John 2:15).

of prayer and the Word. Eufrosinia is of the Parousia. Eternal holy passion is that of the Parousia, as are the oil of myrrh and the Holy of Holies. The whole world belongs to these priests.

With the Pharisees there are only barriers, nets and alienation. There is emptiness behind the facade. There is only a desolate wasteland for an endless crowd of people. It is strewn with litter and goodness knows what. A lone bishop sits like a bald wolf on a pile of stones in his princely chambers, looking into the distance through the wolf-like eyes of the Mafia, whilst biting his lip as he recalls something. He is needed by nobody.

There are chapels, tombs and concrete churches... The saints have been driven from their huts. What is the point of the Aristotelians and the wise eunuchs? The Psalms of Saint Eufrosinia has been replaced with computers and television screens playing their theological pornography.

The terrible truth (of which everyone, from the top, to a simple, deluded, 60-year-old nun, is afraid of), is that the Most High has abandoned the Roman Curia. The Roman harlot has been given a dose of deadly poison. However, the dragon in its dead throws is particularly dangerous. Its fiery jaws produce a poison which is twice as deadly and can poison a knight of the sword of David if he celebrates his victory prematurely.

Lord, there are so many angels heralding the good news from the army of the Archangel Gabriel! The evil villains and magicians of the Psalter know the Archangel Michael and his army. Gabriel is the messenger of the Eternal Gospel and the never-ending Revelation. Gabriel, like Michael, is born out of Divine Wisdom. His army is no smaller than that of his powerful brother, the archangel Michael, to whom now belong many of the cohorts of the Heavenly Host and of the Lord of Hosts.

How many heralding angels accompany those who spread the good news! How do they spread the news? They spread it through letters of fire, myrrh from the heart and the lamp of the soul. Just one enlightened, peaceful and radiant glance is sufficient to reveal the divine potential.

*

'Auntie, something has scratched you on the chest!' (said a five-year-old Seraphite to a nudist on an Adriatic beach).

She wanted to release her divine potential, but she built a throne to an idol from within her breast. She idolised a demon. Her worn out heart slept. Most frightening of all, though, are the sorcerers... They are like a candle which has been blown out: its wick continues to give off a pungent aroma. There is no strength to light it again. One thing remains: the silent stench in a cell accompanied by silent, partly meaningless prayers and outdated rules. So she has become like a dreamy sleepwalker. 'I have lost my mind' (an old woman in confession).

However, as our radiant Lohengrin of Solovki, knight of the Holy Grail, said, the Lamp of the Soul gains its advantage by killing serpents, so that they do not crawl into the radiant light, open their jaws or lay their eggs. According to serpents, the lamp of the soul 'turns a blind eye' towards evil, sin and the deadly plagues of the evil one. It is as if our enemy – the father of lies, allows all kinds of abomination and is free to do as he pleases. Here is the breeding ground for sentimental murdering executioners, jealous people, and Cainites, with their 'everyone is a prophet!' and 'back to Egypt to the holy fathers!' Ironically, it is from Egypt that their 'holy fathers' came.

20.06.2005 Deris Island

***

The Grail is the vessel of the love which is neither of heaven nor of this world. So the Divine Mother has conquered the underworld. This is why Christ, too, descended into the underworld. Only love can defeat the underworld. The internal underworld of the human soul can only conquer with the strength of the love which is neither of heaven nor of earth.

22.07.2005 Deris Island

***

In order to be deified, it is necessary to worship the Lord. You must love Him with all your heart. You must love Him to distraction, just as He deserves. People worship themselves, their relations, the devil or anyone they like. That is why their destiny is emptiness.

23.06.2005 Deris Island

***

Oh My throne of unspeakable mysteries!
Grant me Your blessing, oh Blessed Lady.
Sing, sing, messenger of the Most Pure One! Sing, sing!

There is not one world superpower which would not adopt expansionist plans, such as Russia, the USA, China, and the European Union. The Queen has put Her angels everywhere and blesses the peacemakers with a green olive branch in their hands.

May the peacemakers of the Most High be granted the most fragrant peace. Amen.

*

The mind of a prophet is revealed, and all the mysteries of the Most High have been revealed to the prophet. In front of him there is a book of dates, times, people, names, events, plans, programmes, changes, crowns, creations of the Most High, and His incredible victories over the devil. The Lord's triumphs have become ever greater over time. The greatest victory will be the last, which will be at the end of time. It is as though the devil is just about to triumph with his satanic civilization which is almost complete, when all his plans suddenly collapse. All his work is immediately reduced to smoking ruins.

The Most High knows how to do this. He may only have one method at His disposal, but this is enough to destroy all the plans of the evil one, all his multi-faceted, cunning schemes, insidious thoughts, and so on.

*

Prayer:
The Grail of the sea is both victor and king.
The Grail of the sea is the banner of the Most High.

This prayer is heard by the fish of the sea.
The Grail of the sea is the guardian of mysteries.

*

After the revelation on a mystical hill covered in grey stones near the sea, immersion in water is accompanied by the prayer, 'I am a sacred Fish of the Grail', to the mind which has been revealed.

This is an amazing mystery. The earth would do well to imitate the sea. The mysteries and laws of the sea are greater than those of humanity. The sea is full of evil, cunning monsters, but they only have power over certain species of fish. If fish had shields and bore a certain mark, not one predator would be able to get anywhere near them. The laws and the marks of purity occur much more frequently in the sea than on land. If those who dwell on land knew the power of the shield of primordial purity and the protection of the Most Pure Virgin, they would be invincible when faced with behemoths, leviathans, sharks and other predators with their crocodile jaws and spikes.

The law of purity reigns in the depths of the ocean. The inhabitants of the sea seek protection from the Mother-fish against a host of marine powers. They honour the Virgin Mother like the Mother-fish who brought Ichthus – the Christ-fish – into the world.

When Christ went to the bottom of the sea and preached in the White Castles under the water, He amazed all the inhabitants of the sea. Never before had the King of the *anointed* ones descended to the bottom of the sea. Never before had the elements and the Kingdom of the Sea been so enriched by the great mysteries of Divine Wisdom. The treasury of mysteries had been revealed like an opened ark. Therefore the Saviour prayed at the treasury of mysteries like the high priest at the ark in the temple of Jerusalem. Then, from the mysterious pearl of the Grail He made a scattering of pearls for the fish. Thus, as they swallowed the pearls of the Grail, the fish were transformed into holy priests of the kingdom of the sea.

Those who dwell on the land must be filled with such awe in the face of the wisdom of the sea! Such virginity! Such beauty! Such wisdom! Such perfection!

The sea is one of the twelve immortal bodies. It is followed by those of light, strength, air, the ether, the Eucharist, and sound (as an inside the sea shell).

23.06.2005 Deris Island

***

The key to victory in battle is not to cross paths with the dragon of sin. As soon as it touches you, it will kill you. The True Church does not fight its battles with hymn books, bowing and scraping, curses and exorcism, but rather with the unprecedented rapture in the new spheres, which are inaccessible to the evil one. In fact, the spheres are immaculate and he is not permitted to leave his greasy fingerprints on the spotless clothes there.

24.06.2005 Deris Island

***

How is it possible to be attracted without being in love? How can countless obstacles be overcome without being consumed by divine, profound love?

This is the first commandment in the Kingdom of the Holy Spirit, the third Person of the Trinity. It combines 'love with all your heart', from the Old Testament, with 'I give you a new commandment: love one another as I have loved you', from the New Testament, to form something beyond reason, sacred and eternal.

18.06.2005 Deris Island

***

We are to ascend to the heights of purity and never come back down. From these lofty heights of virginity and virginal love not one blow from the devil can be sustained.

A pure mind excludes all visions of sin and darkness. Repentance begins with tenderness in the form of opening up the heart and thirsting for inner change. Repentance without a desire for change and without the revelation of an appropriate enlightened ideal is like a barren fig tree. The Jews at the time of the First Coming of Christ did not know of the triad of repentance: *metanoia,* the image of perfection and penitence.

*

I love the old tarantass[12],
In it I will sing a Parastas.
I will sing the service of the dead,
As I gaze out of the windows.

*

Just as a person can have perfect pitch in the musical sense, it is also possible to have perfect pitch in the spiritual sense: the ability to hear the voice of the Most High. Others have a relative ear. There are souls who have perfect spiritual pitch.

*

There can be no Christianity without the all-consuming love of holy passion. The religion of the divine King of the anointed ones will lead to other practices and schools. Without virginal love and a heart which is set on fire, it is not possible to receive the Holy Spirit – you will remain an outsider, on the periphery, second-rate and 'in the shadows'.

24.06.2005 Deris Island

***

Oh, it is so important to follow the will of the Most High!

Something reached out to me from inside the box of Catholic graces, when the blessed 'Ave Maria', dressed in white robes, was revealed to me after reading Stefano Gobbi. Mother Eufrosinia anointed me with holy oil according to the Orthodox custom... The ecstasy of *Nightingale Mountain*, though, is beyond compare. The anointing on the Bed of the Assumption is unparalleled.

Anyone who is invited by the Most Pure Virgin to come to this mysterious place of heavenly anointing will become a fervent apostle of the Bridal Chamber and a chosen one of the

[12] Old car.

Most High. He will only eb able to exclaim, 'It is indescribable! Such heavenly rapture! Such perfection! Oh! It is even higher than heaven! Such mystery! There is nothing more exalted...'

Whoever worships the Most Pure Virgin, the Mother of *Divine Humanity*, will receive the highest gifts and special mercies. They will also be granted the most important mission of being a messenger bearing an olive branch, the gift of prophesy and other myrrh-anointed charismata for the conversion of mortals. Theirs are the gift of enlightenment and discernment (in order to sort serpents and chaff from the true grain and potential saints). They are granted the gift of healing, finding their way, *metanoia,* the keys to the Kingdom, sceptre, and countless other blessed gifts, free of charge for the sole purpose of enabling their soul to reach the exalted mystery of Theogamy. And they are granted this gift, so that they can sweetly repeat, along with all the other chosen ones of the new Seraphite race, 'I came into this world to stick to the Most High through the suffering of humanity. Amen.'

*

People love those who serve selflessly, and instinctively avoid spiders that draw them into a web of seduction, so that they can be served by people under the guise of pastoral care of the flock.

*

The Queen protects my sacred calm (seclusion), so that I am not distracted by anything unworthy. Without this, there would be so many interruptions to my work. So much poisonous dust must be swept away! There are so many forbidden mysteries which must be penetrated! The microscopic eggs of serpents and flies' droppings must be removed from it with a scalpel!

Oh Queen, how joyous it is to be counted among those who are chosen, and to have said 'yes' a thousand times to your requests! Out of ten who are called (daily work...) only one is chosen. However, he is amply rewarded for his seemingly futile efforts. Lord, such ecstasy reigns in the heavens of the Grail! Every soul is welcomed with such glorious rejoicing on arriving at the bridal chamber! The maidens of the Grail are so truly pure, innocent and unsuspecting. Its knights, the divine children, are so fine and their hearts are so open!

*

The Grail will crush the head of the Roman Harlot. Another Church exists and is filled with a desire to reveal to the world the truth about the stolen goods, she has bought and the trophies stolen by pirates. The white ships which they captured will return to their harbour, with more passengers than ever before. As they sail the seas, the Spanish corsairs and the one-eyed pirates are no longer waiting for them in the castles of the Grail, like religious conquistadors or Jack the Ripper, plundering and sharing out the spoils with the tacit support of the authorities.

*

Only the naïve can separate a mystic vision of the Most High from spirituality. Every revelation of the Most High is a revelation about those around us. Penetrating the mystery of the Most High simultaneously produces the key to the *metanoia* of His flock.

On the other hand, if a spiritual journey is not confirmed through revelation, it will lead to an impasse and fatal errors. A spiritual mentor makes one mistake after another if he is not guided by the Most High and so he degenerates into falsehood.

25.06.2005 Deris Island

***

Often, in the sonorous halls of the Grail, the sound of an oath rings out, joining father with son and son with father in union. 'The cross of the father is the life of the son. The life of the son is the cross of the father.'

Does this need explanation? Certainly.

In the Grail it is taught that the particles of holy pollen (a treasure which was given to Adam at his creation and which was hidden somewhere in the depths of his mystic composition and structure) join father and son perfectly. The fifth commandment of the Law of Moses is written in the heaven of the Grail: 'Honour your father and your mother so that your days may be long in the land that the Lord your God is giving you'.

In the Kingdom, honour is synonymous with union and becoming as one. Succession and inheritance is passed from a father to his beloved son. The father dies in the son (the mystery of union in holy passion) whilst passing on to him his spiritual wealth and treasure. The son serves his father and dies out of love for him. This is the perfect relationship between the Father and the Son in the Holy Trinity.

The army of the Grail is the embodiment of this through a wonderful motto: THE CROSS OF THE FATHER. The son, having been stuck to the father, sees like nobody else, that the 'yoke' of the Kingdom of Heaven handed down by the anointed father IS THE LIFE OF THE SON.

Is this not surprising? The life of the son does not consist of anything of his own; not marriage to a woman (having a family in the normal sense), not a career, not emotional pleasure (an ultimate rejection of his father, nihilism and patricide), but sharing the cross of his father.

The cross of the father is the life of the son. Did Christ not say this before His incarnation on earth? However, the father is obliged to bring his son back from the brink of temptation and share his cross with him.

Both aspects – the sharing of the father's cross (the life of the son) and the sharing of the son's cross (the life of the father) – occur through chaste and supreme love. Chastity is in no way related to erotic, intimate, idolatrous and sublimated love. The libido and its lustful epicentre within a person is a microscopic demon, infiltrated by the devil, which cannot be called love. Libido is lust. The relationship between the Father and the Son remains chaste and forms a model for all kinds of love. The Father's incredible love for His Son knew no bounds.

He loved Him so much that He sent Him to death and resurrection in glory, and raised Him higher than the heavens. The Son so loved the Father that, seeing His suffering, He yearned to share His cross which was the life of the Son.

The relationship between father and son and brother and sister was the invincible power behind the order of the Knights of the Zaporizhian Sich, the Knights Templar, and many other true brotherhoods based on the father-son and son-father relationship. The father is surrounded by loving brothers. Brothers are joined to each other by bonds of *divine union* and share the cross of their father and by this, they inherit his blessing. And that is the treasure of life on earth. True life comes from the father.

This is the teaching of the Grail and it perfectly embodies wisdom which was incomprehensible to the world and left by it.

*

Terra incognita. The world still does not understand the 'promised land' of the chaste and espoused relationship between the Father and the world.

Divine Wisdom is such a paradox! In Russia, where Stalin, the monster and tyrant with moustache, sent the finest and most noble fathers and sons of the Fatherland to their untimely death in concentration camps; in Russia, with its traditional matriarchal tendencies and its more secret and homicidal inclinations, perfectly portrayed in Dostoevsky's novel 'The Brothers Karamazov'; in Russia, where family life no longer exists and where only one in ten families have a father (many people say 'I don't know what it means to be a father and why you need one anyway'); from this same country which has been abandoned by the Most High and by fathers, a new fatherland of fathers and a brotherhood of Serafimov brethren will be born!

Never before has there been such love between twelve people filled with holy passion, with no rights of their own, and who were not even registered citizens – it was as if they had been erased from the surface of the earth or buried alive in a

Siberian permafrost. The love the Serafimov brethren bore for each other was indescribable; with their tears of fervent tenderness it was as chaste as could ever be imagined.

Solovki extend far beyond the islands of the Archipelago. On a universal scale, it has chastened humanity. Suffering has stifled the repulsive demon of complacency and conformity which has always been encouraged by hierarchic priests. Bonds of union between father and son will also emanate from Solovki through their eternal friendship with Christ, their attitude towards the spiritual testament, which became a guarantee of victory over the spirit of the world, and their attachment to the higher mysteries of existence.

Those who have not reached the heights of the Bridal Chamber and the eternal flame, those who have not achieved the state of ecstatic, heavenly rapture, those who have not risen above the established order of the world, will not come to know the Most High and will not know the purpose to which they were assigned long ago.

*

The bonds of virginal love after death are such a relevant theme for the Adamites!

Those who are in love will never part. Their love will only grow stronger until the end of their days on earth, and it will be made complete in eternity. In fact, there is nothing except this love.

26.06.2005 Deris Island

***

In the Grail there is no definitive teaching. However, every mountain, sphere, castle and summit has its own secret entrances.

One version of the story of Mary Magdalene is that Mary gave birth out of unbearable sorrow. There are no words to describe how she suffered on learning of Christ's crucifixion... Anna, the mother of the Holy Virgin was also overcome with the holy passion of grief.

Immaculate children are born in holy passion. They are the fruit of holy passion. Those who are born without the seed of a man are born out of the blood of suffering. Thus, the child Joseph (or as Tristan is described in the legend of Tristan and Isolde, 'The Sorrowful One and the Weeping One') was born out of the suffering of Christ on the Cross, and his mother.

26.06.2005 Deris Island

***

Have you been captured by the Grail? Wonderful! Take a look at yourself: are you ready to take a vow of unconditional and eternal virginity, and to reject all kinds of evil, lust, abomination, deceit, betrayal, predation, corruption, narcissism and sorcery? If there is any kind of lust in your mind, be it written, refined, sublimated or mental, then do not endeavour to approach the Grail. If the infinite potential of eternal virginity has not been revealed to you, you will not be able to go any further than the knights of King Arthur in their fruitless quest for the Grail.

The Grail fulfils the ideal of the Most High and demands absolute dedication. The Sufis or the followers of Krishna are more suited to this than institutional serpents or the half-hearted. In these times of darkness and general corruption, the Grail is nearer than ever. It is ready to welcome those disillusioned thirteen-year-old girls in Sodom, Lesbos or night clubs.

Adorn yourself with the virtue of virginity. See it as a source of all mercy and grace, just like the Grail. Virginity and the Grail are one and the same. Gauge your proximity to the Grail (or your distance away from It) by your readiness to swear an oath of virginity and to see in it the meaning and the source of the Tree of Life.

This is so difficult when surrounded by corruption, eroticism, narcissism, selfishness, nudism etc., and when all around there is the cult of the body, sweaty, naked bodies, Mammon, Eurobanks and so on. However, it is no less difficult to reach the Grail.

Meanwhile the path to the Grail lies through perpetual virginity and the Most Pure Lady who perpetuates it.

26.06.2005 Deris Island

***

Lord, an anointed one is such a marvel! He comes down from heaven. Where will he appear today? Maria Orlovskaya (my godmother) covered her tracks and nobody knew where she was: a monastery in Odessa one day, a secluded place in Kamchatka the next, and in Pimenovsk Cathedral in the Novoslobodskaya district of Moscow the day after.

Today she is setting a sinner on the right path; tomorrow she will join a general in praying for his wife... When an anointed one comes down from heaven, though, he always appears suddenly somewhere in a forest glade, on beautifully fragranced meadow grass, or in a juniper field where sheep graze.

*

What a joy it is to see the Most High in the flesh! Adam's race is divided into those who tremble, those who see firsthand, those who come forth relentlessly, those who walk in the cloud of His Glory, and those who hear and so on, as well as those who are enveloped in sleep, serpents, and those who rely on hypnosis.

25.06.2005 Deris Island

From Talks in the Grail of the Sea

How does the Grail suddenly dematerialise and disappear like a submarine in the depths of the sea? With the help of the Most Pure One. Having taken the immortal and eternal Divinity into Herself, the Queen of Heaven was granted an exclusive charisma. As the first to be divinised, She became visible, was transfigured, and then suddenly disappeared. She was given the gift of the Divinity Incarnate, not just of Christ, but the ability to constant descending- ascending embodiments.

This gift continued during the Lord's days on earth (and in the next life in the Holy Being). With its help the Saviour was able, unimpeded, (through the Parousia) to come to His thousands of disciples, talk with them, work miracles, heal the sick, and leave behind material objects such as crosses, oils, and beads. He blessed, gave communion, and taught as well as if He had been present in the flesh.

The Grail is His True Flesh and Blood, which is enduring and unchanging. It is not only His Blood, but his Flesh too, as the circulatory system is closely linked to a person's spiritual bodies and integrity. Through the immortal Flesh and Blood of Christ, the Most High has announced that He will always be present on earth – until the end of the world and beyond.

In the last days, the True Blood will appear in a special way and will perform miracles.

The Grail dematerialises with the help of the Most Pure Virgin and with the help of Christ. The True Blood possesses the same abilities as the Lamb who bestowed them. Manifesting itself as the throne of the Most High and the divine bliss of the anointed ones, it lingers in the ethereal waves of the fifth dimension. It comes like a revelation, materialising like the preaching of Christ on Spilled Blood (the pre-Eucharistic holy passion of the Lamb can be likened to His three hours on the Cross). Then it is enraptured by Elyon, it appears again, it teaches, it enters the immortal bodies etc.

This is the only way of explaining the mystery of the dwelling place of the Grail in a different world and a different reality, its elusiveness in the world order and its ubiquity and its omnipresence, like the elusiveness of Christ and the Divine Mother. Where is He? Still, He sends the Holy Spirit, lives in our neighbours, embraces the whole of creation, and is more closely united with it than during His days on earth. The Grail enables this spousal union with Christ. It is a token of His presence and His true altar. The saints of the Grail teach that there are no other altars and no other churches except the altar of the Grail and the place where it resides.

The Templars were not really guarding the Temple of Jerusalem, but Monsalvat, where the Grail was kept. By 'Temple' these holy, virginal knights, the greatest angels ever incarnate on earth, were not referring to a stone structure (an imitation of an ancient place of worship), but a tent pitched by holy Wisdom – a white tent housing a radiant chalice. They called it an ark for carrying around the earth and they believed themselves to be priests of Melchizedek and carried out a wondrous rite in the Holy of Holies – the transubstantiation of the chalice from the Grail into silver goblets and a mystic meal at the Round Table.

*

I was introduced long ago to the miraculous, sacred vessel, filled with every kind of grace and mercy. The Grail revealed to me the secret to overcoming our inborn programming, social complexes and suicidal neuroses, as well as the secret of purging the sinful bowl.

My spiritual mother Eufrosinia, my holy mentor in the Grail, was the only person on earth who presented the unique teaching about the path to the Kingdom (= the Grail) as the gradual purging, and eventually absolution, from all sins and receiving the royal, sovereign Holy Spirit.

I was called to the wisdom of the Grail whilst still a babe in arms. I climbed the 150 stairs along the *yurodivy* and unfathomable path. It led me away from Alexander Blok to Tsvetaeva, from Plato to Karl Jaspers, from Kabbalah to Martin Buber, from Meister Eckhart to 'The Secret Doctrine', from Tolstoi to Nikolai Fedorov, from Berdyaev and Shestov to Barsanuphius the Great, Macarius of Egypt and Nil Sorsky, and from them to Stefano Gobbi, Our Lady of Lourdes, Mother Eufrosinia and Louis-Marie Grignion de Montfort. Each of these pearls of the Grail brought its own treasure, which enriched me as one *anointed* in the supreme mysteries, the miraculous vessel filled with true bliss, the fullness of wisdom and 'every kind of grace'.

The Grail is no stranger to all things that are human, whether it is Beethoven's 9th symphony, Schubert's sublime impromptus, Chopin's nocturne № 20, Vivaldi's 'The Four Seasons' or Tchaikovsky's Pathetique symphony. Nor is It a stranger to the yurodivy canvases of Hieronymus Bosch, Bruegel, or the abstruse and shocking paintings of Salvador Dali... One day, Divine Wisdom will say to each of these accomplices of the evil one and Tibetan spies who were hatched from the eggs of serpents, 'Has the time not come to change?' Then, standing on the throat of the snake, it will point authoritatively to the Grail, the highest of mysteries.

I believe that in some time when Salvador Dali, Pablo Picasso, Andrei Voznesensky, Bella Akhmadulina, Anna Akhmatova and Joseph Brodsky will turn towards the chalice, having heard the call of the True Church. Just as a century ago, at the time of my conversion, the intelligentsia was drawn towards Orthodoxy, so now, at the time of its 'reinventing' and its confusion, when it seems as though the dragon with all of its ten heads is prepared to convert to anything, as long as it can stand up to Mammon. At this time of disillusionment and lack of faith in the Vatican, the people are drawn towards the mystery of the Grail. It attracts people in the same way as it attracted the young and noble Perceval on meeting his grandfather, Sir Bron.

*

...Perceval suddenly felt the attraction of the Grail. Sir Bron only needed to mention the Chalice of Christ before Perceval began asking insistently, 'What is that? What is that? Tell me more!'

The Keeper of the Chalice was cured of his ulcerous affliction, the stigmata of the true Christ who had been distorted. The Spirit of Divine Wisdom and the mind of Christ came down onto Perceval, quickly making him pure, chaste, and later the wise keeper of the priceless Chalice, which is more valuable than all the gifts and treasures in the world.

Oh! Sir Bron told Perceval of so many mysteries in their unbroken three-hour conversation! It is as though this conversation had been prescribed by heaven and then written down and preserved in the archives of the eternal library of heaven.

'The Grail has no parishioners, my child. The maidens and the keepers of the Grail have no audience watching from outside. However, as soon as a holy father, a royal knight, a conqueror of the world, or a priest of Melchizedek raises the radiant Chalice, the faces of thousands and millions of suffering orphans immediately appear in the Holy Being. The Grail comes to all those who thirst and gives them something to drink'.

Although the Service of the Grail is beyond the realms of the visible world, it still exists in the Holy Being – that glorious and miraculous place between heaven and earth. When the constant earthly cries of, 'Help! Let me in! Is there anybody there! Mother! Help Me!' are heard, the eternal light of the

Kingdom becomes one with the darkness of the holy passion of hell.

The white screen of the Grail – the entrance to the great hall through a triumphal arch, decorated with lions and carved from ivory – keeps a record of these groans. The writing on the White Screen (cries for help or of all those in the world in a state of holy passion) is transformed by the vibrations of the Bell of the Grail, rekindling its knights' desire to help those who are suffering.

They are not glorious warriors, filled with a mystical strength and helping the weak. No. They are junior christs, untouchable lambs, and can easily be hurt. They take it upon themselves. They come to help wherever nobody else is able to help. They see what others cannot see. They vanquish the enemy and abolish his fatal plans. In their hands they carry the divine key with which they open the countless gates of the Kingdom of Heaven, bringing comfort to all...

My child, do not feel sorry that you are alone in the desert. The followers of the *starets* Hesychius (one of the ancient hermits) were the birds of the air and mountain goats. The old man did not see another person for years or decades. However, thousands of suffering people drank from his *yurodivy* chalice (like a goblet created by nature itself and retrieved from the bottom of the sea).

The priests of Melchizedek love the liturgy in seclusion. They serve on behalf of the Most High – one on one, or in twos or threes, like the ancient cenobitic brethren (although they do not have congregations of thousands). They are not deterred by evil tongues and poisoned arrows. Their shields of heavenly holy passion and divine ecstasy keep them at a distance from the world. Therefore the devil cannot touch them however hard he may try to leave his greasy fingerprints on their spotless skin.

*

Seraphim the Tender of Solovki, with his gift of dwelling in the Royal Holy Being and talking with those, who are in heaven, those who have died, and people from the future, often went into the archives of the mystical library where he read the mysterious scrolls of the Grail, which are written in 15 languages. The educated Russian emperor understood many of these with ease. He understood Old English, French dialects, German, Spanish, Church Slavonic, ancient Hebrew, Greek and so on. There were also hieroglyphics, which he did not understand. The Holy Spirit dictated the contents of this mysterious charter for the Knights Templar. Then, to his joy, having heard about the most complex mysteries of the sacred Chalice, Seraphim was able to assess the level of anointing of his blessed cellmates – the Seraphimov brethren who were carried away to a divine world during the Liturgy of St. John Chrysostum.

The angels of Divine Wisdom essentially taught them the same thing. There was no need to rummage around in historical archives and look for the Grail based on memories, traces or anything else. Seraphim recognised himself as a keeper of the Grail.

The screen, the curtain, the white ivory lion, the swan the colour of mother-of-pearl, the lance with the Last Drop, the sword of David, the funeral stole, white and crimson cloths, the white screen, the bell and so on: symbol after symbol has emerged from the Grail. The Grail was the architect of the White Castle. The knights had no need of the Gospels, mysteries or theology. The true Blood protected them and guided them.

Filled with the Holy Spirit which far exceeded the grace of hermits and elders, the holy virginal knights instinctively felt their dynastic relationship to the Saviour, their involvement in His life, their common blood and the mingling of His Blood with theirs. What else do you need if you have the Most High?

*

The mystery of the Grail is unlawfully sought after by the 'Roman Villain' and the 'Byzantine Monster'. The Sacred Gifts are only truly absorbed among those of the same race, those of true spirit, and the heirs and Disciples of Christ. In other people they remain dormant. Therefore, multi-million gigantomania and regular communion with the empty Sunday bell-ringing ritual is a marketing ploy on the part of the Catholic priests. Only those bearing the mark of the Grail can approach the true Blood of Christ. They may only exclaim, 'This is the true Flesh and the true Blood of My New Covenant' from within the Holy Being.

A true priest does not run a cult like a theatrical spectacle, but rather he inspires his flock with admiration for heaven and leads them to the Holy Being. Then, from the lofty heights of heaven, the voice of the Saviour can be heard saying, 'I never abandoned you because I was present in the Chalice. Those who drink from it will live forever'. His words are echoed in the Eucharistic Gospel, 'If anyone dies, he will rise again. Then I will take him to my dwelling place and to the Bridal Chamber'.

This is the miracle of the Eucharistic troubadour: they sang a song and it was etched on their hearts with a golden cane in such a way that it was beyond all possibility of commentary, scientific study or dissertation. The Divine Wisdom of the Grail was spread through mysticism. It always appeared to simple orphans, widows, semi-literate twelve-year-old girls, or shepherds in Fatima, and spoke of the Other Church, hardly ever crossing paths with Her rival.

*

It is important to introduce the fifth dimension where the perpetual presence and joy are indescribable. It is not possible to experience bliss without the Holy Being. Philosophical, academic paths and the porticoes of the Areopagus are a sorry imitation of the sacred groves of the Grail, where the birds of heaven sing and where the saints dwell along with other beings unknown to the world.

Sacred fish, sacred birds, sacred meals, sacred brethren, the Sacred King Melchizedek, the Sacred Virgin, and so on... Life has been sanctified and transformed into a constant sacred rite. Outside of this, time passes in emptiness and is considered to have 'a negative value' and a sinful nature.

*

The three secrets of the Most Holy Divine Mother are revealed in the Grail.

(1) Mary is the incarnation of Divine Wisdom, the Mother of the Lord and the mother of spiritual birth. The latter is particularly honoured.

Chivalry arose out of worship for the Eternal Virgin. It is actually a vow to serve Her, and to join Her host on earth and in heaven. Love for the Most Pure One requires total sacrifice. If a knight is always prepared to stand up and give his life for a beautiful lady, then how much more fervently ecstatic is the chivalry of a knight of the Grail, if his Lady is the greatest Lady of all, the Queen of Heaven!

A warrior must be disciplined in order to avoid making mistakes. He is jovial, does not avoid humor, is always in a good mood, strives for perfection, and is not so much ashamed of sin and Divine punishment (obsession with sin is foreign to the virginal robes of the Grail), as of making clumsy mistakes in front of his Lady and thus disappointing Her.

(2) The greatest love, profound love for the Most Pure One, and worship greater than that with which She is honoured in heaven, lead to another mystery of the Grail: The Most Pure One reveals the life-giving Heart of Christ dwelling within Her as the personification of the Tabernacle of the Covenant, and love for Him.

The knights love Christ like a bridegroom loves his bride, like a son loves his father and more besides – more than themselves and more than anything on earth. They know His holy passion and his fervent love with every cell of their bodies and they respond to Him in the same way, through self-sacrificing service, living and dying for His sake.

(3) The third joyful mystery of the Grail is the love for humanity. It namely gives the state of constant ecstasy. The knights constantly love souls from their divine perspective and their undiscovered potential gifts. They see people through the eyes of the Most High and profess an equal love for the Most Pure Virgin and Christ, as well as for the Most High and His creation. In the Grail it is said that, 'love for the Most High is confirmed by love for one's fellow man' and there is no need for other measures to determine whether faith is sincere and true. Sincerity of faith cannot be determined through dogma and belonging to a religious institution. It is enough to watch how the faithful relate to their similar ones or other sons of men in order to draw a conclusion about the greatness of such mystery as faith or love for the Most High.

Christ, the myrrh-anointed, consecrated King of the Grail, spoke of this when He said, 'whatever you do for one of the least of these brothers of mine, you do for Me. I know of no other judgement over you. A person judges according to his love for his neighbour (through the eyes of My love).'

27.06.2005 Deris Island

***

Joseph the Magnificent was a virgin, as were the twelve kings of the Grail after him, who were conceived immaculately of Christ and the Virgins of the Grail; the myrrh-bearing virgins who had taken a vow of eternal virginity. Then, from them came the Royal Messianic Branch (Dynasty).

*

The revelation of the True Church of the Messianic Dynasty of Christ heralds the beginning of the Divine Civilization. The ark of the last days will come out of the true church which was previously kept hidden. Its purpose is to drive out the adulterous harlot and establish the Kingdom of Christ. The saints who have come down from heaven, and whom I have seen on more than one occasion, are the Messianic Melchizedek Dynasty of the immaculately conceived sons and daughters of Christ. They are the sons and daughters of the Bridal Chamber.

*

The Pharisees' restrictions have been penetrated: 'This is Our Race', said the Divine Mother, when She appeared to Seraphim of Sarov, i.e. to the Messianic Dynasty.

Eufrosinia never tired of saying, 'we are His spirit', 'the spirit of the Lord' and 'the true spirit'. By 'true Spirit', mother Eufrosinia meant the spirit of the Dynasty of Christ – the mysterious, inner mystical kingdom, which was kept under cover, beyond external objectification, materialisation and blasphemous distortion.

*

There is a direct connection between the Immaculate Conception of Christ and His coming down from heaven.

Melchizedek, the priest who came down from on high and returned to heaven, when he had completed his mission, was immaculately conceived. So, too, Christ, who came into the world in the same way as the Seraphites (through conception by the Holy Spirit), was given by Divine Wisdom in order to become the origin of a new humanity, i.e. to immaculately conceive, by Mary Magdalene, an *anointed* king, the founder of the new Messianic Dynasty of Junior Christs. From that time on there were no less than twelve immaculate conceptions in the castles of the Grail amongst the Royal Dynasty, including the royal families of Europe.

However, this true history of Europe and of humanity has been erased by the villains of Rome and Byzantium; by the catho-yogi, who practise mortification, and the byza-yogi who practise self-harm. Above all, their practices involved destroying the saints and, in particular, Christ, together with any signs of His presence, every day for two thousand years. For some reason they have not mention this.

The Virgin Mary conceived easily. The woman crying out with the pains and suffering of childbirth (Rev. 12:2) means that the Immaculate Conception of the messianic heirs to the throne occurred in the throes of holy passion: the most painful labour of love. This involved a mortal grief for the Heavenly Beloved, which is the highest state of holy passion (as with the mortal grief experienced by Mary Magdalene when the Lord was arrested in the Garden of Gethsemane).

*

The European monarchs knew that the miraculous and powerful Grail was the key to the strength and the flourishing of their states, as well as to the power of the monarchy. Thus, they sought the Grail as far as they were able, and they strove towards the truth.

To search for the Grail is to search for its secret messengers who manifests yurodivyly.

27.06.2005 Deris Island

***

Nightingale Mountain, the bed of the Assumption of the Most Pure Fifteenth Gospel, moved me completely but somehow left me in a quandary. What exactly is the Altar of Union? How was the Lord united with the Virgin Mother? This is the revelation of the second Immaculate Conception. Just as Mary Magdalene was joined in union with Christ and conceived Joseph, so He joined in union with the Blessed Virgin.

Only Mary gives birth in the Holy Being to souls with the mark of immaculacy on their foreheads. Thus the Messianic Dynasty is perpetuated through both Christ and Mary.

*

The Grail remains hidden from the world even though it is clearer than anything else, because the path of divine love requires extensive trials and preparation. For those souls who are not sufficiently prepared it is a temptation and a short cut into the kingdom of the devil, who also teaches of love, but in his own way.

Without this, the Grail would be intercepted. Therefore, in order not to be forever intercepted, the Kingdom of supreme love prefers always to remain hidden from onlookers. However, whenever an anointed one is found who is capable of mastering its language and climbing the stairs, it immediately reveals itself to him. Then it assigns the inner chalice, after which the ascent to the Grail begins.

*

This is how Solovki is connected with Nightingale Mountain and the Grail. It is the great golden solar triangle. Divine Wisdom brought the last Russian Tsar, Seraphim Romanov, to Solovki, where he was anointed Messianic King of the Russian Grail, and where he was granted the Solovki Grail of the third millennium, the heavenly altar of the divine civilization III.

Both the burning hierarchy of the Seraphimov brethren and the church which came out of the Second Solovki, inherited the origin of Christ through the succession of Seraphim, one of the last great Russian monarchs of the messianic dynasty. Seraphim became the second christ of Solovki through the fiery synthesis of his messianic composition.

30.06.2005 Deris Island

***

Christianity does not know Christ... Nor does it know Christianity itself, or about its beginning or end. The beginning of the Gospel story is the Immaculate Conception of the Most Pure Virgin Mother. The continuation of the story certainly does not end with the Ascension. There is also the Immaculate Conception by Christ of the second Christ, Joseph the Magnificent, the sweetest heir of the Messianic Dynasty.

So what does institutionalised Christianity know about Christ and about itself? It knows nothing. It is a degenerate sect of medieval fanatics, focused on the four official gospels and working them to suit the needs of the machine, providing far-fetched guidance for the saints and paraffin candles in exchange for a widow's mite. There are rounded golden domes like the bellies of priests, sorcerers' bells which serve only to make dogs bark, together with ceremonial magic (worse than a magician's tricks) and extrasensory arts. Moreover, no sorcerer or psychic can curse like these serpents in black cassocks. These small fry must learn from the big fat cats, the great cursed ones from long ago who dug their poisonous proboscis into the flesh of the saints and drank their blood, draining the life from them and taking their throne for themselves.

Christ went out among them virtually in vain. He rose, went away, and left them in His place. However it turned out quite differently. He never did go away – He left His Blood, which was collected in the Grail, and He did not disappear without trace. From the divinely passionate Blood of the sun of Golgotha, He conceived an heir by Mary Magdalene. Wondrously, He chose a 'whore' and rejected those who were supposedly righteous. As a result, the authorities of the righteous ones turned into the 'whore' of Babylon, whereas the former prostitute repented and became a virgin anointed with myrrh and the mother of the new humanity. This is so incredible.

On the one hand, the Most Pure Virgin Mother prepared herself to become the Mother of the God-Man, and on the other, a prostitute was purified, *anointed* with myrrh and prepared for giving birth to the son of the Only Son of the Most High. Who, from among the theological ranks, can possibly define the worth of Joseph the Magnificent? Who knows the history of the royal branch which is directly connected to the Grail and which descends directly from Christ? The evil authorities have placed a ban on knowing the truth!..

*

The heavenly sources have scorned the Pharisees for thousands of years. The time has come to reject them and turn to the life-giving scrolls of the Grail. From these come the continuation of the Gospel story. Those who watch, will see the plan of the Most High for establishing the Kingdom of Christ, for His church of surpassing love, for *anointed* ones, and for the knights who lead the fight against the rabble of the Pharisees, the black mass, the black dogs, the red bloody barons who inflict terror on those around them, and the serpents in human form.

The time has come to bathe in the white font and to read the Gospel anew, to see Christ as if for the first time, and to wonder why there had to be two thousand years of outright lies and deception. Some died and some were saved, but the world did not seem to care about the truth. Meanwhile priests came along who served truth and peace. The ultimate truth was not hidden from them. The Lord counted on them, let them dispel the cloud of lies, and reveal Him to the world as He really is. Just as He revealed the Father two thousand years ago, so the Kings of the Holy Spirit and the anointed ones of the divine civilization will reveal Him, multiplied in the thousands of His true disciples.

*

At the beginning of my conversion I saw the endless potential of purification through repentance. Now I see the equally infinite potential of love which reveals a new universe.

*

Sometimes I asked myself, what is the purpose of constant darkness and the concrete tomb. It cannot be penetrated. The Lord releases a special measure of holy passion in order to help a soul to pass more quickly through the trials along the path to the Grail. Then He calls him, so that the flame is not extinguished, wherever he is: in the damp prison, in Solovki, but always by candlelight in dire situations.

Love is unconditional, but the flame must also burn unconditionally. Supreme love is unconditional, in spite of everything. The flame must burn in spite of everything. This is the condition for entering into the inner Grail.

Tristan and Isolde

In the Kingdom of supreme love,
In the white castles of the divine civilization,
In the bridal chambers

Protect, protect
Tristan and Isolde
As they soar in lofty heights.
Below, at the foot of the hill,
Ants crawl about.
The evil ones hold out their basket
Hermetically confined and sickening.
Oh whatever it takes,
Preserve Chrysostom,
Regardless of any slander and blasphemy
Madman, idiot
Or thrice cursed leper.
With a flame burning in the breast
In the darkness of the repose of holy passion.
It is impossible for two to die together out of love
In your embrace I am divinised.
Do not blow out your lamp
I will come in the night at quarter to three.
Do not sleep, let me in.

*

The Grail was the second thing after the Lord to be distorted by the Pharisees and sorcerers, as if it was something cosmic, so that they could bury their heads in the sand having robbed it of its characteristics. The Grail is more than just slandered – it is completely distorted. The sacred vessel is overshadowed by the ghosts of these sorcerers and Pharisees.

Oh, perfect, sacred holiness of Christ! Reveal yourself to the world. Make the disciples of the true Blood of the Bridal Chamber, Your sons and daughters, into noble knights and the sweetest maidens. They can then guard the entrance to your eternal, white chambers, bring anointing oils to all who are suffering and anoint them until their wounds are healed, they have repented and can enter the Sacred White Castle – the path to heaven.

The Second Solovki showed the path to the Grail, which is inaccessible without holy passion (Fr. Paisius).

*

They have an intense hatred of the sacred vessel, the miraculous vessel and its bearers. The Grail cancels out the hypnotic effect of the church. If the chalice of the Lord is preserved, then they are revealed as a band of robbers and thieves (Fr. Paisius).

The Grail denounces them and deals them a crushing blow on the forehead. All around the Grail... His seed is carried by the Women who crushed the head of the serpent. The serpent tried to kill Christ and feed the people with His Blood, but the Lord left behind the sacred Chalice, the divine vessel of the holy passion of His supreme love, the Myrrh origin of the divine civilization. In it lies the salvation of humanity. The serpent's chalice, the chalice of the harlot, is filled with abominations. They hate the Grail because it exposes the fact that their cup is filled with abominations. They have no idea what it is and where it has come from. Is it really possible to go there to receive communion?

The Most Holy Virgin says:

The Glory of Christ lies in His multiplication into a small kingdom of Christs. We need as many of His disciples as possible, who look the same, exactly like Christ. They are from His origin and His race. They have originated from the Grail family and from *Joseph the Heir* – not from Peter who denied Him three times.

01.07.2005 Deris Island

The Fish-Eye Lens of the Grail

I will never forget the eye of the sacred fish which appeared to me in the waters of the Adriatic near the Island of Deris where we spent a wonderful month in the white castle of the radiant medieval knights of the Inexhaustible Chalice.

Whilst performing the sacred ablutions in the waters of the Adriatic Sea, I said the prayer 'I am a sacred Fish of the Grail...' when a priestess of the sea swam up to me and called the same name. 'I am a sacred fish of the Grail!' she said. Before anything else, I felt her gaze with every bone in my body.

Our eyes met. Her gaze was the fish-eye gaze of the Grail.

Such divine wisdom flowed through her! I was literally set on fire. There is not, and never has been, anything like it on earth.

'Such is the eye of the Most High', said the sacred fish, the sea-priestess of the ivory castle.

How great is the divine wisdom of the Most High and how sought after is the eye of the Divinity! It follows me constantly. It is peaceful. It does not stare, it is not like an X-ray, it does not stray into anything forbidden, it does not force its way into the unconscious mind, it does not shame and it does not judge. It is the gentlest and meekest. It bears the mark of an unearthly spiritual superiority and a level of intelligence which is unattainable on earth. It alone surpasses all human knowledge and capabilities. It is always kind and merciful. It rejects the world. Its kindness is not of this world – neither of the land nor even of the sea.

The fish explained to me that the divine wisdom of the Kingdom of the Seas (spheres) surpasses that of humanity. The earth owes much to her. It was simpler for the Saviour to talk with the fish of the sea and with countless numbers of dead people who had descended to the sea bed. Christ often came down with the Most Pure Virgin to visit the Kingdom of the Seas. But more than just Christ! Sovereign Seraphim the Tender, *Innocent Baltski*, Eufrosinia and other saints were revealed to me before my very eyes and were more real than in their physical state.

I saw Eufrosinia more than when I had known her on earth. I did not write about her life so that I could reminisce and grieve; no, no! I wrote so that I could really meet her; see her with my eyes as she is now, and more besides. Perhaps I might sometimes ask for her protection, and maybe, who knows, I might ask her to help me along my way to the Heavenly Grail.

In Sosnovka, during a revelation in the forest on Her radiant throne the Most Pure Divine Mother showed me St. John Chrysostom, transfigured in the rays of the sun – Chrysostom as he is now. I heard liturgical music of indescribable beauty, but... The last sea apparition, the fish-eye, which is the eye of the Grail – known as the eye of the Most High – created the deepest impression and affected me more than anything else. It contains all the Divine Wisdom for the countless souls of the Kingdom of the Sea as well as for those who dwell on the land.

Oh, do not leave me, sacred Fish of the Grail! Help me to swim in the waters of the world's oceans and to find followers and disciples from all over. I am quite lost, oh sacred Fish of the Grail. Allow me to enter a dialogue with you, Holy Priestess.

*

Earlier, during my conversion, I held real keys in my hands. I knew they could unlock the twelve gates to receiving the Holy Spirit in true Orthodoxy and so I bravely entered with them. Like my mother and mentor, the holy woman Eufrosinia, I never doubted the truth; why had I come to Orthodoxy without repenting, receiving the Holy Spirit and experiencing the bliss of the Paraclete? I laboured in vain, 'in sin and in condemnation'.

My hand was firm and everything seemed clear – although

my cross of holy passion was to be an outsider, a parasite, a *yurodivy* and a schizophrenic at the time when I hated the Soviet leadership.

'May the Most High give you the strength to carry your cross', the Holy Fish of the Grail whispered to me, hardly moving her lips and speaking to me with the gentlest vibrations of the sea which I was able to hear.

'Cross?' I exclaimed. 'How does the Kingdom of the Sea know of the cross? The Saviour was crucified in Jerusalem, on Golgotha...'

The priestess of the sea was silent.

The white cross, the sacred and transfigured cross... I saw it, shining throughout all worlds, at the bottom of the Kingdom of the Sea, in the playing of the light on the water and the blinding rays of the Kingdom of the Sea.

'Tremble before the wisdom of the Kingdom of the sea, you land-dwellers and all creatures under the heavens of the Most High! Use the gifts which you have been given to see before you the Kingdom's mirror of the sea, the transparent mirror of the Kingdom of the Sea. The mystery of the sea as the 'reflection of heaven' is only revealed to a very small number of holy hermits, living in the caves of the mountains near the sea. It is revealed to you as a father and King of the Grail.

Those who dwell on the land crucify and desecrate the Kingdom of the Sea. Only the infinite patience of our holy elders and the watchmen of the sea (at the entrance to the ineffable powers of the divine light known as the Sea Castle of the Grail) can withstand the wrath of our sovereign.

Turn, turn your gaze to the heavens. They are beautiful. Look away from the earth more often, from the asphalt jungle and the roads paved with stones and covered with blood. All around are agonising groans from the dying, cries for help from the living and the wailing of the dead... Turn away more often from the things of earth. Drive out the vile beast from within you – your demon. Set your heart on fire and look heavenwards, as it is fitting. My child, is anything preventing you from lying on the Altar of Union and looking up to Heaven?

'Where is the Altar of Union?' I hear you ask. 'Wherever you like: in a hospital bed, by the sea, or on the grass. Lie down on the Altar of Union and nothing can prevent you from contemplating the heavens – if they are revealed', added the Sacred Fish.

'Now, though, my child, make use of the other privilege your have on your four-week stay on the Island of Deris and your frequent visits to the Kingdom of the Sea. Enter the sea with great trepidation, pray the prayers which have been revealed to you: 'Oh Mother of the Sea who faces the heavens, bless those who enter your holy water', and you will be filled with our bliss. Then the Kingdom of the Sea will wash you clean of dirt, disease and sin, give you one of the twelve immortal bodies of the sea and teach you how to breathe and live under water, never leaving your prayer cell.'

03.07.2005 Deris Island

***

The Ever-Mysterious Neighbour...

I cannot find anything mysterious in my unsuccessful pupil, 'composer' and a former provincial pianist. How can this happen when burdened by the memory of the evil authoritarian grandmother, echoes of generational curses, floating as greasy plastic bags on the surface of a clean pond... what defiler dared pollute the marine area of the inner man in such a way? But if the layers at the bottom of his heart are opened one after the other, and the scars of family traumas are washed away his true qualities emerge, and an angel and a lamb can be revealed in him.

What can be said about my other neighbours?
To me they are endlessly sealed.

I am not shaken by the inaccessibility and supreme potential of the divine treasure chambers – no! There is something more which impresses me: which bodies we are in, or which worlds we exist in. Is it then that if this Supreme Divine potential was freed, we could see each other inexplicably more than we could before and we could hear further afield than we cwere able to before? Are we then no longer delivered here, but rather somewhere into the Grail of the Sea, into a white castle in the air, into the Church of Mystery, or somewhere else?

We still have more than one millennium ahead of working together, of adventures, victories, hardship, yurodstvo, carrying crosses, tears, trials and fighting, rebelling against neighbours, forgiveness, blame, brotherly embraces and fervent prayers... I have possessed this mysterious soul for over a quarter of a century. And what of it? I know so little about it! It is a mystery to me, just like the Lord Himself.

My neighbour and the Most High are one and the same.

Did I recognise the Most High? Is this even possible? Such blasphemy? It takes forever to come to know Him.

Seeing Perceval on his way to the Castle of the Grail, two angels said to him, 'Hail, glorious knight! At last you will find that which you desire, and your quest will come to an end.' Then they added some strange, incongruous and paradoxical words, 'If only it were destined to reach the end at some point, and if only you, too, were destined to reach that end.'

The Psalter. Its original strains are closer to me without the Josephite distortion. When translating the Psalter I did just one thing – I freed its pure, Church Slavonic sun from the Josephite darkness and barbaric distortions. They are not so much the work of angels and saints, but more like that of dogs chained to the walls of execution chambers. No, no! People do not read the Psalms to hear terrible groans, the noise of instruments of torture or the breaking of bones. They read them in order to enjoy their epic great delights.

The music of the 67th Psalm is dearer to me than the 14th Symphony of Shostakovich, Richter's performance of Rachmaninov's Concerto for Piano and Orchestra, or Chopin's nocturne №20, 'Swan Song'. The dearest thing to me about the Psalter, though, is how surprising it is, that it is translated into thousands of spheres and thus is truly infinite.

It is impossible to end completely. If it were not for the final 'conclusion' in a collection of poetry by Anna Akhmatova or Joseph Brodsky, or some theological research – if it was architecturally complete, however bold its findings or progressive outlook, however authentic the language of the author, and however much it corresponds to the truth – if it does not contain that invisible 'conclusion', the book is not destined for eternity or longevity. Eventually, people will get tired of it and it will invoke a kind of rejection, though it began by nourishing people. But later it will be turned into a stubborn prejudice and an obstacle...

I can see this endless, distant perspective in my neighbour. We did not come here to 'carry out our mission' but to venture to the heights of the boundless and the infinite. Perfection is infinite. It is boundless. The indescribable heavenly treasure chamber was only millimetres away from the 'Olympus' recorder I was holding as I dictated this text. It contained more than could be seen from the outside, and it penetrated my nervous system and my whole being to the very core

*

I will tirelessly repeat, 'The Most High is greater even than Himself, and man is greater than himself', and 'The Most High and man are one and the same'.

They have been joined by the covenant of union from time immemorial. They have one friend in common – the cross which connects them.

Is this not why the Bridegroom at the bridal chamber so insistently called His disciples to carry the cross? Alas, they did not understand Him and they transformed the cross into the Inquisition, an 'instrument of torture', or a 'place of torture' for holy, righteous people etc. They did not know the blessing of the cross. Only the great saints knew that.

A person is a mysterious phosphorescent white stone of the Grail; a new stone. Do you not know that, at the heart of a person of the future, there will be a white stone and, is the new name of the Lord written on it, 'Bridegroom', signifying that He is United with the person; the Worshiping and Divinising?

Lord, Lord,
Worshiping and Divinising!
Bless the sons of the Bridal Chamber,
Sanctifying,
Through mysticism surpassing Yourself,
Yurodivy, gentle and honoured,
And glorified and praised
In the Holy of Holies of the True Church!
(From the prayer of petition in the liturgy of the Grail).

Christ's prayer was heavenly, silent, universal and miraculous. In His heart He bore the whole of creation and His Kingdom at the same time. His prayer served as a bridge between them. It is as if the royal retinue had rushed at once from earth to heaven and no-one could stop it. It was led at the front by white horses whose riders called out, 'Make way for the King of Heaven and the royal procession!'

The Hesychasts from Mount Athos chose a silent, wise prayer 'in keeping with the vibrations of the Sabbath'. However, the Saviour knew something even greater than the divinely passionate, ever-present, burning, meditative, contemplative prayer in the spheres of heavenly rapture – He knew the eternal prayer which is greater even than itself which is not possible to render in the here and now.

I call this longed-for type of prayer, the Prayer of the Holy Grail.

03.07.2005 Deris Island

***

The four Gospels were essentially subjected to the 'devil's censor' (Fr. Paisius) which distorted Mary Magdalene as a former prostitute. They were obsessed with her sinful past: she was not the greatest *anointed* one, transfigured, purified and the

Bride of Christ, but a former sinner who was saved and converted. What happened after that, though, is not understood.

As it was with Mary, so it was with the whole of Adam's race. Lucifer, in the form of Judeo-Christian evangelists, distorted Adam's race with its incurable sinfulness (murderers, prostitutes and sinners). It was closed, sealed and cursed forever, and the *metanoia,* which had been called for by the true Christ, was forbidden: change, reform yourself, convert, recognise Me for what I am, stick to the Father, become one with Me (thresholds of the bridal chamber).

Mary was not only 'sanctified and purified', but she also became the greatest of the *anointed* ones and had the honour of being the guardian of the body of Christ and the spiritual labours of Christ. Thus she became a keeper of mystery. The mystery of mysteries, the supreme ritual, and so on, were realised through her. This is the true mystery of the heavenly Jerusalem. She conceived through Christ which was equal to or possibly even superior to the Immaculate Conception of Christ by the Divine Mother. She achieved that which Eve was unable to do in paradise.

On the other hand, Mary Magdalene became the second New Eve after the Most Pure Virgin. The enemy must have had to work very hard to seal off this mystery over the centuries! The Gospel remained open and unfinished. He came, he went, and then what happened? The institution.

Once again we will begin reproducing in sin: and in sins did my mother conceive me. This is where the phenomenon of Sun Myung Moon comes from, accusing Christ of fruitlessness. He says that the Mother of the Lord, and Elizabeth, prevented the Lord from marrying and having offspring. He, Moon, the 'new Christ' did this for the Lord.

These are such unprecedented perspectives! This is a new view of Christian history. It brings such inspiration and such joy! The origin of Christ has played a part in the history of humanity. Moreover, it has reached the summit. Christianity is not a religion which generates outsiders and pariahs, as it is portrayed by the Orthodox Church and the Catholics (i.e. two categories of people: the rich clergy and the poor congregation), but a religion of kings, monarchs and noble knights.

Sir Galahad, one of the keepers of the Chalice, was a direct descendant of Sir Lancelot. Perceval, Lancelot and Galahad are sacred names which have been distorted by poets. The mysterious covenant of the Shema; 'Hear, Oh Israel: the Lord our God is one Lord', is hidden in the name Galahad (kha El Ehad – one Lord).

St. Augustine's caricature of the Kingdom of the Most High's 'offensive' in the 4th century, the frequent euphoria associated with the conquering of land by the Christian emperors, and the ease with which the priests gathered souls, is stolen from real history. As it was the true sons of the Most High, the sons of Christ, replaced the reign of Ben Elohims and themselves became earthly monarchs and rulers.

Whole dynasties of European kings and Russian Tsars were direct messianic descendants of Christ. The world received its messianic inheritance from the Lord, but it was constantly subjected to persecution on the part of the Roman Villain and the Byzantine Monster. These royal, immaculate and radiant dynasties (from which came the Glorious Branch) were opposed by the 'successors of the apostles'. Two thrones emerged: the throne of Peter (the inheritance of vicars, bishops and priests) and the throne of the Immaculate Conception – the throne of Christ, the direct descendant of the Lord. Like the Lord, Himself, His dynasty is superior to that of Peter's vicars.

In the history of Christianity the devil achieved one thing: endless distortion, i.e. erasing the Most High. Mary Magdalene was distorted, although she is such a great saint! Humanity was distorted, as was the heavenly church. The Disciples of Christ were essentially lured into the same trap as Mary Magdalene, the 'former prostitute who was saved by the mysteries'.

The mystery of mysteries, though, is the possibility of Immaculate Conception in the Blood of Christ, and in human blood, through which flow particles of the transfigured divine-human composition, messianic particles and messianic bodies. This divine- humane aspect, which has already entered the composition of the blood of Neo-Adamites, renders the mysteries of the Pharisees superfluous. Thus the institution will be shut down in spite of the vested interests of its brethren and the inquisitors who serve it.

03.07.2005 Deris Island

***

The Desposins (The Messianic Dynasty) suffered directly what Christians were instilled with en masse (sometimes through hypnosis and with a significant dose of guile and institutional cunning).

They are fearless because of their faith in immortality. The Father is the Most High Himself. They, the Desposins are divine incarnations on earth. The devil has no power over them.

The Most High Lord has promised eternal life for His Creation. From them has come a new race of divinely anointed immortal Knights of the Glory of the Most High; knights of the true faith. They have no need for catechisms, confession and other such things which are propagated by those of false blood who come from a different race.

Christ revealed himself to them from within, from hidden sources. They experienced His origin in their blood. Only one thing gave them happiness: the Lord working in them, and they in the Lord. Christ's love for His children was like the Heavenly Father's love for His Son: threefold and indescribable.

Inner Christianity has replaced the external institution with its leadership, rules, encyclicals, papal bulls, and new statutes (the Neo-Jewish variation of faith in a universal Messiah descended from the Jews of Jerusalem).

Christ came to them, heard their confession and talked with them. He was not in any way 'other-worldly' and extraordinary. He did not require medical, psychological or any other kind of tests: a visionary is not insane (as it is customary to believe in the Vatican). His apparitions seemed just as natural and obvious as a loving father visiting his children. The covenant between them was a special one: it was not about an all-powerful Divinity and his flock of sinners, but about a Father and His Children. The latter include not only the likes of great knights who were born immaculately, but also the many families who are part of Christ's race. If anyone among them is found to be harbouring wickedness, he is quickly removed from the list of the heirs of Christ. Thus the dynasty has preserved its amazing and exceptional purity.

*

The Eucharist of the Grail. Anyone who understands this will experience a holy disillusionment with regard to the Roman Eucharist. The Saviour prepares the Chalice not for 'the congregation' or even for His 'disciples', but for those who are of one composition and one blood with Him. Otherwise the Eucharist would be meaningless.

Those who are with the Grail wonder what happens in a church during the liturgy. One formula of transubstantiation and recollection is not enough! Improved compositions and prepared oils are required. The Immaculate Origin injected into blood is needed. 'But what is it then?' they say. 'If there is no Grail and His Blood has spilled into sand, how can wine be transubstantiated into the Blessed Sacrament?'

The liturgy of holy passion lasts for an unspecified time, until the Church of the Round Table enters the divinely passionate experience of the Lord, and a cloud of the Parousia (the presence of His Holy Divine being) envelops the knights and the myrrh-bearing women who serve them.

The Father gives Himself to His Children. Oh, all-consuming love!

This is the other Eucharist. Those who partake of it must believe that they 'will live forever as long as they come to know the Sacred Gifts'. They are already immortal and initiated. The Blood of the Lord is in their blood. Only they are able to understand that the Father has gone away to another kingdom for a while. They continue to be joined with Him, to be born of Him and to renew the bonds of their Covenant of Union with Him.

The Eucharist is the uniting of blood ties in a Covenant with the Divine. There is no other way to understand it. The Saviour conceived through the Blood He shed at Golgotha. He continues to feed with this Blood anyone whom He has led into the world through the most mysterious way without blemish through Mary who anoints with myrrh, the former harlot now purified and raised to the level of the greatest of saints.

Oh, the rapture of the Eucharist! How rapturously it mingles with the blood! Peacefully. Blissfully. Sweetly.

04.07.2005 Deris Island

***

The Grail's vision of a person is very different to that of the eye of the Inquisition. To the Grail, the united soul of a person is innocent, pure, holy and divine. To the Roman inquisition he is a monstrous, shameful sinner and an incorrigible whore.

The True Church defends the honour of the worldly soul which has been slandered and seduced by the false church. For a priest of Melchizedek the inspiration of faith enables him to defend the honour of a slandered soul (Fr. Paisius).

The devil shows the negative side of souls and wants to destroy them through the Roman Harlot's sin-obsessed rituals ('they wallowed in sin'). However, to the innocent eyes of the Grail, the human world is the Golden-haired Elsa, the pure virgin. No-one can defend her, though: there is no-one in the world who can defend her slandered honour.

The diseases which afflicted the lepers and the weak in the Gospels are the ghosts of the slander which the Pharisees spread about good souls. The Lord, as the true King and Knight of the Grail, healed them, i.e. showed them for what they really were. The sun of virtue performed miracles during the Saviour's time on earth. On the other hand, the Saviour returned the ghosts to the Pharisees and, in order to make them feel ashamed, He sent those who had been healed to show themselves to the priests.

The saints said that Christianity is a religion for superior, noble souls. Nobility is a sign of true Christianity. Conformism and double-dealing, though, are signs of evil and substitution: saints are substituted for vampires in disguise.

*

Elsa lost when the thought occurred to her that something might depend on Lohengrin's background. The world is not capable of understanding the concept that the Church has come down from heaven. It needs facts and figures on paper. Lohengrin, the heavenly messenger, was required to confirm his earthly origins. The evil and jealous Count Telramund started this rumour and was defeated by Lohengrin in fair combat.

The legend of Lohengrin shows the conflict between the evil of the Roman villain and the world's souls. Similarly, the Jews demanded documents of John the Baptist when they came to him at the River Jordan, 'Who are you? Why do you baptise? Are you a priest? Prove it! Show us a document bearing the seal of the Sanhedrin'.

04.07.2005 Deris Island

***

Now I have understood what it was that attracted me to Orthodoxy. The Lord revealed it to me. The Institution of Nikon[13]

---

[13] The Institution of Patriarch Nikon (1605-1681) – Patriarch Nikon strengthened the Institute, as an external apparatus of faith, ruined spirituality and the concept of the Church as the Body of Christ. Nikon conducted a brutal and violent church reform, accompanied by torture and executions against the Christians of thc old rite; he sought supremacy of power over the Tsar, following the example of the Pope of Rome. He influenced Tsar Alexis the Quietest, by imposing the Byzantine Orthodox silence, burning all musical instruments in Russia and exterminating Russian troubadours.

was sealed to me. In the church I saw an Immaculate Virgin, a Bride, accepting her blood-covered Bridegroom as the seed of Abraham. The church attracted me as an oasis of original purity, which it had long since lost. I entered the virginal embrace and was led there like an innocent child.

Obsession with sin is an age-old impasse. There is no way out of this sin-centred teaching. This emphasis on sin can only be overcome with the power and the actions of the opposite – the immaculate origin. A person needs a source of original purity beside him, even though it has been blocked up at some point by the church, a holy father, an ascetic, or a brother. He needs an example of some other heavenly or otherworldly origin.

The church praises Christ for His Heavenly Immaculate Conception. The Holy Virgin is likewise praised for Her original purity which She revealed in the depths of Her Immaculate Heart. However, the fiendish inquisitors who 'eliminated' the Most Pure Virgin by means of Her apparitions, adopted Her purity and divine maternal embrace for themselves. Their embrace, though, is nothing more than that of a harlot.

*

Man's creation in the 'image and likeness' of the Divinity is highly mysterious. The potential for Divinization lies within him. Sin is now just a part of divinely passionate history.

One of the aspects of the teaching of Divine Wisdom is taking a step back in order to reach an even higher level. Divinisation, which was intended from the beginning, cannot occur without being tempted by the devil. Having passed through the abyss, and having defeated the devil as well as the serpent in himself, a person achieves a superior relationship with the Most High. Having passed through the bonds of mortality, he then achieves the bonds of union.

The Most High allowed him to be bound by the ties of sin and death in order to introduce stronger bonds of partnership and thus achieve the perfect level to be united with the Divine through divinization.

What did Christianity proclaim? It abolished the sin-centred Judaism in times of decline and apostasy. Christ proclaimed Himself as a different origin reaching beyond 'Lord-have-mercy' and the sin-centred, funereal and reminiscent. Christianity is about descending into the World of the Great Light and the Sun of Suns, which is Christ, the Bridegroom, the One who was immaculately conceived. Then, through Immaculate Conception, He engenders a new humanity.

Original Immaculacy shone from the Throne of the Virgin and lit up the world. However, Christ was sealed as the Redeemer and Saviour within a new framework of sin-centred doctrines and the new law. He was thrown into the trap of obsession with sin and a new institution was created.

The new Christianity must now detach itself from the old tabernacle of theology, filled with mouse droppings, and proclaim a greater, Immaculate Origin – the power of the Virgin who gave birth from on High to a new humanity. Then people will come in search of this faith.

*

The Byzantine Villain stole the understanding of the Body of Christ from the Grail: in a sense the Church is the 'Body of Christ'. The Body of Christ is literally contained within the Grail. The Blood is also contained within It because it is connected with the Body. Therefore the Church became the 'Body' because it partook of the Body of Christ in the Grail. However, the God-Man Body of Christ is also literally present in the Church of the Grail; the Church of the Lord's Chalice. There is no longer any other Church.

In Solovki, all the messianic monarchs who had partaken of the origin of Christ in the Grail consecrated Seraphim and crowned the Solovki Grail with twelve pearls of the spreading Kingdom of the Grail. Then Seraphim gave this Grail to us. Therefore we are the direct heirs of the Messianic Dynasty.

30.06.2005 Deris Island

***

My Lord, My Lord... A frail old woman lies alone and unwanted in a hospice, abandoned by the world. With trembling hands and a hoarse, other-worldly voice she asks, 'May I receive communion?.. I don't have any money though'.

She has taken a Knight of the Grail for an Orthodox priest... What is this? Does she really need the serpent's chalice from the hands of an inquisitor? Through her illness she is faced with a death bed. She does not want the Orthodox Last Judgement with hordes of demonic men with green eyes, terrible tarantulas which approach the death bed and parishioners who have been seduced by them. Rather, she wants this painful disease-ridden bed to be transformed into the Bridal Bed. Then she would hear the voice of Christ:

'My daughter, this illness does not lead to death, but to the glory of the Most High'.

*

Having converted to Christianity through Orthodoxy, I found myself in the shoes of an innocent child clinging to the branch of the 'mother church' like a child clings to its mother's breast. Clearly the Church is also an 'ancient mother'. So, just as, when starting to free yourself from the world order, you must overcome your inherent programming in the family sense, so, too when climbing the stairs along the path to the Grail, you must leave behind all inherent programming in the sense of inherited faith.

Looking more closely, I wondered whether Christ has really abandoned such a Church. There is nothing left of Christ within it. The Gospel has been distorted. The hierarchy has been sold off. Instead of love there is hatred, and instead of mercy there is barbarity. There is no brotherhood; only hypocrisy, lies and magic.

What exactly is going on? Did Christ really abandon the Church of the new Rabbis who had changed into the clothing of Catholic priests and Orthodox clergy?

'It cannot be!' I thought. All these 'ecumenical councils' and theological explanations about the 'face of Nature' and 'hypostasis' by bright young men must be some kind of lie. Perhaps someone may have found it interesting if it were not for the crossing of theological swords in different symphonist councils presided over by emperors, resulting in the persecution of thousands of dissidents. The declaration of 'absolute truth' in dogmatic councils is accepted as something which has come down from heaven. Any objection to it is punished as treason. Therefore the machine of repression worked more effectively against heretics than against thieves and other criminals.

'What exactly is going on?' I wondered. Is Rome the place where Christ is crucified every day?! Instead of the second Jerusalem, the 'Third Rome' was proclaimed, to replace the second one which was 'corrupt Byzantium'. How did this happen? Did they put up with the bad morals of the corrupt Byzantine hierarchy (as early as the 4th century, St. John Chrysostom called them monsters) and believe it to be the Church? Does Christ encourage this? Is there no other church, as they claim? They are 'His body', 'His successors', 'the heirs of the apostles', the 'vicars of St. Peter' and so on.

This is such a massive deception and such a cloud of lies which has been casting a shadow over humanity for thousands of years!

That is, until the Chalice of the Grail and the Church of the Grail are revealed.

Christ left behind his radiant heir; the second divine child. Then His Church took its repose in the white castles of the Grail amongst wondrous lions, eagles (the symbol of royal authority), calves and divine humans (the four apocalyptic animals of John's Revelation), as well as swans, golden boats, the magnificent Galahads, Lohengrins, Percevals, Sir Brons and other noble, royal elders and anointed Christs.

Christ was preserved in thousands of faces in the True Church. The 'history of the Church', as told by Orthodoxy and Catholicism, is false.

It is a great fabrication... For thousands of years they have looked at this copy of the divine original and have accepted it as an original. Lord, this is such deception!

However, in recent times, this deception has been exposed by the Holy Spirit. Thus the Messianic Dynasty of Christ and his disciples will be revealed to the world at the Second Solovki, in the Divine Civilization of *Nightingale Mountain*, on the thrones of Founding Virginity, and everywhere that the Most Pure One speaks. She clothes people in the robes of chastity and the white stole of the quest for the supreme mystery to which a person is called: to love Him more than it is possible even in the heavens.

Thus, to conceive immaculately by Him is far greater than to love him, to enter the Bridal Chamber, to stick to Him and to lie down on the Altar of Union.

Oh! It is not possible to go any further than this...

28.06.2005 Deris Island

***

What can a person possibly know of a conversation between two lovers who are whispering in a neighbouring room? What can he possibly know of the dialogue among the Three Who Love Each Other – the Father, Son and Holy Spirit? Divine Wisdom now reveals the Triple-Hypostatic Trinity as three-fold love. Their counsel and Their thoughts are theogamic. What a prayer is offered up on those thrones amongst the theogamic ones who love Each Other!

'Oh! My beloved! Oh!..'

This 'Oh' is not without significance. This 'Oh' is filled with supreme heavenly ecstasy. It is a prayer which is raised up to heaven and beyond.

...Thus Mother Mary of Heavenly Kindness[14], Who spent over a year, in human terms, in the royal destiny of the Divine

[14] Mother Mary of Heavenly Kindness – passed away in 2003, she was the closest collaborator of the Author. She had been poisoned together with the author, but did not survive. Those who knew her noticed her humbly-meek character and her devoted service to others to the end. She was a dedicated nun and now she continues her spiritual way by helping others who remain on Earth.

Mother, knows of the infinite ascent to the Throne of the Most High. A stairway of fire with 150 stairs stretches out before her. Each step is more wonderful than the last. So far though, She has not been allowed to go beyond the seventy-second step yet.

*

What happened to Christ was very strange. Anyone who did not understand Him went away. Thus, many people left this 'strange' Lord. 'Whoever eats My Flesh and drinks My Blood' sounds strange. Surely this is madness? It was strange to see Him, the All-powerful Messiah, crucified on the Cross.

It was strange with me, Fr. John, too. Everything was new, whether it was the Paraclete, the Immaculate Conception, the Revelation of Lourdes in the far-away concrete jungle of Moscow, or Solovki or the Grail... Each time there was something new! How could I possibly not lose my way? How could I avoid the snakes, scorpions, Dathans and Abirams, false prophets, Cainites and other reptiles hidden in the sand?

However, this mysterious strangeness explains some of the greatest mysteries and mysticism which have been revealed, as well as the mysterious anointing with myrrh as a sign of royalty: a chosen one.

Strangeness and *yurodstvo* in a teacher is a good and positive sign.

Woe to those in who have nothing strange them, who are too formal and normal.

*

From Your Divinely Immaculate womb
A royal dynasty is born.
The sphere of sin and hardship is closing.
Satan is defeated on his throne of hypocrisy
In the guise of a monarch.
In the Jewish temple is proclaimed
The glory of those Saint Nicholases
Who have descended from Heaven.
Let the organ sing
A song of their glorious victories!
Prayer of petition from the Liturgy of the Grail (Deris Island).

*

I pass the night in rapturous prayer.

Lord, the Grail presents such prospects! The air is so fragrant!

There is no White Cross in front of me. There is a limestone terrace with high concrete walls and marble benches. Within these walls there is a village well, a rocking chair, a bucket on a chain and a refectory table with another bench underneath it. At the side, a neighbour's toilet shares an adjoining wall. On another terrace, Croatian washing is hanging out to dry.

There is no cross of white marble with which I can immediately ascend to heaven and to Gethsemane... The Grail is here, though. I am not surprised when, on the first floor of the house where we are staying, I notice a chalice with rays of sun flowing out of it, together with the inscription, 'Christ is the King of the Grail', beautifully etched on the wall by the builders long ago.

I tremble in my prayer of ecstasy. No soul has ever entered such a sphere...

What is this? It is the perspective of the Grail.

A fire is burning within me as if I was serving an endless liturgy. Oh! Inspired, I soar higher and higher. A flock of migrating birds join me as we fly up to heaven and then continue soaring.

03.07.2005 Deris Island

Glossary

Akathist – a chanted prayer performed in the Orthodox Christianity.

Anointed (one) – one of God's chosen ones in whom the Divinity is manifest and God is fully present.

Ben-Elohims – (Ancient Hebrew: 'sons of God') – dark spirits (archons) who rebelled against the Heavenly Father of Pure Love (Genesis 6: 1-2,4).

Eufrosinia – a holy woman (female *starets*) who was granted the honour of sainthood and acquired the Holy Spirit during her lifetime. She was the mentor of Blessed John of the Holy Grail. Following her physical death God rendered her relics incorruptible and fragrant.

Dabak particles – myrrh divine particles of sticking to the Most High, particles of Theogamy and of the Wedding Chamber.

Divine humanity, divine civilization III – the approaching divine civilization of transfigured humanity which will be established on earth in the third millennium.

Divine Union – the great moment (for people who have dedicated themselves to God) of transition to the state of God-Human, at the divine marriage of the love which is not of this world. The soul ascends to the Heavenly Bridegroom (God) at the altar of union, often during the final moments of life, through the last drop of blood which flows from the Divine Grail.

The Holy Being – this term was coined by the teaching of the author, which defines the mystical and fragrant spheres of the true Church, where the Chalice of the Grail with its 144 castles remains.

Innocent Baltski – a great saint and anointed one of God from the 19th and 20th centuries. He was persecuted by the Pharisees of official Christianity. He possesses the special power of supreme love and immunity from the Pharisees. His mission will be revealed in the future.

Immaculacy, Original Immaculacy, first generative immaculacy – a divine attribute, as well as being the gates through which immaculate souls come down to earth without the burden of original sin. Original sin results in a fatal reorganization of the human composition which is sealed with heavenly light and a spiritual heart before birth. Original immaculacy, as a gift of the Virgin Mother, is called to help people overcome sin and begin living in the bosom of an immaculate and holy existence.

Joseph the Heir – the immaculately-conceived son of Mary Magdalene and Christ. As the First of the Dynasty of the Desposins (Messianic Dynasty), He is the keeper of the Grail Chalice and the representative of the new, radiant, seraphitic, divine humanity.

Metanoia – a change of consciousness and transfiguration of the man, the feat of victory over the self who we were yesterday and the thirst for a new life, new breath; the wish to be born from above, to live in new bodies, to shine with a new face, to become a new being descended from Heaven.

Mikhail Romanov – See Seraphim Romanov.

Nightingale Mountain is the mountain where the Altar of Union and the Bridal Chamber were revealed to the Divine Mother. The mountain where Supreme Love, which is not of this world, was revealed. It is situated near Izmir in Turkey.

Parusia – the inseparable and mysterious presence of the Divinit.

The Russian Orthodox Church and the True (Russian) Orthodox Church – the True Orthodox Church (also known as the Church of the Catacombs) was opposed to and persecuted by both the atheist Soviet authorities and the Russian Orthodox Church – those priests who sided with the Soviet authorities; the current official church in Russia is the Russian Orthodox Church, i.e. from a canonical point of view, the official church is in no way related to the Church in Russia before 1917. The modern-day official Church, (the Russian Orthodox Church) claims that the True Orthodox Church does not exist and never has; it is not difficult to guess why the Russian Orthodox Church adopts this stance.

Second Golgotha – the greatest people of Russia were sacrificed at Solovki: honest and trustworthy priests and laity. The repressive machine of the GULAG slaughtered innocent people on a massive scale. Therefore, the events which took place at Solovki can be called the Second (Solovki) Golgotha.

Seraphim Romanov – Seraphim Romanov was, by blood, a member of the Romanov royal family in Russia. He was the brother of Nikolai Romanov. He was called to preserve the spiritual hierarchy of the church in Russia as Patriarch of the Church of the Catacombs. He is an apostle of supreme love and the head of the new burning spiritual hierarchy.

Solovki, Solovetsky Archipelago – the Solovki Islands are located in Northern Russia. During Soviet times they were the home of Solovetski Special Purpose Prison (see 'Second Golgotha').

Solovki startsy, Solovki elders – the martyrs of the Solovetsky Archipelago. Mainly priests who, during Soviet times, were subjected to immense suffering and deprivation, yet remained faithful to God and to supreme love. Now in heaven, they are the founders of the Russian church of the new martyrs.

Starets; starchestvo – in Orthodoxy this is a special spiritual school or calling, particularly in Russia. The main aims are perfecting oneself through service, sobriety, acquisition of the Holy Spirit, and the deification of a person. In a wider sense, a starets may belong to a non-Orthodox faith.

Third Testament – God's covenant with the new seraphitic humanity. Many mystics and philosophers have spoken about the Third Testament (such as Joachim of Fiore, Merezhkovsky, Vladimir Solovyov etc.).

Yurodivy; yurodstvo – a person who is not of this world and behaves in a manner which worldly people consider abnormal.

The Knight of Divine Love

about the Author

Blessed John of the Holy Grail is the worthy representative of the intellectual elite, who has acquired the archetype of its virtues: high erudition, un-compromising viewpoints, bright intellect and ability of a profound perception.

The inimitable originality of style, bright aphoristic character of the language, stupefaction of new images reliably allow his 350 books to be the part of the spiritual masterpieces of the great thinkers of the third millennium.

In total have been published a million and a half copies by Blessed John of the Holy Grail, and have found their readers from England to New Zealand and from Japan to the Americas.

Blessed John of the Holy Grail has put an end to the image the old god with his angry doctrines of awful judgment and inevitable recompense for the sins, and opened up for mankind the presence of a new God – the Father of Pure Love.

The anointed one confirms that only pure Love without any selfish motives, violence and usurpation can transform the world towards peace and a harmonious way of life between the different religious streams and nations.

The mankind goes through a hard, spiritual crisis. Blessed John of the Holy Grail reveals to the society of this world a wonderful way out, a great union beyond nations – the birth of the new mankind united in this new God – the Divine civilization.

It is called upon to establish this unprecedented society on the Earth, living with higher principles than the democratic ones – the principles of the Divine civilization III.

In order to understand Blessed John of the Holy Grail, it is necessary to go beyond the stereotypes of ordinary human thinking and existing images of obsolete traditions; centuries old.

Every speech, book, or revelation of Blessed John of the Holy Grail is the unique, new word that has been revealed to mankind for the first time. The ode to the magnificence of the Human Being, of its divine potential resounds from the pages of the books by Blessed John of the Holy Grail.

Directing humanity to the mysteries of the forthcoming Divine civilization, Blessed John of the Holy Grail reveals the dazzling heights of the spiritual mission of humanity towards a promising future.

The mission of Blessed John of the Holy Grail cannot be related to any of the adopted clichés, like being a pastor, poet, writer, revolutionary or teacher. He rather is a modern mystic and prophet, spear-heading this new civilization.

He is a true representative of the new epoch, which the ancient prophets have proclaimed. He is the anointed one, whom the God sends to the humanity in the times of great crises, on the eve of the changing of the epochs and civilizations.

His prophetic and epistle devotion can hardly be limited to words, books and preaching.

With absolute personal dedication for this mission he follows his credo and constantly reaches for higher levels of kindness, of love, wisdom and purity, and to excel in this permanently.

This is what he teaches to his numerous disciples and followers.

His ecumenical contacts, not only with branches of Christianity, but also with other religions such as Islam and Buddhism, etc are particularly notable.

Many people are inspired by his dedication to complex theological, philosophical and social questions. The keen interest in preserving peace in the world has allowed Blessed John of the Holy Grail to become a special consultant of the UN International non-government organization 'Educators for World Peace', which has its offices in more than 90 countries. He has given numerous interviews on TV and radio, communicates with people through articles, published in mass media.

One of his greatest spiritual gifts is the ability to find positive and constructive solutions, practically for all circumstances in the modern world.

Charles Mercieca, PhD. President
International Assodation of Educators for World Peace,
Professor Alabama A&M University says:

'In his work Blessed John of the Holy Grail qualifies as the man who was born like heavenly angel, who has come down to the Earth with a mysterious aim. But where is the mystery?

It manifests in a man, descending from on high, who came to triumph with Love, where there is no Love. In this respect he is unanimously (unequivocally) united with the medieval Cathars – poets, ascetics and martyrs of Love, who were slandered and extirpated by the Medieval Roman Inquisition.

Blessed John of the Holy Grail is a devoted successor and heir of the Cathar's L'Eglise D'Amour (the Great Church of Love), uniting all righteous and loving souls of the Earth without any institutional framework.

The blood of perfect *bonshommes* (good people) who went to the stake with the words "God is Love", are transfigured and metamorphosed in his poetry. Their voices sound in his lines. The memory of them engages him in an uncompromising struggle against original bearers that are hostile to Love – first of all, against world hypocrisy of any form.'

Zoya Krahmalnikova, Russian writer, was jailed
in a Soviet concentration camp for her faith:

'Blessed John of the Holy Grail's ideas, directed towards universal values through eternal ideas of the sacred, everlasting and kind, are one of the modern teachings of the mystical revelation leading to 'God inside us'. They are absolutely suitable for the revival of the true spirituality the texts of Blessed John of the Holy Grail are deep inquiring of the soul, leading towards God without any sluggish dogmata or ideological orientation. Lucid language and brilliant simplicity of his thoughts make books by Blessed John of the Holy Grail fully claimed by the modern spiritual man. Considering vital necessity of the mankind perished by oddities of the material culture, barefaced pragmatism and evident conjuncture, Blessed John of the Holy Grail's diaries are pearls of spiritual values and divine ideáis. They should be accessible to the European society and therefore translated into English.'

In 1998 **The International Bibliographical Centre (Cambridge, England)** included his name into 13th edition of the encyclopedia 'Who is Who among the Intellectuals' as a recognition of his special achievements.

All who wish to learn the teaching and practices of the Spiritual School of John of the Holy Grail are invited to the seminars

With the help of spiritual guides, you can learn the practice of catharsis, metanoia, fasting, meditation, contemplative and breathing prayer, sacred reverences, healing ablutions in holy springs.

In our centres you can meet cathars of today, to know the art and the way of the author of this book, Blessed John of the Holy Grail. There are catalogues of books published by the Cathar Association, which can be ordered. We also invite you to meditative music, played by Blessed John in a new spiritual interpretation of Mozart, Beethoven and Tchaikovsky. This music is available as CDs from the same source.

Contact our Spiritual Centres:
www.theogamy.com
tel: +44 758 3949 766